DATE DUE FOR RETURN

CAMBRIDGE LANGUAGE EDUCATION
Series Editor: Jack C. Richards

This series draws on the best available research, theory, and eduational practice to help clarify issues and resolve problems in language teaching, language teacher education, and related areas. Books in the series focus on a wide range of issues and are written in a style that is accessible to classroom teachers, teachers-in-training, and teacher educators.

In this series:

Language Teaching Awareness

A guide to exploring beliefs and practices

Jerry G. Gebhard
Indiana University of Pennsylvania

Robert Oprandy
Monterey Institute of International Studies

CAMBRIDGE
UNIVERSITY PRESS

PUBLISHED BY THE PRESS SYNDICATE OF THE UNIVERSITY OF CAMBRIDGE
The Pitt Building, Trumpington Street, Cambridge, United Kingdom

CAMBRIDGE UNIVERSITY PRESS
The Edinburgh Building, Cambridge CB2 2RU, UK   www.cup.cam.ac.uk
40 West 20th Street, New York, NY 10011-4211, USA   www.cup.org
10 Stamford Road, Oakleigh, Melbourne 3166, Australia
Ruiz de Alarcón 13, 28014 Madrid, Spain

First published 1999

Printed in the United States of America

Typeset in Times Roman [AG]

Library of Congress Cataloging-in-Publication Data
Gebhard, Jerry Greer.
Language teaching awareness : a guide to exploring beliefs and
practices / by Jerry G. Gebhard and Robert Oprandy.
p.   cm
ISBN 0 521 63039 8 hardback
ISBN 0 521 63954 9 paperback
1. Language and languages – Study and teaching.
I. Oprandy, Robert.   II. Title.
P51.G4   1999
418′.007–dc21   98-48366
                                                 CIP

*A catalogue record for this book is available from
the British Library*

ISBN 0 521 63039 8 hardback
ISBN 0 521 63954 9 paperback

To John Fanselow, our mentor and friend,
who has liberated so many of us from the
usual ways of looking.

Contents

Contributors

Jerry G. Gebhard, Indiana University of Pennsylvania
Laura Golden, Teachers College, Columbia University
Mio Hashimoto, Indiana University of Pennsylvania
Jae-Oke Joe, Indiana University of Pennsylvania
Hyunhee Lee, Chungbuk National University, South Korea
Robert Oprandy, Monterey Institute of International Studies
Kayoko Shiomi, Teachers College, Columbia University
Helen Collins Sitler, Indiana University of Pennsylvania
Zubeyde Tezel, University of Illinois, Urbana-Champaign

Series editor's preface

A current theme in teacher education is to view teacher development as a process that involves both the acquisition of practical knowledge and skills and the examination of beliefs, principles, and theories and how they influence the way teachers teach. Teaching involves both thought and action, and the interaction between the two forms the focus of recent approaches to teacher development. Teacher education also has to face the issue of linking the content of teacher education to the contexts in which teachers work. Much of what occurs in campus programs is soon forgotten or discarded when teachers enter or return to schools; hence teacher educators are constantly exploring ways of making their curriculum and the activities they make use of relevant to the immediate and long-term concerns of student teachers.

In *Language Teaching Awareness* two scholars at the forefront of second language teacher education and their collaborators describe the rationale and practice underlying what they term an *exploratory approach* to teacher development. This refers to activities that seek to develop deeper understanding of teachers' beliefs, theories, principles, and attitudes in order to better understand the nature of classroom second language teaching and learning. The authors' agenda is not to present a body of information that is intended to help change or improve teachers' practices. Rather, they make a strong and convincing case for exploring teachers' beliefs and practices and using the knowledge and awareness that result from this process to make informed decisions about one's own teaching.

Crucial to the process of exploratory teaching proposed in this book are the observation and description of teaching events and processes, investigation of teaching through action research, using journal writing to write about and explore teaching, and using conversation to examine teaching from different perspectives. These activities are intended to help teachers understand their own practices as well as those of other teachers, to explore alternative approaches to teaching, and to see teaching in different ways. The book presents accounts of how these and other activities can be used within an exploratory approach to teacher development. Procedures for using each activity are carefully illustrated, and ideas on how to use the information or insights gained are given. At the same time, new and challenging insights about each of these processes are presented. The set of first-hand accounts and case studies in Part III describe how these processes have been successfully used and how they helped teachers achieve new insights about teaching and about themselves as teachers. *Language Teaching Awareness* thus makes a valuable contribution to the field of second language teacher education and will provide a valuable resource book for teachers and teacher educators who seek to better understand and manage their own professional development through the application of the principles of exploratory teaching.

Jack C. Richards

Preface

This book is about how teachers can explore their teaching in order to gain awareness of their beliefs and practices. There are several ways in which we consider our exploratory approach to be different from that in other language teacher education books. Some books with a teacher *training* emphasis focus on ways teachers can improve their teaching by mastering prescribed ways to teach. That is not the purpose of this book. Other books do not present *best* ways to teach but concentrate on how teachers can develop knowledge and skills about second language teaching. For example, Richards in *Beyond Training* (1998) discusses six content domains of second language education that teachers should develop. These include theories of teaching, teaching skills, communication skills and language proficiency, subject matter knowledge, pedagogical reasoning skills, and decision making and contextual knowledge.

Teacher educators who follow such a *developmental* approach provide a variety of activities for teachers to construct a knowledge base in the six domains. These include, according to Richards (ibid., 17), experiencing teaching (e.g., practice teaching, microteaching, internships), observing (e.g., peer observation, use of video protocols), reflecting on teaching and learning (e.g., journals and other written activities, language learning experience), investigating teaching and learning (e.g., analyzing classroom processes, establishing databases), focusing on critical events in teaching (e.g., by analysis of case studies, doing role plays), doing project work (e.g., action research, curriculum and materials development), information-oriented approaches (e.g., lectures and large-group teaching, discussions), communication activities (e.g., student oral presentations, skills training), and proficiency-focused activities (e.g., analysis of classroom language and discourse, practice of classroom functional language).

We see much value in this developmental approach to teaching and have made great use of such activities in our own teacher-preparation programs.[1]

---

1 Although we see value in the developmental approach to teacher education, we also recognize that development is not always beneficial. Tanizaki (1967), for example,

We also recognize that there has been much progress made in second language teacher development (see, for example: Edge 1992; Freeman 1989; Freeman & Cornwell 1993; Freeman & Richards 1996; Johnson 1999; Li, Mahoney, & Richards 1994; Richards & Nunan 1990). Through our experience, though, we feel compelled to forefront several ways to promote an *exploratory approach* to developing teacher awareness. Our emphasis on exploration overlaps with the developmental approach to (language) teacher education. Similar to those touting that approach, we agree that teachers need to take responsibility for their own teaching and that they can benefit from the cooperation of colleagues, students, and others. However, we set ourselves apart in certain ways from the usual approaches to teacher development.

Unlike one of the goals of development, that of improving teaching, the aim of exploration is, in our view, simply gaining awareness of teaching beliefs and practices. Improvement implies that some ways are better than others in teaching. Searching for such ways can limit teachers from looking beyond the concept of effective teaching, possibly blocking them from becoming more aware of teaching possibilities outside of what is considered *improved teaching*. In contrast, the goal of exploration is simply to gain awareness of teaching. As Fanselow points out, the aim of exploration is "seeing . . . teaching differently" (1988: 114). Being open and attempting to see and understand what is going on between the teacher and students and among the students themselves liberates teachers from the pressure of finding a better way. Trying alternatives just to see what happens, exploring to gain awareness, is energizing. The more elements of the teaching-learning dynamic that reveal themselves to us, the more we want to explore. Thus, a cycle is created; increasing awareness makes teachers curious to explore further, leading again to fresh insights and new questions to explore.

points out how modern lighting has eroded the aesthetic quality of traditional beauty in Japan. As Tanizaki puts it, "This was the genius of our ancestors, that by cutting off the light from this empty space they imparted to the world of shadows that informed there a quality of mystery and depth superior to that of any wall painting or ornament" (p. 20). Examples of the risks of development are everywhere. For example, an article in the Science and Environment section of the *Pittsburgh Post-Gazette* (Glausiusz, June 22, 1998), reads: "Growing disaster? Genetic engineering can improve crop yield, and may create aggressive plants that are super-resistant to disease and insects" (p. A-6). The article is about how genetically engineered crops can increase food production in the developing world. But, there is the risk that "ecological and evolutionary forces could turn these crops into disasters" (ibid.). Perhaps the plants will prove to be so robust that they will grow aggressively, like weeds, to overrun other surroundings, including other farmlands. Antibiotic-resistant genes might escape into soil bacteria and end up infecting humans. Crops engineered to carry Bt-toxin genes might trigger the evolution of Bt-resistant bugs, and so on.

An appreciation for the intricacies of teaching takes over, and the search for *better ways* or *the best way* to teach something is less pressing than discovering new choices.

Quite similar to this point is the second distinguishing feature of our approach – seeing nonjudgmental description as preferable to prescriptions of how teaching *should* be done. Detailed descriptions of teaching can provide explorers with a wealth of knowledge that can result in a great deal of awareness of what is. We do, however, recognize some value in prescription within an exploratory framework. For example, while working with a preservice teacher who spoke about 85% of the time during class and who expressed interest in cutting down the amount of his teacher talk, his supervising teacher said, "I wonder what would happen if you were to feign laryngitis the next class you teach. Try it and tell me what happens." The realization that came from being silent and noticing how much the students were able to communicate without him transformed the teacher's view of classroom interactional possibilities. In this case, the teacher was seeking some direction from his supervisor, and the prescription was given in the spirit of exploring what might happen if the teacher were to "lose his voice."

A third feature of our exploratory approach is the need to pay attention to language and behavior. In regard to language, usual conversations about teaching are filled with high-inference words and ambiguities. To counteract such tendencies, we promote the use of metalanguages, discussions among teachers of the ambiguities of the usual words used to talk about teaching, and awareness of the ways that teachers use judgmental as well as descriptive language during such discussions. We also explore how crucial listening is in opening up channels of communication and creating understanding among educators.

A fourth characteristic of our approach is our emphasis on going beyond usual ways of understanding teaching, especially that of problem solving (i.e., identifying and overcoming a problem area in one's teaching). Although problem solving can provide much awareness, as Chapters 4 and 10 demonstrate, there are a number of other avenues that teachers can travel. These include seeing what happens by trying the opposite of what we normally do (e.g., asking open-ended questions instead of ones we already know the answers to), by seeing *what is* by contrasting what we do with what we think we do, by considering what we believe in light of what we do, and by exploring other avenues discussed in Chapter 1.

We also see value in exploring connections between our personal and our professional lives. This is often neglected in the literature on teacher development. Therefore, a fifth highlight of our approach is our interest in having teachers consider *connecting questions,* that is, questions connecting who they are as people with who they are as teachers. Examples of such questions, discussed in Chapter 7, are: "How does language teaching fit into my vision of who I am (becoming) and how I'd like the world to be?" and "Am I REAL in and out of school?"

Sixth, we recognize that a number of teachers and teacher educators understand the importance of process as it relates to teacher development. Bailey (1990), for example, discusses the process of keeping a teaching journal. Wallace (1998) elaborates on the process of doing action research. Gaies and Bowers (1990) present a process of clinical supervision. Lange (1990) offers a blueprint for teacher development programs. We choose to highlight the importance of involving teachers in processes through which they can make more informed decisions. As Jarvis pointed out in 1972, we need to shift "the responsibility for decision making to the classroom teacher. . . . It is perhaps time to train the teacher to analyze his situation and make his own decisions for his situation" (p. 201). By knowing and experiencing ways to process their own teaching, the goal of Part II of this book, teachers can more easily "construct, reconstruct and revise their own teaching" (Fanselow 1988: 115). This frees teachers from others' recipes and prescriptions, which can not only limit their awareness of how they (can) teach, but also block them from constructing their own set of beliefs,

Paradoxically, for teachers to make more informed decisions, we feel it is important for them to start with "a beginner's mind" (Suzuki 1970), the final distinguishing feature of our exploratory approach. This means we enter conversations, observations, and other teacher education activities with an open mind, unclouded as much as possible by preconceived notions about what we think *should* take place in classrooms and other teaching settings.

We invite you to try our exploratory approach to teacher awareness if you are a student or a teacher educator in a teacher-preparation program, a teacher in a language-teaching program who wants to further your awareness of teaching or of how to do classroom research, or a supervisor or administrator working with language teachers in the field.

If you are willing to suspend judgment, not be overly concerned with improving your teaching, explore avenues to awareness that are off the beaten path, pay attention to your use of language and behavior, make connections between your personal and teaching lives, try out processes of exploration that may be new to you, and start with a beginner's mind, then we invite you to explore your teaching beliefs and practices through the readings and tasks in the pages that follow.

Jerry G. Gebhard
Robert Oprandy

Acknowledgments

We owe a special thanks to students who gave us feedback on our book, including Joan Brill, Tim Cauller, Maria Estrada, Gail Pizzola, and Mark Putnam; to students in Observation of English Teaching (EN 694) at Indiana University of Pennsylvania, including Muhamed Alkalil, Abdulaziz Alnofal, Ali Mohammad AlSehri, Maria Luciana Beltramo, Chin-hui Chen, Katherine Lai, Noh-shin Lee, Frances Lin, Patricia Miller, Yuji Ogura, Hyeong-Kyun Oh, Robert Palmer, Jennifer Ritter, Paige Tomkinson, Mi-Lim Ryoo, Nancy Shepardson, Akiko Suzuka, Patricia Tompkins, Lu Xu, and Dorothy Yoo; to students in Language Teacher Supervision and Language Teacher Education at the Monterey Institute of International Studies, including Michelle Bettencourt, Mary Chang, Maria DaCosta, Komal Deshpande, Ruth Dilsiz, Noel Harris, Brian Howell, Deanna Kelley, Esther Kim, Jonathan Langley, Heather MacLean, Erin McDermott, Debie Mirtle, Marissa Monty, Adam Myers, Rachel Nason, Julie Pfeffer, Allison Rainville, Kyla Stinnett, Stephen Tharp, Linda Wade, Gordon Walker, and Toni Washuta.

We thank David Thorstad and Olive Collen for their careful editing. We also thank Ida Roman and Geraldo Contereros for their research assistance, Mio Nishimura and Pat Tirone for their graphic design help, and Peter Shaw for going the extra mile at MIIS. We would particularly like to thank John F. Fanselow for his feedback on Chapters 1 and 2, Leo van Lier for his feedback on Chapter 4, and Jim Roth for his contribution to Chapter 6. We also thank the Japan Association for Language Teaching for granting us permission to republish parts of Chapter 11 and William Acton and Taeko Kamimura for their roles in making this happen.

We also offer our loving appreciation to our wives, Yoko Gebhard and Pat Tirone, for their unswerving patience and understanding.

PART I:
INTRODUCTION TO AN
EXPLORATORY APPROACH
TO TEACHING

In the Preface we highlight how we set ourselves apart from other approaches to teacher education. In Chapters 1 and 2, we discuss our *exploratory approach* to gaining language-teaching awareness. Framing the book, Chapter 1 spells out the assumptions underlying our approach. In Chapter 2, we present an overview of several processes through which teachers can explore their beliefs and practices. Chapter 2 also illustrates how two teachers-in-training carried out explorations in distinct ways that combined several of these awareness-raising processes. Tasks accompanying the content of both chapters allow readers to gain experiential awareness of what we mean by exploring teaching.

1 Exploring our teaching

Jerry G. Gebhard
Robert Oprandy

If the teacher agrees to submerge himself into the system, if he
consents to being defined by others' views of what he is supposed to be, he gives up his freedom to see, to understand, and to
signify for himself. If he is immersed and impermeable, he can
hardly stir others to define themselves as individual. If, on the
other hand, he is willing . . . to create a new perspective on what
he has habitually considered real, his teaching may become the
project of a person vitally open to his students and the world. . . .
He will be continuously engaged in interpreting a reality forever
new; he will feel more alive than he ever has before.

—M. Greene (1973: 270)

Have you ever discovered something new in a place with which you are
very familiar? Perhaps a secret compartment in a desk you have used for
years? Or, in an attic box, love letters written by an ancestor or photos of
family members from past generations? An out-of-the-way alley or street
in a city where you have lived for years? Whatever it is, what was it like to
make this unexpected discovery? Were you surprised? Delighted? Perhaps
a little sad? Why do you think you never saw this thing before?

In this book we invite you to explore a familiar place – classrooms – and
the interaction within them, their pulse. We invite you to share in the excitement, fun, and challenge of discovery and rediscovery of your teaching
beliefs and practices and to find things in your teaching and classroom interaction that have been hidden from view. We invite experienced and inexperienced teachers alike. If you are an experienced teacher, you likely
have explored aspects of your teaching already. We will show you how to
go beyond your usual ways of looking. If inexperienced as a teacher, you
are not new to classroom life. After all, you have participated in classrooms
as a student since you were very young. You have probably spent thousands
of hours observing classroom behavior from the unique position of the student. As such, we invite you to rediscover classroom life from a different
perspective, that of the teacher, so that you might have opportunities to become aware of new things in a very familiar place.

Of course, an exploration may not merely be of some *thing* that is new, but also of an insight about yourself, about others, or about the bigger context in which our teaching lives are situated. About climbing Mount Everest, Thomas Hornbein wrote, "at times I wondered if I had not come a long way only to find that what I really sought was something I had left behind" (in Krakauer 1997: 51). When we explore teaching, we simultaneously probe ourselves and the larger meaning of our endeavor. Although we will stay close to the classroom in what we cover in these pages, we occasionally will stray into the more personal as well as the sociopolitical realms.

To begin this journey of discovery and rediscovery, in this chapter we offer our answers to the following questions:

- What do we mean by exploration of teaching?
- What beliefs and assumptions underlie exploration of teaching?
- How can we go beyond superficial awareness?

While addressing these questions, we also highlight several distinctive features of our exploratory approach to teacher awareness.

What do we mean by exploration of teaching?

The central reason to explore is to gain awareness of our teaching beliefs and practices, or, as Fanselow puts it, to see teaching differently (1988: 114). In assuming the role of teacher as explorer, we carry out such activities as collecting and studying taped descriptions of our own teaching through self-observation, as well as observing in other teachers' classrooms. We also work on action research projects, talk with colleagues about teaching, write in teaching journals, and reflect on and relate personal experience and beliefs to our teaching. How to carry out such explorations is central to this book.

Before providing guidelines for how to explore, as we do in Chapter 2, we first address the beliefs and assumptions that underlie our exploratory approach to developing awareness of teaching.

What beliefs and assumptions underlie exploration of teaching?

We build our approach to exploration around nine beliefs and assumptions:

1. Taking responsibility for our own teaching
2. The need for others

3. Description over prescription
4. A nonjudgmental stance
5. Attention to language and behavior
6. Avenues to awareness through exploration
7. Personal connections to teaching
8. Attention to process
9. A beginner's mind

Taking responsibility for our own teaching

As you read our assumptions underlying our approach to exploration, notice that we use the first person plural *we* to include not only you, but also ourselves as explorers. One reason for doing this is that we genuinely like to explore teaching beliefs and practices and prefer not to distinguish ourselves from other teachers in this regard. Perhaps more experienced than most of our readers, especially considering our combined half century of teaching, we are every bit as much learners as you are. In fact, the activity of writing our ideas, constructing what we think is a coherent text, and then discussing it with each other has forced us to internalize our learning of the ideas in this book at a very deep level. Much of what we have learned in our co-construction of knowledge is evident not only in what appears in these pages, but also in what we chose to modify or leave out of earlier drafts of the book.

A second reason for using the first person plural is our belief that each of us has to take responsibility for our own teaching. The desire to explore must come from within each of us. When we turn John Donne's *Meditation XVII* upside down, as Lou Forsdale (1981) does, we have "Every person is an island, isolated from all others in his or her self, forever physically separated after the umbilical cord is cut" (p. 92).

Not dismissing Donne, who wrote in 1624 that "No man is an island, entire of itself," Forsdale goes on to say, "The anxiety, the loneliness of the isolation moves us to create bridges between our islands . . . transitory bridges, pathways of signals, that carry delicate freight of meaning" (ibid.). We believe, then, that we must, all of us islands, take responsibility for our own teaching. Nevertheless, we must also reach out to others in the process.

The need for others

Exploration cannot be done in a vacuum. As Fanselow (1997) suggests, seeking to explore by ourselves, alone, "is like trying to use a pair of scissors with only one blade" (p. 166). In other words, and as Edge explains

I want to investigate . . . my own teaching. I can't do that without understanding it, and I can't understand it on my own . . . [I] need other people: colleagues and students. By cooperating with others, we can come to understand our own experience and opinions. We can also enrich them with the understandings and experiences of others. (1992: 4)

Another reason to explore something with others is the joy of seeing it through another person's perceptual filter, one who has a fresh take on it. A former student once told one of the authors, Robert Oprandy, of her young son's first visit to Washington, D.C. They looked down the mall from the Lincoln Memorial at the Washington Monument. When she told her son that was the next place they would visit, he stared at the vertical height of the obelisk and whined in a somewhat scared voice, "I don't want to go into space!" Seeing the monument as a spaceship, the boy gave a fresh perspective that made sense when seen through his eyes. Undoubtedly, he had seen TV and photographic images of spacecraft liftoffs. Perhaps he and his mother had earlier visited the National Air and Space Museum at the Smithsonian Institution and images of its spacecraft and airplanes were fresh in his mind.

In our teacher education programs, we relish having novice teachers mixed in with experienced ones. Fresher observations and thoughts about classroom practices and teaching theories rubbing up against the reality checks provided by more experienced visions of teaching make for rich discussions and more topics and questions to explore. Differing perspectives provide choices.

Others help us to explore our own teaching through the consideration of such choices. Fanselow explains:

The need I have for others to enable me to travel roads on my own at first seems to be paradoxical, if not contradictory. But I feel I need others to have experiences with so I can make choices. The insights, knowledge, and advice of others provides me with choices as well as stimulation. With choices I can compare. (1997: 166)

In writing this introductory chapter together, for example, each of us had to be responsible for our own thinking. At the same time, though, we had the need for our cowriter to attach himself to our thoughts and words and bridge the gap between our styles of writing, the relationship we are trying to establish with you the reader, and the ideas we wish to communicate to you.

Description over prescription

Before discussing our preference for a descriptive approach to exploring, we begin with a story that illustrates prescription:

I had taken a part-time job at a well-known language school, and as a part of that job I was expected to be open to being supervised. One day a person I had never seen before walked in and sat down as I was in the process of teaching a reading lesson. I was trying out a few new ideas and wanted to see the consequences of not going over vocabulary before having the students read. Instead of presenting vocabulary, I was having the students read a story several times, each time working on a different task such as underlining words which described the person in the story or crossing out words they did not know. The supervisor sat in the back of the room taking notes, and I became nervous. After the class, the supervisor came over to me. She smiled and whispered that she would like to meet with me at her office after the class. At this meeting, she opened by leaning over, touching me on the arm, smiling and saying, "I hope you don't mind. I'm not one to beat around the bush." I sank a little further into my chair. She proceeded to tell me that I should always write difficult vocabulary on the board and go over it before the students read, that students should read aloud to help them with pronunciation, and that in every class there should be a discussion so that students have the chance to practice the new vocabulary. (Gebhard 1984: 502–503)

You can likely identify with the teacher's experience of being supervised. The supervisor believes that she knows the best way to teach and tells the teacher, in a prescriptive manner, how he should be teaching.

Whether it is a supervisor who is prescribing, or other teachers or even ourselves, we see several problems with the use of prescriptions. To begin with, there is little evidence that any one way of teaching is better than another in all settings. Research on the relationship between teaching and learning does offer some interesting and relevant ideas that we can try out in our teaching, but research has not, and likely never will, produce *the* methodology we should follow to be effective teachers (Kumaravadivelu 1994).

A second problem with prescriptions is that they can create confusion within teachers. Some teachers might want to experiment by trying something different just to see what happens, but they might refrain from doing so because they (or others, such as the supervisor in the story above) believe that there must be a *correct* or *best* way to teach. This quandary over exploring versus teaching in the best way could very well lead to a feeling of "half-in-half-out engagement"[1] in which the teacher has mixed feelings over conforming to someone else's preferred way of teaching and exploring his or her own way.

A third problem concerns the rights of teachers. When others tell us how we should teach, we lose the "right to be wrong."[2] The right to teach the way we want to is very important for teachers. If we lose this right, we may

---

1 This idea of "half-in-half-out engagement" is mentioned in Rardin (1977), who describes ESL students who do not feel fully accepted into a class.
2 This idea of having the right to be wrong comes from reading Rowe (1974).

lose the courage to try new ideas, to explore more than one alternative, to explore freely.

A fourth problem is that prescription can force us to comply with what those "in authority" believe we should be doing in the classroom. This does not allow us, as teachers, to become our own experts and to rely on ourselves, rather than on others, to find answers to our teaching questions.[3] As a result of others making decisions for us, we also lose the chance to discover awareness of our own teaching beliefs and practices. Such experiential knowledge can liberate us and build our confidence so that we can indeed make our own teaching decisions based on our teaching context and knowledge about students, teaching, and ourselves.[4]

Rather than encourage teachers to follow prescriptions, we urge them to collect descriptions of teaching. Descriptions provide a way of portraying what happens in classrooms that can be useful to us. They can provide a mirror image for us to reflect on our own teaching, as well as to talk about teaching possibilities. If we have a detailed description of classroom interaction, we can analyze what went on in the classroom, offer interpretations about the value of what went on, and generate alternative ways we might teach specific aspects of the lesson. Throughout this book, we offer many ways to collect, analyze, and make use of descriptions of teaching. It is through descriptions, more than prescriptions, that we can gain deeper awareness of our teaching and empower ourselves to know how to make our own informed teaching decisions. We have found that descriptions are more powerful than prescriptions in fostering the spirit of exploration we seek to promote.

A nonjudgmental stance

In addition to believing that exploration is both an individual and a collaborative endeavor and that there is more value in description than prescription, we strongly believe that as teachers as explorers, we need to let go of our judgments about our own teaching or the teaching we observe because such judgments can get in the way of seeing teaching clearly. In other words,

---

3 The idea that teachers need the opportunity to become their own experts, rather than to depend on others, is not new. Jarvis (1972) was one of the first teacher educators we know of to emphasize this need. Fanselow (1977a, 1987, 1997) and Fanselow and Light (1977) have also voiced this opinion and have shown ways that this can be done.

4 Mehan (1979) points out that prescribing is oppressive. However, providing people with ways of looking reminds them that they are capable of acting on the world, and that these actions can transform the world.

Task Break[5]

1. Choose a topic you know a lot about. Discuss it in as descriptive a way as you can and see if your detailed descriptions help you explore some aspect of the topic in a novel way.
2. Why do we recommend descriptions over prescriptions? Are prescriptions always wrong? Can you think of any situations inside or outside a teaching context where prescriptions might be useful?

---

judgments, whether positive ("Good job!") or negative ("I'm not very good at teaching grammar"), can raise emotions that interfere with a focus on description.[6] In this regard, we have found the ideas of W. Timothy Gallwey (1974, 1976) to be useful.[7] He emphasizes that we need to let go of our human inclination to judge ourselves and our performance as either "good" or "bad." He suggests that tennis players replace such judgmental remarks as "What a lousy serve!" and "I have a terrible backhand" with descriptions that allow the player "to see the strokes as they are" (1974: 30). For example, the player can pay attention to the spot he or she throws the ball during the serve before making contact with the racket, the direction the ball goes, and so on. Gallwey makes the point that when the judgments are gone, so are the feelings that are associated with them, feelings that can create tension and take attention away from gaining awareness of what is actually going on. The mind, he says, can be "so absorbed in the process of judgment and trying to change this 'bad' stroke, that [the person might] never perceive the stroke itself" (ibid., 32).

Over the years we have related Gallwey's tennis examples to exploration of our own teaching, as well as introduced his concept of *nonjudgment* to other teachers. Our message is that, rather than make judgments about our own or others' teaching, we prefer to explore by describing teaching, something we emphasize throughout this book.

---

5 We encourage you and other teachers you know to do the tasks on your own and then to share your ideas with one another.
6 Simon and Boyer (1974) first brought our attention to the effect both negative and positive judgments can have on describing teaching.
7 Earl Stevick (1980) was one of the first to relate Gallwey's (1974) ideas on judgment to second language teaching. Fanselow (1987) also discusses Gallwey's ideas on judgment.

Task Break

1. Besides the verbal use of language, list other ways we express or demonstrate judgments. Can silence be judgmental? If so, can you think of an example?
2. Do you feel you are capable of achieving Gall-wey's state of nonjudgment (*a*) in regard to your teaching, and (*b*) in other aspects of your life?
3. Listen to conversations in everyday places. Jot down short dialogues you hear that include lines that show judgment. If needed, add intonation markers and sketch or write a description of non-verbal behaviors, for example, a facial expression that shows judgment. Analyze your descriptive notes. What did you discover?

Attention to language and behavior

In addition to nonjudgmental description, we see value in paying close attention to the use of language and behavior. We have listened to and participated in a multitude of conversations about teaching, and one thing that is obvious is that teachers and teacher educators often use vague words to talk about teaching.[8] We have heard teachers say such things as "My instructions weren't very clear," "The students need more encouragement," and "I like the atmosphere in the class." We have also heard teacher supervisors say things such as "Get the students more involved," "Show more enthusiasm," and "Try to get the students to be more interested in the class." As we listen, it is apparent that such language is vague and, as a result, discussions about teaching seem to be based on a great amount of miscommunication.

Words such as "encouragement," "clear," "atmosphere," "enthusiasm," and "interested" are *high-inference* words. In other words, they have different meanings for different people. For example, when one teacher hears the word "involved," she might think of a class of students attentively listening to a teacher lecturing from the front of the room. Another teacher might think that "involved" means students talking loudly in groups and the

---

8 For years, Fanselow (1977a, 1987, 1997) has pointed out the vague language that teachers use to talk about teaching. His ideas have directly influenced our understanding of the problems associated with the use of general vague words to describe teaching.

teacher walking from one group to the next. A third teacher might envision students deeply engrossed in reading silently at their seats.

Task Break

Study the following lines from M. M. Bakhtin's book *The Dialogic Imagination*:

"The word in language is half someone else's. . . . [It] is not a neutral medium that passes freely and easily. . . . It is populated – overpopulated – with the intentions of others" (1981: 292). What do these lines mean to you?

Recognizing a need to have a common language that can be shared by teachers, some educators offer observation systems that can be used as a metalanguage to talk about teaching. One such system that has gained some recognition for its usefulness is Allen, Fröhlich, and Spada's (1984) COLT (Communicative Orientation of Language Teaching). The most detailed we know of is Fanselow's (1977a, 1978, 1982, 1987) FOCUS (Foci for Observing Communication Used in Settings), which is discussed in detail in Chapter 3. Such coding and observation systems raise awareness through the precision of the metalanguages they provide for teachers in talking about what they do. Teachers trained in the use of such systems can get beyond the vagueness of high-inference words such as "atmosphere" and "enthusiasm." Good and Brophy concur with us when citing one of the reasons why teachers are often unaware of what happens in their classrooms: "Historically, many teacher education programs have failed to equip teachers with specific teaching techniques or with skills for labeling and analyzing classroom behavior. Too often they gave teachers global advice (e.g., teach the whole child, individualize instruction) without linking it to specific behavior" (1997: 35). They agree that "*Conceptual labels* are powerful tools in helping teachers to become aware of what they do" (ibid., 36) and cite research findings that point to instances in which teacher education programs have failed to give teachers the metalanguage for labeling and monitoring their classroom behavior. Terms such as "quarterback sneak" in U.S. football or "checkmate" in chess have unique meanings in the context of playing or discussing those games. Participants or observers have a limited understanding of those games if they do not understand such terms. Why should teaching be any different?

FOCUS, for example, provides a common language to talk about teaching. Such a specific shared language can make communication among educators easier because it facilitates the sharing of meaning. Without this, teachers and their supervisors have to play internal guessing games about the vague words usually used to talk about teaching. Take, for example, the following statement in FOCUS terms: "I see a pattern in my *reacting* moves to their *responses* with 'very good,' even when a *response* misses the mark." It is less likely that miscommunication will take place when this precise metalanguage is used rather than vague statements such as "I seem to dominate the class." Also, in the former case the conversants are focused on describing what is happening, whereas in the latter example, a more judgmental tone creeps into the conversation.

Such specific descriptions not only make communication easier. They also allow us to describe teaching in such a way that we may more easily generate alternatives in our teaching. The supervisor working with the teacher in the example above might suggest or brainstorm with the teacher the following alternatives: "You could change the *source* of the *solicits* from yourself to the students by having them write down questions to ask you and each other"; "You could *react* to the student *responses* by being silent to see if other students react verbally." The idea here is to use a metalanguage to talk about teaching rather than to use general statements and words. Going beyond general words provides a means for teachers to increase comprehension (to be "on the same page," so to speak) and to have a language through which to generate teaching alternatives. Another important element here is in generating alternatives. The words "You could" are not usually meant as directives or as better ways to teach. They are, instead, meant as alternatives worth exploring for the sake of learning more about classroom dynamics. (We go into the use of FOCUS and how to generate alternative teaching behaviors in more detail in Chapter 3.)

We also recognize that teachers (with or without their supervisors) often follow a particular pattern of discourse when talking about teaching. We discuss this in Chapter 6, where we introduce the idea of how teachers (and teacher–supervisor pairs) can explore other ways than the usual ones when they converse about teaching. An example of three teachers breaking the mold (to some extent) is the subject of Chapter 8.

One important ingredient in changing the nature of the discourse is the role that listening plays. In paying attention to communication, teachers and supervisors need to consider how crucial listening is in opening up the conversational space (Edge 1992; Oprandy 1994b; Rardin, Tranel, Green, and Tirone 1988).

Rardin et al. emphasize how essential listening, or what they call *understanding*, means in relation to communication:

It is not only the basis of a sound interpersonal communication process but also of human belonging, which is essential to a learning community. A sense of secure belonging, regardless of one's difference from others or inadequacies, is the "glue" of the teaching-learning relationship. It is what holds the relationship together and gives it life and meaning. (1988: 53)

Establishing an understanding relationship is central in creating the kind of learning community in which learners are recognized as knowers in their own right and in which their unique learning process is acknowledged. "By genuinely becoming learners of them, the teacher conveys a deep regard for them as persons" (ibid., 22), not just as learners. This enables both teachers and students or teachers and their supervisors to explore one another's contributions to their co-construction of knowledge.

Avenues to awareness through exploration

In this section we address the following four *avenues to awareness,* which suggest different ways to explore our teaching:

1. problem solving
2. seeing what happens by
   a) trying the opposite or
   b) adapting random teaching behaviors
3. seeing what is by
   a) contrasting what we do with what we think we do or
   b) considering what we believe in light of what we do, and
4. clarifying our feelings

The first of these is a heavily traveled route; the others are roads less traveled. We encourage you to try different routes from time to time in expanding your awareness of teaching.

To focus your attention on *exploring through problem solving,* please imagine that you teach an 8 A.M. class and many of the students consistently come late to class. This presents a problem of trying to understand what causes the students' behavior. Are the students partying too much and cannot get out of bed in the morning? Are they studying late because they have too much homework? Don't they see the value of the class? Then, you try to solve the problem. You might have a heart-to-heart talk with the tardy students to let them know how you feel and discover why they come to class late. Based on what you find out, you change some aspect of the class or your behavior and see what happens.

Such a problem-solving process is a normal part of teaching. Certainly, each of us gains a certain amount of awareness about our teaching beliefs and practices as we work out problems. Besides this common avenue to awareness are at least three others, ones that most teachers we have worked with find very useful, even fun.

One not-so-usual avenue to awareness is to *explore simply to see what happens*. To do this, Fanselow (1987, 1992a, 1997) suggests we try the opposite to our usual modus operandi. For example, if we are aware that we say "very good" after most student responses, we can be silent. If we find we give our instructions verbally, we can try writing them down for students to read. If we always teach from the front of the classroom, we can try teaching from the back. The idea is to discover what we normally do and to try the opposite to see what happens.

Another way to explore, adapted from Fanselow, is to see what happens by adapting random teaching behaviors. This can be done by writing down different teaching behaviors on slips of paper, including behaviors that we do not normally use. The idea is to select one or two of these slips of paper randomly and to adapt our teaching to include the behaviors written on them. Just for fun, it is also possible to select several slips of paper and to design an entire lesson based on what is written on them. Besides being fun and tapping our imagination and creativity, this can lead to some surprising discoveries. One way to select behaviors is to use categories from an observation system such as FOCUS. The categories and subcategories are rich with possibilities. Of course, it is also possible to use nontechnical words, such as "students ask questions to teacher," "students ask each other questions," "silence," "overhead projector," "candle with lights out," "bottles," "lesson content about students' lives."

In addition to exploring simply to see what happens, another avenue to awareness is *exploring to see what is*. This is at least a two-lane avenue to explore. One is *exploring what we actually do* in our teaching *as opposed to what we think we are doing*. To accomplish this, we need to become aware of what we think we are doing by keeping a record, perhaps writing in a journal. We then need to collect descriptions of our teaching relevant to the areas of our teaching under study. For example, if a teacher thinks that she has designed group work activities in which students are spending a lot of time working on the task, she could check this by tape-recording students during group work. (The trick is to get natural interaction, with students not doing things differently because of the tape recorder.) By taping and analyzing several groups interacting over the tasks the teacher gave them, she can determine if what she thinks is going on is indeed occurring.

A second lane to explore on the same avenue is considering *what we believe as teachers in relation to what we actually do*. Do our beliefs match our actual practices? To illustrate what we mean here, we will use a master's thesis research project carried out by Jimenez-Aries (1992). Among other things related to error treatment, the investigator was interested in learning about what ESL teachers who taught at the university language institute believed about error treatment in relation to how they treated errors. She interviewed two teachers to learn about their beliefs about treatment of oral errors. She also observed them teach. She discovered a variety of consistencies and inconsistencies. For example, she learned that one of the teachers believes in minimal error treatment, but in actuality, she corrected very often. She also discovered that the other teacher, who said she believed in treating errors as soon as they occur, as long as the treatment is not disruptive, consistently treated errors as soon as they occurred. This same teacher also stated that she explored a variety of techniques, depending on the situation. In fact, however, she consistently used the same technique to treat most errors. Jimenez-Aries's study shows that much can be gained by defining our beliefs about teaching, then seeing whether or not our behavior in the classroom matches them.

Finally, we can *explore to gain emotional clarity*. By exploring our feelings, we can gain awareness about things we feel deeply about or do not really care about, or are ambivalent about. This affective side of teaching is often neglected. Our feelings about things can affect our behavior, so we see a need to explore the emotional side of ourselves, including how we feel about ourselves, the students, teaching, and more.

We see personal journals (as opposed to dialogue journals that are read by others) as particularly suited for this type of exploration. Private journals are a place we can express our feelings without the threat of having to bring them out into full view. And, such exploration of feelings, coupled with other ways to explore, such as self-observation, reading, and talk with other teachers, can raise awareness of links between our personal and our professional lives (discussed in Chapter 7). It is through such exploration of feelings, for example, that some teachers discover a strong belief while writing in their journal after reading Jersild's (1955) classic *When Teachers Face Themselves*. Of the connections they make, Jersild says: "A teacher cannot make much headway in understanding others or in helping others to understand themselves unless he is endeavoring to understand himself" (p. 14).

Personal connections to teaching

Another distinguishing feature of the exploratory approach to teaching awareness is having teachers connect who they are (becoming) as teachers with who they are. We recognize that we all have unique connections to make, given the diverse contexts we live out at work and elsewhere. As such, we feel we can greatly benefit from formulating *connecting questions*, that is, questions that connect our professional teacher persona with our personal, out-of-school selves. We might, for example, think about how we label students and people in general – and then explore whether a tendency to do so in class carries over to those we relate to in nonschool settings and vice versa. Or we might consider simpler, easier-to-see connections – for example, who and what we can bring into class from the outside community that will engage our students. Another area to explore is what we notice when we study or just pick up new skills and knowledge in a variety of subject areas (carpentry, dance, aerobics routines, and so on) that have lessons for us as teachers.

These links between who we are as people and as teachers are rarely dealt with in teacher education programs. We feel that they should assume more importance in the lives of those of us who want to gain awareness of our teaching. Teachers' contexts – especially given how mobile so many of us are at this time in history – change quite often, and at times dramatically. As a result, the same may be true of our connecting questions.

Personal connections to teaching allow teachers to relate anything in their life experiences to teaching, thus encouraging explorations well beyond the teaching act itself. The central aim is to foster reflective exploration that makes teaching come alive in whatever we do and wherever we go. Such personal exploration may go further in the long run in opening up awareness of our teaching than mastery of the latest techniques and methods of language teaching. After all, teaching fads come and go, but teachers remain in their classrooms, facing new challenges and students to work with every time they begin a new class.

Attention to process

We see value in teachers being attentive to the process of exploration. It is through understanding the process of exploration that we know how to explore. Also, by practicing exploration we deepen as well as expand our understanding of the process. Attention to the process of exploration is a key to continuing our professional development. Without a process to follow, we cannot be systematic in our efforts to gain awareness of our teaching, and, as a consequence, we will likely end up gaining this or that glimpse of our teaching practices and beliefs without being able to gain any real depth.

Throughout this guide, we provide several processes through which we can gain awareness of our teaching beliefs and practices. For example, in

Chapter 3 we show a process of observation adapted from Fanselow (1988), which includes how we can observe, analyze, and interpret our teaching. In Chapter 4 we adapt ideas from Crookes (1993), van Lier (1993), Wallace (1998), and others to show how to use action research as a way to explore teaching. In Chapter 5, adapting ideas from Bailey (1990) and others, we show how to use a teaching journal to process our teaching.

We want to emphasize, however, that although each of these processes is different in some ways, our adaptation of them includes important salient characteristics related to exploration of teaching. We feel that these processes contribute to the development of an exploratory approach to teaching when they are grounded in the assumptions about exploration we sketch out in this chapter. As we mentioned earlier, these include an understanding that we are each responsible for gaining awareness of our own teaching, but at the same time, we still need to collaborate with others; that we study descriptions of teaching, rather than follow prescriptions; that we pay attention to language and behavior; and that we consciously follow different avenues to exploration.

A beginner's mind

We feel that it is important for teachers to explore, as much as possible, with a beginner's mind (Suzuki: 1970). This means that we try to begin our conversations, observations, conferences, and other teacher education activities without preconceived ideas about what we think should be going on in the classroom. We agree with Fanselow (personal communication), who illustrates how he wants to approach his communications with other teachers from a beginner's mind:

What level is the class? Don't tell me. What is the goal of the lesson? Don't tell me. What is the type of activity you are going to use and what content are you teaching? Don't tell me. Let me try to hear what the students say and what you say. And let me try to see some things you and the students do. Let me not try to think of comprehension questions, or focused listening, or warm-up, or role play. Let me try to see and hear what communications are taking place and what communications seem not to be taking place.

The point is put another way by the Zen master Shunryu Suzuki:

When you listen to someone, you should give up all your preconceived ideas and your subjective opinions; you should just listen to him, just observe what his way is. We put very little emphasis on right and wrong or good and bad. We just see things as they are with him, and accept them. (1970: 87)

How can we go beyond superficial awareness?

The four concentric circles shown in Figure 1.1 illustrate the central thrusts of this book. The chief aim is for each of us – and the colleagues we choose to work with – to gain a heightened awareness of who we are as teachers. (The inseparability of who we are as teachers and as people is indicated in the illustration by parentheses around "teacher.") Achieving this aim requires a greater than superficial awareness of our teaching beliefs and practices. Such a level of awareness is fostered by our attention to exploratory processes, which is what most of the chapters emphasize. The assumptions underlying exploration, as explained in this chapter, provide a ground-

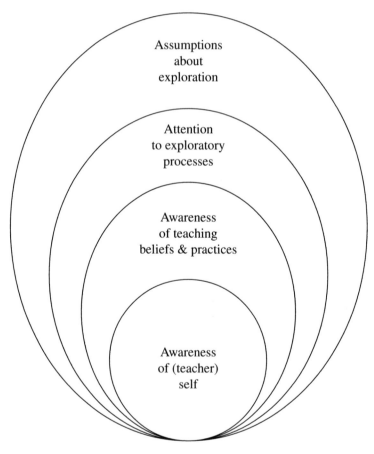

Figure 1.1

ing or backdrop for being more systematically attentive to exploring and being more aware of our teaching.

Jon Krakauer, mountain climber and author of *Into Thin Air*, describes the essence of exploring:

I dreamed of ascending Everest myself one day; for more than a decade it remained a burning ambition. By the time I was in my early twenties climbing had become the focus of my existence to the exclusion of almost everything else. Achieving the summit of a mountain was tangible, immutable, concrete. The incumbent hazards lent the activity a seriousness of purpose that was sorely missing from the rest of my life. I thrilled in the fresh perspective that came from tipping the ordinary plane of existence on end. (1997:23)

Teaching has been a major focus of our existence, and one full of hazards as well. How receptive will classes be to the activities planned? Will personal energies and interpersonal chemistry allow for the unfolding of events intended in our lesson plans? Will the arrangements we make for students to receive, work with, and construct knowledge be sufficient, and will we be flexible enough to move the group closer to our goals and their needs? Every time we walk into a classroom to teach there is a fresh perspective similar to what Krakauer finds on mountains, "tipping the ordinary plane of existence on end." Our commitment to teaching remains very much alive, even after our combined half century of teaching, because there is so much more to explore.

2 *The process of exploration*

Jerry G. Gebhard
Robert Oprandy

> On a crystal-clear night I was struck by the crescent moon
> appearing so three-dimensional, so much like a ball, that it
> was the first time I realized experientially that it was really
> round. Before that night, I had merely seen the moon as a
> two-dimensional object in space. Transfixed by this "dis-
> covery" and perplexed by why I had not realized this sooner,
> I stared at the moon on and off for a couple of hours that
> night.
>
> —R. Oprandy

We liken the child described here, who discovered something new in a familiar place, to the teachers and teacher educators interested in our exploratory approach to teacher awareness. Having explained the assumptions underlying this approach in Chapter 1, we turn now to the process
of exploration and how it can lead to more than a superficial awareness of
teaching. In doing so, we address two questions:

- How can we explore our teaching?
- How can exploration lead to awareness?

While addressing these questions, we also direct your attention to the content of the subsequent chapters of this book.

How can we explore our teaching?

Each chapter in Part II treats a different means of exploration. What follows
is a road map of the five pathways you will travel in Chapters 3 through 7
and for which we provide examples of actual teachers' explorations in
Chapters 8 through 11.

Exploring through observation

One way we can explore our teaching is to observe other teachers. In Chapter 3 we illustrate a detailed process of observation that includes describing, analyzing, and interpreting observed teaching. Many of the ideas in Chapter 3 are based on the thinking of John Fanselow, a leader and innovator of exploratory teaching who highlights how observation can contribute to our awareness of teaching. By observing others, Fanselow points out, each of us has the chance "to construct, reconstruct, and revise our own teaching" (1988: 116). He makes it clear that we can gain self-knowledge and self-insight by observing what teachers and students do in classrooms and other settings. He also makes the point that when we generate our own alternative ways to teach based on our observations of what others do, we are constructing our own knowledge.

Fanselow (1977a, 1987) also sees value in observing ourselves teach.[1] To gain awareness of our teaching, he advocates that we first understand the patterns or rules we follow in our teaching by taping, transcribing, and analyzing interaction in our own classrooms. Once we understand those patterns, we can generate alternative ways to teach. As mentioned in Chapter 1, we can explore by trying the opposite to see what happens or by replacing one teaching behavior with another. For example, if a teacher discovers that she is always the source of information when doing dictation, she might have a student be the source while she writes the information on the board. If the teacher asks mostly questions about language, she might try asking questions about students' personal lives. If the teacher has students read aloud, she might have them read silently. No matter which alternative is used, the idea is to try something different to see what happens.

As we pointed out in Chapter 1 about exploration in general, generating alternatives, whether based on self-observation or observation of other teachers, does not have to be concerned with fixing problems. We can try out alternative techniques to explore simply to see what happens. It is through an awareness of what and how we teach, and the consequences

---

1 In addition to Fanselow, there are others who promote second language teacher-observation. Dick Allwright (1988), for example, gives a history of observation as a teacher education tool, including ways that observation has been used to provide feedback to teachers. Allwright and Bailey (1991) give an understanding of observation as it relates to research. Allen, Fröhlich, and Spada (1984) provide an observation scheme they call COLT (Communicative Orientation of Language Teaching), which can be used to better understand the communicative nature of classrooms. Day (1990) provides different approaches to observation, while Fanselow (1992a), Gebhard (1996), Nunan (1990), and Wajnryb (1992) provide a variety of observation tasks.

of our teaching on classroom interaction, that we can continue to see different ways to teach, as well as form our beliefs about the relationship between teaching behavior and student learning. An illustration of the process of teachers observing their own teaching, as well as their reported comments on the value of self-observation as a way to develop, are presented in Chapter 9.

Task Break

Can you remember a time when you consciously decided to break a pattern you had become accustomed to? What made you aware of the pattern and what caused you to break out of it? What happened as a result of trying out an alternative to the old pattern?

Exploring through action research

Another way we can explore our teaching is through action research, which is discussed in Chapter 4. Action research includes (1) posing problems and addressing concerns based on what goes on in our own classrooms, (2) systematically working through the problems or concerns by creating and initiating a plan of action, and (3) reflecting on the degree to which the plan works. Often action research is a community effort, in other words, discussed with other teachers who offer their support and experience. In addition, as Crookes (1993) demonstrates, action research can take us beyond the confines of the teacher's classroom. When we discover that we share similar problems (e.g., large numbers of students across the program cutting classes, complaining about the curriculum, and not doing homework) and that these problems cannot be solved easily within the walls of the classroom, it becomes an institutional or school problem, one that requires collaboration among teachers, students, and administrators.

Action research is not always associated with exploration because of its narrow "problem-solving" approach to teaching. When the objective of doing action research is just to find a solution to a problem or a best way to teach, then it cannot be considered as exploration as we defined it in Chapter 1. However, if we take on a nonjudgmental descriptive stance and approach problem solving with the idea of learning more about our teaching beliefs and practices, the process of doing action research can provide us with opportunities to explore our teaching.

A number of books and articles have been written on action research, although there are surprisingly few published action research studies done by ESL/EFL teachers investigating problems in their own classrooms.[2] However, Burns (1997) illustrates the usual "problem-solving" way action research is done. Having helped lead a national action research project in Australia, she describes a collaborative cyclic research process in which small groups of teachers supported one another as they each raised their own questions, refined issues, posed problems, planned actions, collected data, and reflected on and interpreted what they found. Burns reports on the action research experiences of one of these teachers. The teacher, who taught very diverse groups of students in her Adult Migrant English Service classes, was concerned about the wide variation in levels of the students in her classes. She was uncertain how to manage the class and felt that her planning was "hit and miss." Therefore, she read the literature on managing disparate learning groups and talked to teachers who had experience teaching such students. As a result, she decided to develop materials and create activities at different levels and then to observe how the students responded to them. After doing this, she recognized that students needed freedom to interact with her materials in their own way, that they seemed to get more out of the materials when she relinquished control over how they were supposed to use the materials in their learning.

Burns's research did not end there. Changes in and reflections on classroom interaction allowed her to raise new concerns and pose a new problem. She observed that students would not cooperate during joint activities. Some expressed boredom, irritation, or exasperation, although the teacher thought her activities would engage the students. Recognizing this new problem, she wanted to know why students felt like this, so she decided to consult with each student and to document their comments. She discovered that students did not like activities and discussions that revolved around cultural and social differences, a theme that ran throughout many of the activities she had created. She discovered that students were already deeply aware of ethnic, religious, and political differences from their life experiences and that they did not want to expose and discuss their strongly personal beliefs and values.[3]

2 Burns (1996, 1997) and Burns and Hood (1997) have published a variety of action research projects done in Australia. Although there are not many published action research studies, there are a growing number of detailed non-action-oriented teacher-research studies, such as those found in Bailey and Nunan (1996).

3 To illustrate a different kind of project, one done independently of a collaborative action research group, Cardoza (1994) studied four quiet women in the back of the classroom. Like many teachers, Cardoza was concerned about whether or not quiet

We see the project just described as a usual way of doing action research, but one that takes a limited exploratory avenue toward awareness. The teacher attempts to understand the consequences of her actions and build on her previous knowledge. The teacher's focus is on her recognizing, understanding, and solving a problem in her teaching.

In Chapter 4 we provide several additional examples of action research that aim at both solving problems and gaining awareness of teaching through exploration, and in Chapter 10 two ESL teachers, Helen Collins Sitler and Zubeyde Tezel, describe the action research processes they went through in attempts to pose and work through problems in their teaching within collaborative supportive settings. They also highlight what they gained from doing these projects as it relates to their own beliefs about teaching.

Exploring through journal writing

We see journal writing as contributing to exploration in two unique ways. First, journals can provide a way for us to work through the emotional part of our teaching. By writing in a teaching journal, we can "criticize, doubt, express frustration, and raise questions" (Bailey 1990: 218). We can even accept a journal as a place to vent our frustrations and to work through our judgments. Doing these things allows us to then focus more on exploring our teaching beliefs and practices.

Second, journals can provide a place to articulate and explore such beliefs and practices. They can be used to keep a record of such things as our self-observations and observations in other classrooms, our conversations with other teachers, our teaching ideas, our teaching questions and answers, and the personal connections we make between who we are as teachers and who we are.

As we will see in Chapter 5, journals can be either intrapersonal or dialogic. Intrapersonal journals, in their purest form, are very private, and entries are usually read only by the writer. As with a personal diary, the intrapersonal teaching journal can be used as a place to write freely without fear of

---

students such as these were learning. Posing this problem, she explored these students' true abilities with English and discovered that they were quite capable of expressing themselves in their jobs (where they use their second language, English). One thing we like about the study is that the author gained a fresh perspective on the idea that not voluntarily speaking in class does not necessarily mean not learning. The research project also illustrates that not all perceived problems are actually problems, and that sometimes we need to dig a little more deeply into the students' lives to understand what is actually going on.

others reading it. The fact that the journal is so private creates a wonderful opportunity to openly explore thoughts that we might not be comfortable revealing to another person or to a larger audience.

There is also value, however, in keeping a dialogue journal in which, as teachers, we can read and comment on one another's entries. When we write in a journal and read and comment on entries of other teachers, we can see that we often share some of the same feelings (doubts, frustrations, joys), issues, accomplishments, and problems. A new awareness of such feelings, concerns, and teaching possibilities, as well as ideas for working through issues or negative feelings, might also surface from reading others' journals. Likewise, we can learn about the explorations of others from reading the descriptions and analysis of teaching from their observations, their action research projects, and what they learned from conversations with other teachers.

Exploring through talk with a supervisor

Another way we can explore our teaching beliefs and practices is through talk with a supervisor. But, as with other activities in this book, we promote talk that is exploratory in nature. With this in mind, we agree with researchers of supervisory behavior (Acheson & Gall 1997; Arcario 1994; Waite 1993) who have been proclaiming that the one-way transfer of knowledge, skills, and even attitudes and beliefs that once was characteristic of supervision is limited. In our lengthy experience as supervisors, we have discovered that many teachers prefer to be partners in the discussions of their teaching. They also want to take some initiative in structuring such conversations in order to explore their teaching more fully than the usual discourse structure in teacher–supervisor conferences allows.

In Chapter 6 we make use of our supervisory experience to provide several lenses through which you can take such initiative and possibly gain more control over the nature of the talk you have with supervisors. These lenses also provide willing supervisors insights into how to empower the teachers they work with, leveling the playing field on which they play the roles they do. Both players can thus play a variety of roles and assume a range of stances in their work together.

Consider for a moment this analogy – supervisor : teacher :: teacher : student. Supervision promotes teacher learning, similar to the way teaching fosters student learning. If this assumption has some validity, then much of what we have learned about teaching and learning should also transfer to what supervisors do with teachers. One thing we have learned about classroom interaction is to shift away, at least some of the time, from the "recitation model" of instruction: a teacher solicits students to answer questions, gets students to respond to their questions, and then follows up by evaluating the students' responses. A report of the National Center for Research on Cultural Diversity and Second Language Learning at the University of California, Santa Cruz (1992: 1), states that classroom researchers "have advocated shifting from recitation to more 'real discussion' or classroom 'talk in which ideas are explored rather than answers to teachers' test questions provided and evaluated'" (Cazden 1988: 54). Why should such a shift not also occur in the conferences between supervisors and the teachers they work with?

If we free ourselves from the didactic, formal nature inherent in the roles supervisors and teachers have traditionally assumed, we can more readily explore ideas in the way Cazden (1988) and Barnes (1976) would have teachers do. In the shift toward a more "constructivist" approach to education, learners are encouraged to "actively construct their own knowledge and understanding – by making connections, building mental schemata, and developing new concepts from previous understandings" (National Center for Research on Cultural and Second Language Learning 1992: 1). Similarly, the co-construction of ideas, attitudes, and beliefs about teaching and learning can occur in supervisory sessions if supervisors can loosen the reins and if teachers will take more responsibility for shaking the reins a bit looser themselves. Chapter 6 offers ideas on how to accomplish these goals.

We are fully cognizant of the difficulty of breaking out of the usual prescriptive mold that characterizes such conversations. As much as we try to break the mold, the expectations and previous models of such sessions continue to trap us into sharing clichés and popular jargon about teaching rather than exploring its mysteries in fresh, genuine ways.

In Chapter 6, we first look at the nature of talk teachers usually engage in with supervisors, as well as the roles that are congruent with such talk. Then we encourage you, as teachers, to assume more responsibility for the kinds of talk you have with supervisors while urging supervisors to share such responsibility. Finally, we explore a variety of contexts and activities that promote talk between teachers and supervisors.

Beginning with an understanding of the "canonical conversation of post-observation conferences" reported by Arcario (1994), we encourage you and your supervisor to use such awareness to try something different. You might take a closer look at decisions you can make regarding pre- and post-observation discussions, as well as options available during observations. You can also consider varying the 5 Ws and H of your talks – that is, who will talk, what will be talked about, how discussions will be structured and when, where, and why they will take place. The central goal is to expand the repertoire of possibilities open to you and your supervisor when discussing teaching and learning. Teaching need not be the "lonely profession" it is often said to be (another theme touched on in Chapter 6). Armed with a plethora of possibilities, you can "talk shop" with your supervisor the way we envision craftspeople may have done when the apprenticeship model of education reigned.

Exploring through personal experience

Having focused in Chapter 6 on an interactive way of exploring our teaching, in Chapter 7 we turn to a more introspective approach. The idea of *connecting questions* is introduced – that is, questions that connect who we are as teachers with who we are. Such questions have us relate life experience outside of school to what we do within the walls of the workplace. We will demonstrate how to do this by "thinking aloud" about a series of our own connecting questions. These range from "Do I play the 'believing game'?" and "Am I developing myself personally as well as professionally?" to "How does language teaching fit into my vision of who I am, who I am becoming, and how I'd like the world to be?" As readers, you will be asked to come up with your own connecting questions, both at the beginning of the chapter and after reading about how Oprandy made his own connections.

The kinds of experiences we promote in Chapter 7 are in some ways similar to the one that confronted the artist Georgia O'Keeffe at age 29. Locking herself in her studio, she analyzed all her canvases in as detached a way as she could. In so doing, she became aware of which professor she had tried to please or which well-known artist she was emulating with each painting.

Then an idea dawned on her. There were abstract shapes in her mind integral to her imagination, unlike anything she had been taught. "This thing that is your own is so close to you, often you never realize it's there," she later explained. . . . "I could think of a whole string of things I'd like to put down but I'd never thought of doing it because I'd never seen anything like it." . . . She made up her mind. This was what she would paint. (Lisle 1980: 81)

Thus began what would emerge as her unique contribution to the history of art. Her personal discovery influenced her work in the way that we will invite you to do by working on your personal development. Through such development, and the connections we begin to make with our professional lives, we can see not only who we are (becoming) as a teacher, but also who we are becoming as a person. The two facets of our lives rub up against each other, each informing the other. That is the process we invite you to begin as a result of reading and doing the suggested tasks in Chapter 7.

Task Break

Of the five processes for exploring our teaching – observation, action research, journal writing, talk with a supervisor, and connecting personal experience with teaching – which attracts you the most? Why?

How can exploration lead to awareness of teaching?

We believe that if teachers are given multiple opportunities to develop teaching, they can more easily gain awareness of their teaching. We believe that teachers gain much from doing individual teacher-development activities, such as observing other teachers, keeping a journal, working on an action research project, talking with a supervisor, or working on a personal development project. Each activity alone certainly offers an opportunity for teachers to explore their teaching. However, teachers are provided with even more opportunity to develop when they process teaching through multiple activities, especially if given chances to relate the experience of one activity to that of another.

To illustrate how exploration through multiple activities can lead to awareness, we relate the exploration experiences of two teachers. The first teacher, June, was in a preservice teacher education program in an MA TESOL program and learned to explore teaching through her program of study.[4] The second teacher, Akiko, was a Japanese teacher at an American university.[5] She was a graduate student teaching assistant, and she taught beginning-level Japanese and worked closely with a supervisor who taught her how to explore her teaching.

June's exploration

A novice teacher in a teaching practicum, June was required to team-teach an ESL class, observe her own teaching through video recordings, observe other teachers, do an action research project, discuss teaching with other novices and an experienced teacher (the teacher educator) in a seminar and during supervisory sessions, and write about teaching and observation ex-

---

4 Here we draw from Gebhard (1985, 1990), Gebhard, Gaitan, and Oprandy (1987), and Gebhard and Oprandy (1989).
5 Here we draw from Gebhard and Ueda-Motonaga (1992).

periences in a dialogue journal. In other words, she went through all the processes we explain in Chapters 3 through 6.

As June experienced these activities, she was faced with a number of teaching issues. One was whether or not to treat language errors. She was one of the student teachers who did not treat student oral errors at the beginning of the practicum. June stated that she believed that error treatment does not help students master the second language and can even interfere with their acquisition process. However, she had the opportunity to observe her peers teaching, and they were treating student errors. The topic of error treatment also came up during talks with her supervisor, as well as during discussions with other teachers. June also read an article on error treatment by Fanselow (1977b) that outlines different strategies for treating errors.

Having had these opportunities, June began to question her beliefs about error treatment. She wrote in her journal: "Shall I correct students now or not?" and "Error correction is really like cutting off communication, isn't it?" When listening to a group of teachers talk about how they treat errors, she asked, "Isn't error correction really like changing the subject?"

June received several responses to her questions, all dealing with how to treat errors without cutting off communication. During a seminar, for example, one student teacher suggested she collect sentences with errors, write them on the board, and have students correct them. Another student teacher suggested she tape-record the class, go home and listen to the students' use of language, and design a lesson based on common errors. The teacher educator suggested that she write down sentences with errors on slips of paper while eavesdropping on small-group discussions and give them to individual students to correct for homework.

As a possible consequence of this set of activities over time (observing, reading, talking with her supervisor, writing in her journal, talking with other teachers), June worked through the personal issue of whether or not to treat student errors, and at some point she made a decision to do so. Accordingly, her attitude toward the question of whether or not to treat errors changed, reflecting the development of her beliefs about treatment of student errors. Instead of asking questions about whether or not to treat student errors, June began to ask questions such as "How do you get students to care about the corrections?"

Akiko's exploration

Akiko, a native speaker of Japanese, was hired as an instructor through a university-supervised assistantship to teach beginning-level Japanese to undergraduates. The aim of the course was to teach students to use Japanese for communication purposes to accomplish everyday things – for example, to shop, talk about the weather, and handle basic functions of language, such as apologizing, greeting, and asking for information. Akiko was assigned a text, *Japanese: The Spoken Language* (Jorden & Noda 1987), which included a book and audiotapes. Akiko, along with an undergraduate volunteer native Japanese speaking teaching assistant and seven students, followed the text in a routine way. At the start of class, students broke into pairs to practice dialogues (called *core conversations*). This was followed by pattern practice drills in which students practiced language structures introduced in the dialogues. This led to situational drills that focused on longer dialogues in specific situations.

Akiko met with her supervisor weekly. They saw these meetings as a chance to learn more about teaching and processes of exploration. During their first meetings, they studied short transcripts made from audiotapes of Akiko's class. They also coded the transcripts with FOCUS (Fanselow 1987), the observation system discussed earlier and designed to capture multiple aspects of communication. (See Chapter 3 for a summary of this observation category system.)

At the same time that Akiko was learning to code and analyze coding for patterns, she talked with the supervisor about what was going on in her class. The supervisor listened carefully, careful not to judge her work or to suggest how he would go about teaching her students. Through analysis of the transcripts and coding, coupled with talking through her teaching with the supervisor, Akiko recognized a communication pattern going on in her classes. She found that the members of this class were not genuinely engaged in communication. She asked the majority of the questions, and students only asked questions when she told them to (e.g., "Mr. Miller, ask Ms. Brown a question using the pattern in the book"). She also mostly asked questions to which she already knew the answer, and there was very little reaction to responses to questions from the students, contrary to what frequently happens in everyday communication outside classrooms. She concluded that most class time was spent studying *about* Japanese, rather than learning *to use* Japanese to communicate, and that the goals of the course were not being reached.

Based on this awareness, she raised the question, "How can I provide chances for students to communicate in Japanese?" To move toward a more communicative type of classroom interaction, she decided to ask students questions that contain what Fanselow (1987) calls *life-personal content* (questions that ask about people's lives). She hoped to get students to communicate in Japanese through the use of such questions. Because she knew that many of the students went to a nearby city during spring break, she decided to ask them personal questions about their trip, hoping that such questions would inspire them to communicate in Japanese. On an impulse, she also decided to bring a map of the city so that the students could point out where they went. She audiotaped the classroom interaction to study later whether or not she was successful at getting students to communicate in Japanese through her personal questions.

As planned, she began the class by asking students in Japanese where they went during the spring break. As predicted, a number gave the name of the nearby city. She then asked where in the city they went, and she brought out the map so that they could show her. Then, something new happened. Students started to ask one another questions and to react to one another's comments in Japanese. They asked where different places on the map were, if they went shopping, how expensive things were, whether or not they had fun, and so on. It was the first time that students communicated with one another in Japanese.

Akiko was very happy with how the class went. She learned that small changes in teaching behavior can have big consequences. She also gained further interest in how *life-personal content* can become a part of the interaction in the language classroom, and in pursuit of this interest, she read Fanselow's (1987) and Nunan's (1988) ideas about studying interaction outside the classroom for the purpose of relating natural ways of interacting to teaching. She believed she could glean insight into how she could make changes in her teaching behavior so that her classroom lessons might better prepare students for their "real world challenges" (Johns 1985). In this pursuit, she explored further by tape-recording conversations between Japanese friends (with their permission), making transcriptions of the conversations, coding some of them, and studying them for patterns. She discovered that the sociolinguistic patterns of interaction used in these conversations differed greatly from those in her classes, and she decided to create lessons that would teach students how to interact with one another in appropriate ways. For example, she would teach them appropriate things to say and how to bow when meeting someone for the first time.

A paragraph from Akiko's research report highlights what our book is about:

As I explore my teaching by describing – recording, transcribing and coding communications – rather than by seeking prescriptions and judgments from others, patterns are broken both consciously and unconsciously. I have sought alternatives in teaching and found them. After I found that I have alternatives, I felt freer and securer about deciding on activities for the students. Throughout this experience, I have learned how to see teaching more clearly and differently through a variety of activities. (Gebhard & Ueda-Motonaga 1992: 190)

In short, participating in multiple activities provided both June and Akiko with opportunities to explore and gain awareness of their beliefs and teaching practices. Although these are only two documented examples of the value multiple opportunities have for teachers to explore their teaching, they do support the commonsense notion that the more opportunities we have to explore, the more likely awareness will take place. Increasing awareness, in turn, whets the appetite for further exploration. Such movement is evident in the studies we include in the final four chapters of this book, all of which illustrate the interplay between the teachers' explorations and raised awareness.

We offer this book as a guide to a wide range of activities that should provide opportunities for your own exploration, as they have for teachers like June and Akiko. We hope the ideas and tasks sprinkled throughout these pages result in your gaining awareness about your teaching beliefs and practices, and that your insights will be a catalyst for continuing exploration.

PART II:
PROCESSES FOR
EXPLORING TEACHING

In line with the characteristics of our exploratory approach to teaching, as explained in Part I, Part II presents and illustrates a variety of processes that teachers (including teacher educators) can use to explore their teaching beliefs and practices. Chapters 3 through 7 detail and provide tasks for how to explore through observation, action research, teaching journals, talk with supervisors, and making connections between our personal and professional lives. The processes explained in Part II also serve as a bridge to the illustrative examples in Part III.

3 Seeing teaching differently through observation

Jerry G. Gebhard

> Here I am with my lens to look at you and your actions. As I
> look at you with my lens, I consider you a mirror; I hope to see
> myself in you and through your teaching.
>   —J. F. Fanselow (1988: 114)

Have you ever considered the value of observing other teachers, as
Fanselow suggests in the quote above? Because there is so much all of
us can learn from observing others, this chapter, after defining the complexity of observation, explains and illustrates an observation process
which has been adapted from Fanselow (1987, 1988, 1992a). The process
includes collecting descriptions of teaching, as well as analyzing and interpreting these descriptions. The goal of this process is to construct and
reconstruct our own knowledge about teaching and thereby learn more
about ourselves as teachers. I explain this process by addressing the following questions:

- What is classroom observation?
- What are the purposes of observation?
- How can teachers collect and analyze descriptions of teaching?
- How can teachers interpret descriptions of teaching?

What is observation?

Following the lead of those who have written about observation (Allen,
Fröhlich, & Spada 1984; Allwright 1988; Allwright & Bailey 1991; Day
1990; Fanselow 1977a, 1988, 1992a, 1997; Wajnryb 1992), I define classroom observation as nonjudgmental description of classroom events that
can be analyzed and given interpretation.

35

By "judgment" I mean forming an evaluative opinion or conclusion. This opinion can be negative ("That lesson was terrible today!") or positive ("Great class today!"). A judgment can be conveyed in words or nonverbally – for example, by shaking the head from side to side while frowning to show a negative judgment. "Nonjudgment" is the opposite, that of withholding an opinion or postponing a conclusion. (See Chapter 1 for another discussion on judgments.)

By "description" I mean a verbal or written account of classroom interaction. Later in this chapter, I go into detail on the kinds of classroom interaction that can be described and ways to collect and analyze such data, including the use of prose descriptions and notes, sketches, checklists, tally sheets, transcriptions, coding systems, and photographs. In addition, I discuss how to collect such data through nonparticipant and participant observation.

Finally, by "interpretation" I mean understanding what went on in the classroom in a particular way, to give meaning to the observed descriptions of teaching and classroom interaction. I discuss interpretation in detail in this chapter, including the kind of knowledge we can use to help us in our interpretations, the value of giving our observations multiple interpretations, and how the purpose of the observation can affect our interpretations.

What are the purposes of observation?

Following the lead of Murphy (1992), in this section I discuss the purposes of observation, consider some of the problems associated with these purposes, and highlight the purposes that observation has in regard to the content in subsequent sections of this chapter.

One purpose of observation is to evaluate teaching – a purpose with which most of you are no doubt familiar. A supervisor (usually an experienced teacher), for example, observes the teacher to identify strengths and weaknesses in teaching behavior. The goal is to help the teacher to improve and to become a more effective teacher. As discussed in Chapter 1, however, one problem supervisors face as observers is defining improvement. This is because the relationship between teaching and learning is complex and not enough is known about how the teacher's behavior results in student learning to specify improvement as it relates to student learning in all contexts.

Gaies and Bowers (1990) suggest that there is more than one way to perceive improvement. Rather than basing the concept of improvement on the relationship between teaching behavior and learning activities, improvement can be based on what teachers are expected to be doing in a specific teaching context (as defined by teachers and teacher educators/supervisors within this context), as compared to what they actually do. For example, if the teacher and supervisor within a particular teaching context value teacher movement in the classroom, and if the teacher stands in one spot for the entire class, improvement could be realized if this teacher moved more freely about the classroom.

A second purpose of observation is to learn to teach. Unlike with a supervisory purpose in which the teacher is observed, when the goal is to learn to teach, the teacher is the one doing the observing. This purpose is often used in preservice teacher-education programs. Inexperienced teachers are given chances to visit experienced teachers' classrooms to "pick up the tricks of the trade" (Murphy 1992: 217). The experienced teacher is seen as an expert who acts as a model for the inexperienced teacher.

Inexperienced or novice teachers can learn much from such observation, especially if the models and prescriptions are "presented and seen as samples of possibilities or prods to question what we do" (Fanselow 1997: 167) rather than as prescriptions of what we should do. This is not always how models of teaching are presented, however. In fact, some supervisors and experienced teachers sometimes give the novice teacher the idea that there are best ways to teach, for example, the way the "expert" teacher teaches; and, when teachers build their way of teaching wholly on models, they miss opportunities to learn to make their own informed teaching decisions. As I discuss in this chapter, teachers who can process their teaching by gathering descriptions of teaching (rather than looking for best ways to teach by observing "experts"), analyzing these descriptions, and interpreting or applying meaning to these descriptions, free themselves to be able to make their own informed teaching decisions rather than blindly follow what others say and do.

A third purpose of observation is to learn to observe. In this chapter, I focus attention on visiting classrooms to learn to collect, analyze, and interpret descriptions of teaching in unobtrusive and nonjudgmental ways. (In Chapter 9, teachers discuss and illustrate what they learned about self-observation.) Whether visiting other teachers' classrooms or observing our own teaching, learning to observe well takes time, effort, and practice. As with other things, learning to observe can be a lifelong pursuit. But those teachers who find interest in learning to observe are more aware of teaching than those who do not learn how to observe.

A fourth purpose of observation is to collect data for research purposes. I do not propose that teachers learn to be researchers in the formal sense. I do, however, see the benefits for teachers who are interested in gaining knowledge and experience through research. My own experience and interest in ethnography and other forms of qualitative research have certainly added to my abilities to describe, analyze, and interpret classroom interaction. Later in this chapter, I briefly discuss how teachers can make use of participant observation and ethnographic concepts to gather holistic and contextually relevant descriptions that can provide meaning from the point of view of the participants in the language classroom. (In Chapter 4, I also discuss issues related to observation as a part of doing action research.)

A fifth purpose, one that is central to this chapter and to an exploratory approach to teacher education, is to observe to become more self-aware. Based on Fanselow's (1977a, 1987, 1988, 1992a, 1997) ideas, the goal of observation is for teachers to see teaching differently. The goal is to observe other teachers to construct and reconstruct our own knowledge about teaching and thereby learn more about our teaching attitudes, beliefs, and classroom practices. The more we observe and develop our teaching, the freer we become to make our own informed teaching decisions. With this in mind, let us turn to how teachers can collect and analyze descriptions of teaching.

How can teachers collect and analyze descriptions of teaching?

In this section, I offer discussion on ways to collect and analyze descriptions of teaching from two perspectives. The first is a nonparticipant perspective in which the observer joins the class, but has no plan to take on roles outside that of observer. The second is a participant perspective. Unlike the nonparticipant observer, the participant observer plans to be involved with the class in some way in addition to being an observer. For example, the observer might join students as they interact during small group work, talk with them about the class, or participate as a tutor. A participant observer takes on any number of roles and uses the experience of being a member of a class or group of learners to capture descriptions of teaching. I further define the participant observer in the second part of this section.[1]

---

1 I use these two perspectives, participant and nonparticipant observation, to show two distinctively different approaches to observation. I realize that observation is not always so much one or the other approach but, rather, it is often a combination of participating and not participating, depending on the context and the invitations of those around us.

Collecting and analyzing descriptions of teaching as a nonparticipant observer

Nonparticipant observers can collect descriptions of teaching they observe in a number of ways. One usual way is to take continuous descriptive notes of observed events. Sketches can also be added.

Task Break

1. Locate a place outside classrooms to observe interaction, for example, a coffee shop, home kitchen or living room, library, shopping mall – anywhere people are interacting. Observe what is going on for five minutes.
2. While observing, describe what you see and hear going on. Draw sketches as well.
3. After the observation, study your notes. Write up a report describing what you observed.
4. Consider the kinds of things you were able to describe. How much of the interaction do you think you were able to capture? How much do you think you missed?
5. If possible, compare your observation notes with others' and read one another's reports. Then, answer the questions again in number 4.

After gaining experience describing interaction (outside and inside classrooms) through notes and sketches and comparing their descriptions with other observers, teachers have told me that they are amazed at how varied their descriptions are. This is not surprising when we consider how selective we are in our decisions about what to describe. For example, when I asked a group of teachers to observe interaction at a fast-food restaurant, but gave them no specific kind of interaction on which to focus their attention, some focused on the way the food was ordered and served; others observed the way adult customers ate and talked with each other; one observer focused on the behavior of two children waiting in line to order their food; another paid attention to the way customers come in and go out of the restaurant door.

When observing classroom interaction, much the same thing happens: one observer focuses on describing students' nonverbal behaviors, another prefers to observe the kinds of questions the teacher asks; still others attend to the way language errors are treated, the interaction between students during group work, how students enter the classroom, and so on. It should be obvious that many possible things can be observed in a classroom, not to mention the degree of detail that can be given to any one description.

As our observations are so selective, most observers prefer to make decisions about an aspect of interaction that they will describe before observing a class. Such plans are especially useful if observations are to be shared and compared or if the teacher being observed wants descriptive feedback on a particular aspect of his or her teaching. Likewise, planning what will be observed provides a means to be more systematic in our explorations, to add some control over what it is that we are interested in learning more about. To give an idea of how teachers narrow the focus of their descriptive observations, here is a partial list of some of the areas of teaching that teachers have observed:

- Amount of time teacher waits after asking a question and getting a response.
- The source and target of questions.
- The number and types of questions the teacher and students ask (e.g., either-or, yes-no, Wh-, tag).
- The number of display questions (questions the teacher already knows the answer to) and referential questions (questions to which the teacher does not know the answer).
- The content of the teachers' questions (e.g., how many questions contain content about procedures, general life events, personal issues regarding the students, study of language, study of other subjects besides language).
- The space the teacher uses in the classroom (e.g., where the teacher walks, who the teacher looks at).
- The way the teacher gives instructions (e.g., writes on the board, gives them orally, has students repeat them) and students' reactions to them.
- Amount of time students stay on task during group work.
- Error treatment: Who treats errors, when, how, what kinds of errors?
- The teacher's use of praise behaviors.

This partial list should make it clear that, if left to our own devices, there are a great number of possible aspects of teaching we could focus our attention on while observing. If we do decide to describe some specific aspect of classroom life before observing a class, we can create or make use of predesigned observation instruments to guide our observations, and there are a number of observation vehicles through which to make our descriptions and analysis more systematic and focused, including checklists, tally sheets, notes with short dialogues, transcripts, and category systems.

A *checklist* allows the observer to check off teaching behaviors as they occur. Below there are a few items from a longer checklist to observe vocabulary lessons. This checklist sample was developed by Mutsuko Akamine (1993), a junior high school English teacher in Okinawa. While studying in the United States, she decided to increase her awareness about how vocabulary can be taught. She began by selecting items from a checklist designed by Fanselow (no date), and based on her teaching experience, she created her own short list. Then, while observing vocabulary lessons, she added behaviors to her list, expanding it to several pages of possible teaching behaviors. At the end of the experience, she not only had a comprehensive list of behaviors to draw from and apply to her own vocabulary teaching, but a very useful system to discover and expand her knowledge about how other teachers teach.

A partial checklist: Observing vocabulary Lessons

1. Teacher introduced new vocabulary by   Yes   No
    a. giving definition   _____   _____
    b. giving synonyms/antonyms   _____   _____
    c. teaching prefix/suffix   _____   _____
    d. giving translation   _____   _____
    e. having students guess from context   _____   _____
    f. writing the word in a sentence   _____   _____
    g. demonstrating meaning through gesture   _____   _____
    h. other: _____   _____   _____
2. Teacher used audiovisual aids
    a. realia (things we use every day)   _____   _____
    b. tape recorder   _____   _____
    c. flash cards   _____   _____
    d. overhead projector   _____   _____
    e. handouts   _____   _____
    f. computer   _____   _____
    g. other: _____   _____   _____
3. Teacher taught vocabulary through
    a. drills   _____   _____
    b. Total Physical Response   _____   _____
    c. a game   _____   _____
    d. crossword puzzles   _____   _____
    e. information gap activities   _____   _____
    f. translation/explanation/lecture   _____   _____
    g. other: _____   _____   _____

(Reported in Gebhard 1992)

Another way to collect descriptions of teaching is to *tally behaviors*. This works like a checklist except that each time a behavior is observed, a tally mark is used. Tallying behaviors is fairly easy to do and can provide some very interesting discoveries. I personally find it interesting to tally when students use the target language and when they use their native language in class. When I share my observations with the teachers whose classes I observe, they are often surprised to find out how frequently students use their native language. I also like to tally wait-time behaviors. To do this, I use a watch to count the number of seconds teachers wait between asking a student a question and deciding to intercede with a prompt or even their own response to the question. I often find, as Mary Budd Rowe (1974, 1986) found, that some teachers wait less than one second. Likewise, I have found that some teachers wait about one second after a student answers the question before reacting to the answer. In agreement with Rowe, I also have discovered that for some teachers, increasing wait time to several seconds can also increase the amount of student interaction in class. But I believe that those teachers who are able to do this by waiting also genuinely are interested in what the students have to say. I will always remember what Arno Bellack, who taught me Classroom Centered Research at Teachers College, Columbia University, said to me: "Don't wait in a mechanical way. The purpose of waiting is to give the student time to organize thoughts, and to show you respect this student and are interested in the answer."[2]

Another way to gain descriptions of teaching is to jot down *notes with short dialogues* of interaction. These dialogues do not need to be long, as the example in the Task Break on the next page illustrates.

Through my analysis of this dialogue and others like it, I concluded that June's way of treating Anna's errors was not working. June attempted to treat Anna's errors twice. The first time, she used rising intonation when saying "Two sisters," trying to draw attention to the error and perhaps get Anna to correct herself. Instead, Anna elaborates. Then, when June puts the correction into a question and emphasizes "died" ("She *died* when you were three?), Anna did not catch the correction. Rather, she took June's question as a request for clarification. Fanselow (1987) and Buckheister and Fanselow (1984) call this a "miss."

As a result of this observation, I decided to explore the "hits" and "misses" in my communication with students. To my amazement, I discovered that I do not always communicate with students as clearly as I thought I did. There were lots of "misses" in my own communications with students, not only with

---

2 *Language of the Classroom* (Bellack, Kliebard, Hyman, & Smith 1966) is still a classic on classroom observation.

Task Break

Here's a short dialogue from an ESL class I observed. The teacher, June, is correcting Anna's language error. Analyze this transcript. What happened?

Anna: I have only two sister.
June: Uh-huh.
Anna: I have no brother.
June: Two sisters (June uses rising intonation).
Anna: Because my mother she dead when I was three years old.
June: She *died* when you were three?
Anna: Yes. She dead when I was three years old.

(From Gebhard, Gaitan, & Oprandy 1987)

our error treatment interaction, but in other communications as well. I have been working ever since to have more "hits" than "misses" when I teach!

It is also possible to audiotape or videotape a class – of course, only after gaining permission from the students and the teacher. The advantage of taping is that the observer can have what Mehan (1979) calls "a retrievable database." Said simply, this means that the observer can later review what went on in the class. Although this certainly takes a little more time, it can provide opportunities to study classroom interaction in more depth. For those observers who believe that listening to tapes is too time-consuming, I suggest popping a cassette into the car tape player or Walkman. Even listening to 10 minutes of a class can prove to be interesting and useful.

One additional thing that can be done is to make short *transcriptions* from a tape. These transcriptions can be studied as they are (as you did with the short dialogue of June and Anna) or can be *coded with a category system*. Allen, Fröhlich, and Spada's (1984) COLT (Communicative Orientation of Language Teaching) and Fanselow's (1987) FOCUS (Foci for Observing Communication Used in Settings) are two category systems designed specifically for language teachers. Although it is out of the scope of this chapter to go into great detail about these systems, here I can briefly introduce FOCUS and illustrate how a short transcript can be coded and analyzed for patterns through the use of this system. I also can show how this knowledge can be used to make decisions about alternative ways to teach.

The first major category of FOCUS is the *source and target* of communication. For example, a teacher, a student, a group, a bird, words in a book, a cereal box, a map, a movie are all possible sources of communication. Almost anyone can be a target.

Task Break

Study each set of possible sources and targets of communication. As you study each set of possible combinations, imagine classroom situations or lessons in which the source/target combination might be used. For example, based on set one, I can imagine a lesson with a student, the *source*, telling a group of students, the *target*, about her life. I can then see this same student writing down the story in a letter to a pen pal, a second *target*. If possible, do this task with a partner or as a small group. Also, see if you can come up with additional source/target combinations.

A sample list of source/target possibilities

Possible Sources: **Set One**	Possible Targets: **Set One**
teacher	whole class
student	group of students
	individual student
	self
	pen pal

Possible Sources: **Set Two**	Possible Targets: **Set Two**
textbook	whole class
students' essays	group of students
video recording	individual student
newspaper	
photograph	

The second category of Fanselow's FOCUS is the pedagogical purpose of communication or *move* type, and there are four basic moves. We can *structure* communications, for example, by setting the stage for what will follow (e.g., "Today we will . . ."), by lecturing, or by putting a visual aid on the board. We can also *solicit*, by asking questions or using language that aims at getting a response, *respond* to solicits, and *react* to what is communicated. The third category is the *medium* used to communicate content.

This category includes a *linguistic* medium, such as spoken words or print; a *nonlinguistic* medium, such as things we smell, touch, see, and hear that are not linguistic and that communicate something to us (the smell of fresh coffee, a cold gust of wind, a thick black cloud, a chirp of a bird); a *paralinguistic* medium, such as a gesture, eye contact, facial expressions; and *silence* used purposefully to communicate a message. The fourth category is the *use* of communication to *attend* to mediums around us, as well as to *present, characterize, reproduce, relate,* or *set* content. The last category is the area of *content* that is communicated, including *study, life,* and *procedure.* Each of these major categories has subcategories, allowing for a very detailed description of interaction going on inside or outside classrooms.

Although teachers, including myself, report that it takes some time and effort to understand Fanselow's coding system, many have also said it is well worth the effort. In fact, some teachers, particularly those with an interest in detail and analysis, have told me that FOCUS is not only useful as a way to see patterns of interaction, but can be fun to use. I agree.

The short transcript and coding given below illustrate how FOCUS can be used to code interaction. The interaction is from an intermediate reading class taught in an intensive language program in the United States. There are eleven students in the class, and they are sitting in a circle, the teacher along with them.

A reading lesson	S/T	Move	Medium	Use	Content
O: (Reading passage)	O-C	str	lv	set	so + sl
T: Okay./Wei, please read.	T-S	str/sol	la	ps	p
S1: (Reads)	S-C	res	la	ps	so + sl
T: Okay. What does moonlighting mean?	T-C	sol	la	pe	sl
S2: To work in the nighttime.	S-T	res	la	ps	sl
T: That's right./But, not just nighttime. Daytime, too.	T-S	rea	la	ce/ps	sl
Anything else?	T-C	sol	la	pe	sl
S3: Extra time job.	S-T	res	la	ps	sl
T: That's right./A person who moonlights already has a job.	T-S	rea	la	ce/ci	sl

[O = other (e.g., text object); S = student; T = teacher; C = class; str = structures communications; sol = solicit a response; res = response; rea = reaction; la = linguistic aural medium (e.g., speech); lv = linguistic visual medium (e.g., print); ps = present state (giving information directly); pe = present elicit (asking a question you already know the answer to); ce = characterize evaluate (indicating correctness); ci = characterize illustrate (giving an attribute); p = procedure; so = study of something other than language; sl = study of language.]

Task Break

1. Study the transcript and coding for "A reading lesson" above. Can you identify a pattern in the classroom interaction? For example, what does the teacher consistently do? The students?
2. If possible, compare your analysis of the interaction with that of others who have also studied the transcript and coding.
3. Compare your analysis with the one I give below.

My analysis of the coding shows that the teacher asks all the questions (solicits), the students respond, and the teacher reacts to their responses. The medium used in all the interaction is linguistic aural (speech) or visual (print). In other words, no nonlinguistic or paralinguistic mediums are used purposely to communicate messages. The teacher asks questions that he already knows the answers to, and the content of the questions is mostly about the study of language. In other words, no content is related to life-general issues (those related to groups of people) or to the lives of the students and/or teacher (e.g., if the teacher had said, "I used to moonlight by giving guitar lessons").

This pattern is quite familiar to most teachers, and this kind of teaching pattern can be seen in many classrooms. Yet, it is through description and analysis like the one we just did that we gain the awareness to ask such questions as "How much of my teaching uses this pattern of communication?" and "How could I break this pattern so that students have more chances to ask questions and react to my responses and to those of their classmates?"

FOCUS also provides a means to generate ways to break this pattern of classroom interaction. When I asked a group of novice teachers who had briefly studied FOCUS what they would change to break this pattern of interaction, they came up with the following suggestions:

Ways to break a traditional teaching pattern

- The teacher could ask *life-general* or *life-personal* questions in the *content* category. For example: "Do people in your country moonlight a lot?" or "Have you ever moonlighted?"
- The teacher could change mediums. Instead of using all linguistic aural (speech), the teacher might also include nonlinguistic mediums, such as pictures of different jobs that people take to moonlight.
- The teacher could add silence as a medium. After a student responds to a

question, the teacher could allow time for another student to say something. If the students get the idea that they can react after a response, they might do so more often.

- The teacher could change the source/target of communication by having students do reading tasks in groups by answering questions on a handout or writing their own questions for other groups to answer.

Task Break

As discussed and illustrated, there are a variety of ways that nonparticipant observers can collect and analyze descriptions of teaching. We can use checklists, tally sheets, jot down notes with short dialogues, tape and make short transcripts, and code transcripts with a metalanguage. Which do you find the most interesting? Which do you feel is the most complex? Which do you think will generate useful knowledge about what is going on in the classroom? Which would you like to try out?

Before discussing how teachers can collect and analyze descriptions of teaching as participant observers, allow me to explain a process of cooperative classroom observation that has proven quite useful to a number of teachers. When I first experienced cooperative observation while studying with John Fanselow and Robert Oprandy at Teachers College, I found it to be very informative for both the person being observed and the observers. Over the years it has continued to be instructive while working with teachers in various settings in Japan, the United States, Hungary, and China.

To help explain one way to do cooperative observation, I like to use a set of guidelines I have developed, "Procedures: Live Classroom Observations."

Procedures: Live classroom observations
1. A number of teachers are willing to have you observe their classes. These English teachers teach a variety of subjects and student levels. Sign up to visit a class. At least two, preferably three, observers should sign up to visit a class.
2. Make an appointment and then meet with the teacher to be observed. Ask the teacher what aspects of teaching she or he is interested in learning more about. Feel free to give the teacher a list that includes areas of teaching that can be described (e.g., questioning behaviors, instructions

and students' reactions to them, what students do during group work, use of native and target language by teacher and students, praise behaviors). Also talk with the teacher about proper protocol. For example, can you audio tape, move around the classroom, talk with students? Agree on a day and time to visit the class.

3. Using the teacher's observation interest(s), meet with those who will observe the class to design and/or select observation instruments and ways to collect descriptions of teaching. For example, you could create or locate a tally sheet or checklist, take freehand notes and draw sketches, jot down example dialogues, make tape recordings (only with permission), and plan to use a category system, such as FOCUS.

4. Observe the teacher. Follow the protocol the teacher gave you.

5. Together, as a group who observed the class, meet to analyze your descriptions. Then, write a group report for the teacher. Include a description of the activities that went on in the class relative to the teacher's interest(s). Do not give your interpretations. Let the teacher decide on the meaning of her or his own teaching. But, do give a few alternative ways to teach related to the teacher's interest. Avoid telling the teacher how she or he should teach. Simply point out that these are ideas for the teacher to consider. If possible, meet with the teacher. Give her or him the report. Spend some time talking about the report with the teacher.

Here is an example of how collaborative observation took place in Japan. While on sabbatical in Japan, I taught a speaking practicum to a large group of experienced EFL teachers studying for their M.A. TESOL degree at the Tokyo branch of Teachers College, Columbia University. The students in this practicum were from Japan, Canada, and the United States. All of the students were teaching, for example, at an area high school, a private language school, or in business. As a part of the course, the teachers were expected to observe three classes taught by their classmates and to be observed one time.

One of the observations took place at a YMCA (Young Men's Christian Association) where one of the students in the practicum, a Japanese high school teacher, was moonlighting. Four teachers (including myself) signed up to observe this teacher. We met with her during our weekly seminar for about 20 minutes, and she told us that she wanted to learn more about her way of praising students and students' reactions to her praise. After the meeting, we selected an observation tally sheet designed by Good and Brophy (1997) (and discussed in Day 1990). Because this sheet lists praise behaviors (e.g., teacher praises progress, effort, success, good thinking, imagination, compliant behavior, neatness, thoughtfulness), we discussed the words and what they mean. We also decided to jot down example dialogues of the teacher's praise behaviors, as well as to write down what the student does after being praised (e.g., smiles). The four of us then distributed our observation tasks, two of us would tally behaviors and two would write down "praise behavior" dialogues and notes.

After the class, the teacher joined us for dinner at a nearby Cambodian restaurant and we took turns describing the praise behaviors we saw. The teacher added her own self-observations. By the end of the meal, we concluded that the teacher followed a pattern. She praised students a lot. She especially praised their effort, progress, and success. However, she also praised students when they did not put forth effort, did not give the right answer, did not make progress, and made language errors. The students reacted to her praise without much expression at all; for instance, they did not smile or say "Thank you." Rather, they simply kept talking or sitting or writing. Based on our descriptions and analysis, the teacher was able to give several interpretations of what was going on in relation to praise behaviors in the class. One interpretation she favored was that students were confused about when they were actually being praised because she praised so often, and praised so many things, including wrong answers, errors, and lack of progress!

In the spirit of exploration, we were also able to generate alternative ways she could use praise behaviors. She could, for example, praise students only when they do outstanding work, put forth exceptional effort, make obvious progress, get the right answer, and so on. She could also not praise students at all to see what happens. She could use award symbols, such as pasting stars on students' written work for an outstanding job or give class awards to those students who made the most progress in certain areas. It is worth mentioning that the teacher did explore her use of praise behaviors by only praising students when they were truly outstanding, and she later reported that students seem more accepting of her praise and some even more motivated to work to gain her praise.

Task Break

If possible, locate a teacher who is willing to invite you to observe his or her class. Using as your guide the collaborative observation guidelines given earlier in this section, meet with the teacher to learn what aspect(s) of his/her teaching should be explored, design or select ways to collect descriptions of classroom interaction relative to the teacher's interest, carry out the observation, and analyze what went on in the class. Then, meet with the teacher (if possible), and give him or her a written report.

Collecting and analyzing descriptions of teaching as a participant observer

Whereas nonparticipant observers want to observe classroom interaction as unobtrusively as possible and without taking on additional roles, *participant observers* want to become active participants in the setting they are observing, taking on membership roles. Participant observers can be rather peripheral in the roles they take on or they can be active members who "become involved in the setting's central activities, assuming responsibilities that advance the group, without fully committing themselves to members' values and goals" (Adler & Adler 1994: 380).

The roles participant observers take on depend on what is possible for the observer to be and do as a member of the group. For example, Bailey (1983), in her pursuit of understanding competitiveness and anxiety in an adult foreign language classroom, joined a French class as a student. Szarska (in process), a teacher with years of teaching experience and a desire to gain empathy with foreign language learners, also decided to observe from the student participant observer's point of view by joining a Japanese language class in the United States.

In a different pursuit, I decided to join a practicum for inexperienced teachers in order to understand changes that novice teachers make (or do not make) in their teaching and how their experiences in the practicum seemed to provide or block them from changing the way they teach (Gebhard 1985, 1990). Although I was an experienced teacher, I was given the privilege of being accepted into the practicum as both an observer and a participant. I participated in many of the required activities. I team-taught a class with an inexperienced teacher, participated in a weekly seminar, was observed by classmates, and observed classmates teach (both with classmates in an observation room with a one-way mirror and solo in student teachers' classrooms). At the same time, I tape-recorded (with participants' permission) seminars, classes, and informal talks with classmates in the observation room and over coffee or lunch, and kept an ongoing journal of my observations.

Interns provide another example of the roles that participant observers can take on. For example, interns who do an internship with me in the MA TESOL Program at Indiana University of Pennsylvania are asked to be participant observers. They keep an observation journal in which they describe and interpret the teaching and other interaction they observe, and they take on a variety of member roles. Those interns who are placed at the American Language Institute are sometimes teaching assistants, administrative assistants, tutors, paper graders, trip organizers, special events coordinators, and listening/computer lab supervisors. They attend staff meetings, organize parties and sports events, and go on field trips.

Participant observers collect descriptions of interaction in the same ways that nonparticipant observers do. It is still possible to take notes, draw sketches, use checklists, tally behaviors, collect short dialogues, make and study transcripts from tapes, and code and analyze patterns of interaction. But participant observers have additional ways open to them, mostly because they are more deeply involved in the classroom and the larger community and are likely to spend more time observing.

Some participant observers make use of a personal dairy to keep a record of their observations. This is what Kathleen Bailey and Maria Saryusz-Szarska did to keep a record of their observations and thoughts in French and Japanese classes, respectively. Some participant observers include interviewing as a way to complement their observations. For example, after audiotaping or videotaping a class, some participant observers get together with the teacher or a group of students to listen to or view parts of the tape. As they listen, the observer asks the teacher or students to clarify, explain, and expand on what is going on.

Some participant observers study and use concepts from ethnography to guide their observations. Briefly stated, ethnography is the study of people's behavior in natural settings, such as classrooms, neighborhoods, or communities. In line with the basic process discussed in this chapter, the goal of ethnography is "to provide a description and an interpretive-explanatory account of what people do" (Watson-Gegeo 1988: 576).

As Hornberger (1994) reminds us, the value of ethnography is found in its *holistic* and *emic* view. The holistic view refers to the goal of "creating a whole picture of the particular culture, cultural situation, or cultural event under study – a picture that leaves nothing unaccounted for and that reveals the interrelatedness of all the component parts" (p. 688). As such, it is not enough for participant observers who want to gain an ethnographic description, for example, of a whole language approach to teaching and learning, simply to observe what teachers do. In addition, the ethnographer might pay attention to the relations between the teacher and the administration, parents, and others. The observer also needs to do such things as observe what students are doing, study the interaction between the teacher and the students, study how the materials are used in the class, and consider the proxemics of the classroom. The observer might also informally interview many of the participants within natural contexts, photograph interaction, read students' written work, and study teachers' lesson plans and other pertinent documents. The idea here is that if participant observers want to capture descriptions of teaching from an ethnographic perspective, these descriptions need to be holistic.

Ethnography also encompasses an emic point of view. This means that observers want to describe the culture "as its members understand it and participate in it" (Hornberger 1994: 689). For example, what does communicative language teaching and learning mean to the teacher? the students? the administrators? The totality of their views will provide an understanding of what communicative language teaching and learning means in the particular classroom context being studied.

Task Break

The purpose of this task is to understand what happens in the classroom from a student's perspective. Visit a class, preferably one with which you are already familiar. Sit next to a student. Draw a line down the center of your paper to make two columns. On one side write down what the teacher does. On the other side write what the student does. At the end of the observation consider the class from the student's point of view. Here's an example:

What the teacher does	*What the student does*
Asks the class the question, "What did you do that was fun over the weekend?"	Looks out the window.
Waits one or two seconds, then calls on a student.	
Listens to the student say, "I saw a good movie." Asks another student, "How about you, Mario?"	Looks down at his book. Pulls a letter out, written in Spanish. Reads.
Asks, "Do anything fun over the weekend?"	Looks at teacher. Appears puzzled. Is silent.

For those of you who are interested in learning more about ethnography, I recommend the following references: Agar (1980, 1985), McDermott, Gospodinoff, and Aron (1978), Smith (1992), and Watson-Gegeo (1988).

How can teachers interpret descriptions of teaching?

At the beginning of this chapter I defined interpretation as a means to understand what went on in the classroom in a particular way. By making interpretations, we give meaning to the observed descriptions of teaching and classroom interaction. But how can we give meaning to our descriptions?

Actually, almost any knowledge can be used to make sense of what we observe. For example, methodologists now emphasize that classroom communication should closely resemble communication in settings outside classrooms. Thus, after describing communication patterns both in and out of classrooms, teachers can interpret to what extent interaction in their classrooms matches that found in other settings.

Some observers interpret the descriptions of teaching they gather through theories of second language acquisition. They ask if students have opportunities to process language in a way that allows for acquisition to take place. Some observers also like to use learning theory or research on effective teaching and learning. My own view is that the more knowledge we have, the more ways that are open to us to interpret the descriptions of teaching we collect and analyze. This provides a panoply of possibilities for explorations.

My approach to interpretation is to ask, "Through this classroom interaction, how are opportunities possibly provided for students to _____?" and "How are opportunities possibly blocked through the classroom interaction?" I fill the blank with my area of investigation. For example, if I discover that a teacher I am going to observe is interested in getting students to develop their spoken fluency in the second language, I will collect descriptions of interaction, and analyze this interaction, for example, for the amount of student and teacher talk, student-initiated interaction, and the length of student utterances. I will then interpret my descriptions by asking, "How are opportunities possibly provided for students to develop fluency? How does the interaction possibly block them from doing this?"

To make sense out of descriptions of teaching, without being limited to our preconceived notions, Fanselow (1988) encourages teachers to provide at least one interpretation that is seemingly outlandish or different in intent from the usual interpretations. For example, if an observer discovers that there is a lot of teacher praise, and this is thought to be a positive behavior, interpretations about how praise is negative could be made. "The goal is simply to try to remind us that each event we see can be interpreted in ways different from our usual ways of doing it because we are each limited by the ideas of reality we have" (Fanselow 1988: 122).

Task Break[3]

One of my favorite books is *Balinese Character* by Margaret Mead and Gregory Bateson (1942). Most of the book has sets of photographs that show the way people in Bali live their daily lives. For example, one set shows a mother and two children. One child is nursing and the other is playing on the ground. Each photograph shows a slightly different view of this setting and topic. On the opposite page there is a corresponding discussion for each photograph that explains the respective aspects of Balinese character, for example, about nursing children. Mead and Bateson offer their interpretations of what the interaction shown in these photographs means to the Balinese.

1. Locate a set of photographs, for example, of a birthday party, a tour, or some other event.
2. Study the photographs. Then offer your interpretation of these photos by answering the question, "How are opportunities provided for the people in these photos to _____?" (Fill in the blank with, for example, "have fun at the birthday party.") Also ask, "How are opportunities possibly blocked for these people to _____."
3. If possible, meet with others who have sets of photographs. Ask them to answer your "opportunity" questions while you answer theirs.
4. Consider how you could do the same thing with photos of classroom interaction.

As a way to show a link between description, analysis, and interpretation, I would like to give an example of an observation I did with a group of preservice teachers. We observed a class using SCORE (*S*eating *C*hart *O*bservation *Rec*ord) created by Acheson and Gall (1997). SCORE allows

---

3 A similar task using photographs is given in Gebhard (1996).

observers to capture descriptions of questioning behaviors in the classroom through the use of sketches of classroom seating arrangements. Using a seating chart, the observer records the occurrences of observed behaviors.

This particular observation was done in an advanced-level ESL class. The teacher introduced a topic for discussion through the use of overheads, gave out short reading passages, spent time reading them, and asked questions about the content under discussion. Our purpose and way of narrowing our observation was to consider how the teacher provided or blocked opportunities for the students to learn English in the classroom through his questioning behaviors.

Task Break

1. Before reading our analysis, take time to do your own. How many questions did the teacher ask the whole class? individual students? Who answered these questions? How many responses are there in relation to the number of whole-class questions? Individual questions?
2. Read on to see if your analysis is the same as ours.

Here's what we discovered (see Figure 3.1). During the one-hour class, the teacher asked fifty-five questions. Thirty-one questions were to the whole class and twenty-four to individual students. There were twenty-six responses to the teacher's whole-class questions, indicating that for some questions, no one volunteered to answer. We also discovered that when the student could not answer a question, the teacher redirected it to another or answered it himself.

In addition, we noticed that eight of the sixteen students answered the teacher's whole-class questions and that most whole-class and individual questions were answered by only five students (1, 2, 5, 10, 16), three of whom sat in the front row. We also observed that the teacher asked nine students individual questions, and that the teacher called on those students who answered whole-class questions more than students who did not. Furthermore, the teacher interacted with all five male students in the class but only with five of the eleven female students.

Since our purpose in doing the observation was to consider how the teacher provided opportunities for students to use English through his questioning behavior, we interpreted what we observed by asking, "How did the teacher's questioning behavior possibly provide chances for the students to learn English? How did it possibly block them from learning English?"

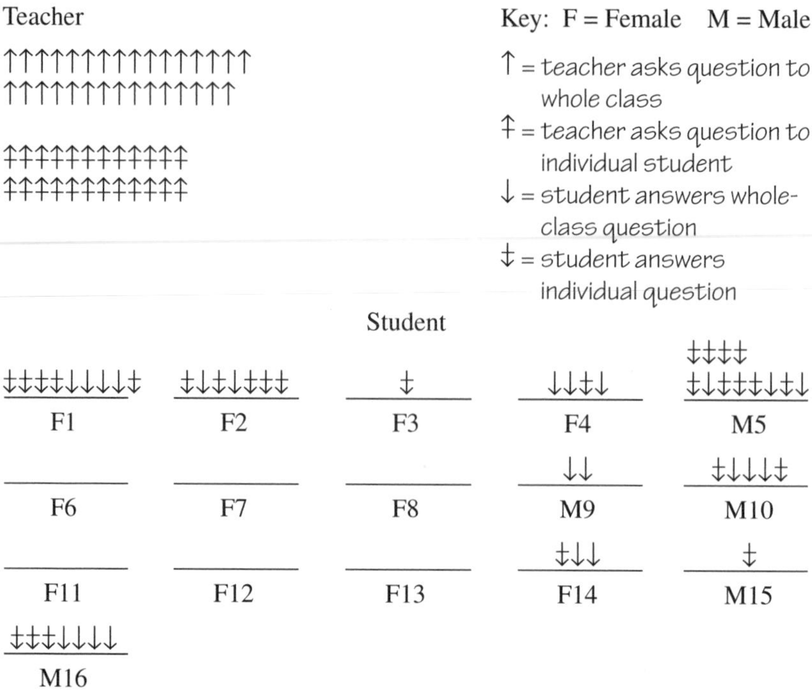

Teacher   Key: F = Female   M = Male

↑↑↑↑↑↑↑↑↑↑↑↑↑↑↑↑↑
↑↑↑↑↑↑↑↑↑↑↑↑↑↑↑↑

↟↟↟↟↟↟↟↟↟↟↟↟↟
↟↟↟↟↟↟↟↟↟↟↟↟↟

↑ = teacher asks question to
    whole class
↟ = teacher asks question to
    individual student
↓ = student answers whole-
    class question
↡ = student answers
    individual question

Student

				↡↡↡↡
↡↡↡↡↓↓↓↓↡	↓↡↓↡↓↓↓	↡	↓↓↡↓	↡↓↡↓↡↓↡↓↡
F1	F2	F3	F4	M5
			↓↓	↡↓↓↓↡
F6	F7	F8	M9	M10
			↡↓↓	↡
F11	F12	F13	F14	M15
↡↡↡↓↓↓↓				
M16				

Figure 3.1   The teacher's questioning behavior: SCORE.

Some observers, including me, decided that students really did not have many chances to learn English in this class. The kind of interaction that promotes language learning was missing from the interaction. For example, many of the students were never directly involved in the questioning process. Instead, they sat passively. In addition, the teacher's questions were mostly display questions (ones the teacher already knows the answers to), inter-action that did not generate much real negotiation of meaning, something we considered important to the language-learning process.

On the other hand, other observers thought that many of the students had chances to learn English, especially those who were actively answering the teacher's questions. They thought that the quick pace and many questions held the students' attention. They referred to their own experience as lan-guage learners, saying that even the students who were not answering ques-tions were involved in following the meaning in the interaction, and that this provides an opportunity to process and learn English.

We all agreed that students sitting in the front of the classroom had more chances to learn English because the teacher selectively called on them. Likewise, we thought that the males had proportionately more chances than the females in this class because the teacher interacted more with males through the questions, even though eleven of the sixteen students were females.

As for outlandish interpretations, we surmised that the students who never answered questions were actually learning the most because they were daydreaming in English, having conversations with people in their heads. Likewise, the students who never volunteered to answer questions were already so good at English that they really did not need to be there. They were too bored to participate. Another outlandish interpretation is that the teacher was selecting those students whom he knew needed the most practice. Outlandish interpretations such as these lead, in my experience, to fresh perspectives on teaching and learning. They thus create new conversations from the usual ones, which is congruent with the kinds of exploration we promote in this book.

Task Break

1. Based on your understanding of what went on in this class, answer the questions "How did the teacher's questioning behavior possibly provide chances for students to learn English in this class?" and "How did it possibly hinder them from learning?"
2. If possible, meet with others to discuss your answers (in other words, your interpretations).
3. Add at least one "outlandish" interpretation. In other words, give answers to the questions in number 1 that would seem quite bizarre to the average teacher.
4. Read what we say about the way the teacher's questioning behavior possibly provided or blocked opportunities for students in the class to learn English. Compare your interpretations with ours.

Concluding remarks

Nonjudgmental descriptive observation of other teachers is one way to explore teaching. We can observe at a distance through nonparticipant observation or we can join others in the context in which we want to observe as a participant observer. We can describe and analyze the teaching we observe through a selection of observation instruments (checklists, tally sheets, prose, photos, sketches, transcripts, coding) and techniques (taking a one-down position, videotaping and audio taping, free writing, no writing), as well as interpret the teaching in a variety of ways (through theory, research, common sense, outlandishness). Through describing, analyzing, and interpreting the teaching we observe, we can construct and reconstruct our own teaching and thereby learn about ourselves as teachers.

The skills developed while doing the kinds of activities described in this chapter can serve you well in expanding your awareness through action research, the subject of the next chapter.

4 *Problem posing and solving with action research*

Jerry G. Gebhard

> Action research has been proposed as an "empowering" pro-
> cedure. But, as Widdowson (1993: 267) has pointed out, if it
> becomes another top-down requirement, it turns into the re-
> verse: not only is it an additional burden upon teachers, but
> it also creates a new kind of dependency on (non-teaching)
> "experts."
>
> —M. J. Wallace (1998: 17)

Action research has grown in popularity, and is considered by some teachers and teacher educators to be an essential part of our professional lives.
This is because it provides a way of looking that helps us to reflect on our
teaching. The problem-solving, as well as problem-posing, aspects of action
research place it squarely in the developmental approach to language teaching discussed in Chapter 1. At the same time, action research can provide
us with a way to gain awareness of our teaching through the kind of exploration that Robert Oprandy and I discuss in this book and I will, at times,
point out where I feel suggested activities fit more in the exploratory realm.
After discussing what action research is, I detail how it can be done as a way
to explore our teaching, through the following questions:

- What is action research?
- How can teachers go about doing action research?
- What are examples of action research?
- How much research skill is needed to do action research?

What is action research?

Imagine the following: Agnes teaches at a private language institute and is
a member of an action research group interested in gaining awareness of

what goes on in their classrooms, institute, and community. Like the others at the institute, she is especially interested in posing teaching problems and exploring ways to resolve them. The group consists of three other teachers and a curriculum coordinator who acts as a guide to the research process. Further imagine that Agnes has met with this group every 2 weeks for the past 3 months.

At the start of the process, Agnes identified a problem, specifically that a large number of students cut her classes. She also raised questions: "Why are students cutting class? Does their behavior reflect what we do in class? Does it reflect a problem or problems outside this class? How can I learn about the reasons students cut class?" After talking with group members, she developed a plan of action aimed at solving the class-cutting problem: to write letters to those students who cut class to express her heartfelt concern, as well as to ask them to correspond with her about why they aren't coming to class. She implemented her plan and studied what happened.

Agnes found that some students did not write back, while others came to class and wrote back to her. Some expressed their discontent with the class, especially about the way class time was spent. These students pointed out that they enrolled in the institute to gain entrance into the university and this required them to pass the Test of English as a Foreign Language (TOEFL). They saw class time as being spent playing games, activities they felt did not prepare them to pass the exam. Agnes reported the results of her investigation to the group and discovered that other teachers believed they had the same problem.

Based on her reflection and collaboration with group members, Agnes decided to talk with the students about the importance of gaining fluency and accuracy in English by using English to accomplish things, as well as about the limitations of trying to do better on the TOEFL only through practice with the exam itself. She also decided to devote 15 minutes of each class to TOEFL preparation exercises and test-taking strategy pointers. In addition, the group members decided to introduce the students' voiced concern about the TOEFL exam at the next staff meeting to see if other teachers had heard students voice this concern. They also wanted to talk to the program director about adding a TOEFL preparation class to the curriculum.

Task Break

Based on the example just given, do you see the value that action research can have for teachers and the school or institute? If possible, meet with others who

> have read this example of action research. Based on
> this example, discuss what you believe action research
> is. Then go on to read my explanation.

What is action research? The concept of action research originated in the work of Kurt Lewin (1948, 1952), a social psychologist who brought together experimental approaches to social-science research and the idea of "social action" to address social issues. Two ideas were central to Lewin's work: group decision and a commitment to improvement. A distinctive characteristic of Lewin's action research model is that those affected by planned changes can be responsible for deciding the kind of action that will possibly lead to improvement, as well as for evaluating the results of what was tried out in practice. Stephen Corey (1952, 1953), a Teachers College, Columbia University professor, was among the first to use action research in the field of education. He argued that formal research following a scientific method had little impact on educational practice. Through action research, he argued, changes in educational practice are possible. Teachers supported Corey's action research emphasis. By studying their own teaching through action research, they stated that "our teaching is more likely to change" than it would from "reading about what someone else has discovered regarding the consequences of his teaching. The latter is helpful. The former is almost certain to be" (Corey 1953: 70).

At one level, action research is about teachers identifying and posing problems, as well as addressing issues and concerns related to the problem. It is about working toward understanding and possibly resolving these problems by setting goals and creating and initiating a plan of action, as well as reflecting on the degree to which the plan works. As Cohen and Manion (1985) put this, action research is "a small-scale intervention in the functioning of the real world and a close examination of the effects of such intervention" (p. 174). In the example given above, a problem was identified (students cutting class), a goal was set (to resolve the cutting problem), and a plan of action (or intervention) was created (to write personal notes to the students). The group then considered the results of this initiated plan: some students continued to cut class and did not write back; others came to class and wrote to tell the teacher they did not like the class activities because they were not preparing them for TOEFL. Through reflection, the teacher modified her goal (to meet the TOEFL needs of the students) and created a new plan (to add TOEFL lessons; to talk with students about TOEFL preparation). She tried out the plan, observed what happened, reflected on the results of the action, and continued to explore solutions to the problem.

I see action research as being more than this, however. At another level, it can be about addressing educational practices that go beyond each teacher's classroom. For example, the teachers in the example above decided that the problem extended beyond the classroom and that they needed to explore whether other teachers outside their group realized the same problem and whether or not some reform in educational policy at the institute was needed. They also decided to involve the program director by requesting the addition of a TOEFL preparation course to the program curriculum. As Crookes (1993) and van Lier (1993) postulate, action research can go beyond the teacher simply identifying a problem and solving it. Rather, action research can be "a cyclical program of reform, whose results are reflected on and further refined and developed in collaborative investigative communities" (Crookes 1993: 134).

An important component of action research is collaboration between or among a variety of different people. This includes a willingness for us to talk with each other about problems and find solutions, as well as assist each other in implementing classroom centered action research projects. Likewise, if we see the need for a plan of action that involves the school, institute, or community, this plan needs the collaborative efforts of teachers, administrators, and, perhaps, public officials, who together implement the plan, observe what happens, reflect on the how the plan worked, and revise the plan. For action research to be successful, the students also need to be involved in collaboration. Students need to know that they are a part of the planning decisions and that they can contribute to the quality of their second language education by their willingness, for example, to be videotaped while participating in classroom activities or interviewed about their concerns, problems, accomplishments, and unique perspective on the program.

As mentioned in Chapter 1, action research as a problem-posing process is not always exploration in the way we define it in this book. When the objective of doing action research is just to find a solution to a problem, rather than to discover and rediscover our teaching beliefs and practices and to gain awareness of our teaching related to our problem-solving processes, then I do not consider action research to be exploration. Similarly, if action research is aimed at finding *the best way* to handle the problem as opposed to exploring the consequences of different ways of addressing the problem, then it does not fit into the exploratory approach we highlight in Part I. If, however, we approach problem solving in a nonjudgmental descriptive stance, in a search not only to solve the problem but also to learn about our teaching behavior and beliefs in relation to the problem, then doing action research can provide opportunities for us to explore our teaching. In so doing, we may heighten awareness of our teaching beliefs and practices. This is especially true if we have chances to describe our teaching and generate teaching ideas while doing such things as talking with other teachers or a supervisor or writing in a journal.

How can teachers go about doing action research?

Action research is carried out as a cyclical process that follows a series of repeated steps. The cycle includes setting a goal, planning an action to reach this goal, acting on this plan, observing the action, reflecting on the observation, and setting the next goal.[1]

In the rest of this section I explain this cyclical process. I bring in an example of what an EFL high school teacher in Japan went through as she did her first action research project on the use of English and Japanese in her teaching. A student in an M.A. TESOL program in Japan, she did her project to fulfill a requirement of a practicum for experienced teachers on the topic "speaking." In addition to meeting this requirement, however, she seemed to be genuinely interested in addressing a very real concern, as well as in exploring her teaching to gain awareness of her teaching practices. In addition, she chose to wrestle with her beliefs about the use of the target language, English, and the students' and her own native language, Japanese, in her teaching.

Setting a goal

Goal setting includes identifying and posing a problem or concern, as well as seeking knowledge about the problem or concern. At the start of the process, a search for a problem is often based on intuition and questioning. The teacher asks, "What goes on in my classroom, at the school, or in the community that are areas of concern or that seem problematic? If not problematic, what aspects of classroom, school, or community life would be interesting to investigate and might contribute to the quality of the students' education?"

Keeping a teaching journal (Chapter 5) and talking with members of an action research group can provide chances for teachers to answer, or at least address, such questions, and to identify problems or concerns they would like to investigate. Some teachers also benefit from videotaping one of their classes. The tenth grade EFL teacher in Japan, for example, got involved in her action research project after videotaping her class, viewing the tape,

1 See Kemmis and McTaggart (1982) and Strickland (1988) for similar processes.

and talking about classroom interaction with a group of teachers in the speaking practicum. This raised awareness of the considerable amount of Japanese used by her and the students in her English classes.

The videotape also offered this EFL teacher a chance to seek knowledge about her concern, an important step in the action research process. She studied the interaction on the tape to see when she used Japanese, which she found was about 75% of the time. She used Japanese to give instructions, explain points of grammar, vocabulary items, and homework assignments, as well as to discipline students. She used English to greet students when they arrived, to praise, and to read passages and ask questions from the text. This personally bothered her because she wanted to offer them more experience with English. She also believed that, in addition to preparing students to pass exams, her job was to provide chances for them to experience the use of English to communicate their thoughts and feelings.

Ways to learn more about a problem or concern
- Audiotape or videotape a lesson and listen to or view the tape while focusing on the problem.
- Listen to or view the tape while taking notes, sketching, or tallying behaviors that focus on the problem. (See Chapter 3 on observation.)
- From the tape, make short transcripts centering on the problem area and analyze them.
- Informally interview students, focusing on the problem.
- Join students for lunch. Listen in on their problems.
- Create a short questionnaire that addresses the problem or concern and have students fill it out.
- Correspond with students about the problem or concern through letters or notes.
- Correspond with students about the problem or concern through a dialogue journal.
- Take sets of snapshots that focus attention on the problem (e.g., use of space in the classroom; nonverbal behaviors of students during group work).
- Have students create a collage as a learning activity in class that addresses the problem or concern.
- Read journal articles or book chapters that focus attention on the problem.
- Talk with other teachers about the problem.

As this list shows, there are other ways to seek knowledge that the EFL teacher could have used. She could have searched for journal articles from practical professional journals. She could have given students a short questionnaire asking them for their opinions about using English in class, such as what reservations they might have about expanding the use of English and whether or not they would be willing to try using English on a limited basis. This could also have been done through informal interviews with small groups of students or through dialogue journals with the students. The teacher could also have written letters or notes to students (as the ESL teacher in the first example did), asking them for their opinions and support. When one is open to exploring, there are a lot of possibilities!

Task Break

Meet with two or three others at a place you teach or study. Together, do the following:

1. Identify a teaching or school problem one or more of you have.
2. Decide how you will seek more knowledge about this problem.

Planning an action

A plan must "by definition be prospective to action – it must be forward looking" (Kemmis & McTaggart 1982: 7). We see such a plan as one that includes predictions about what will happen when the plan of action (or intervention) is implemented. For example, the high school EFL teacher in Japan planned to expand her use of English in the classroom in two ways. First, she decided to give instructions to activities in English. Second, she decided to ask students questions that are based on the content of the readings but that are outside of the textbook questions that students could read. For example, she would ask, "We read about food in England. If you went to England, what would you like to eat?"

The teacher as action researcher predicted that most of the students would not understand her instructions in English. Most would probably not even listen at first, expecting her to follow up by giving the instructions again in Japanese. As for the use of her own questions related to the content of the textbook, she predicted that some students would comprehend the question but answer her in Japanese. Some might give nonverbal cues that they do not want to be called on or to volunteer. Others might sit in silence when called on. A few would use English, but would take a long time to come up with the answer. In cases where students insisted on speaking in Japanese, the teacher decided to translate their responses into English. This would not put any student in an embarrassing situation, yet at the same time promote the use of English in the class.

A plan also needs to include ways to observe by collecting and analyzing descriptions relative to the planned action. Ways to collect descriptions of teaching, for example, include making audiotapes or videotapes of classroom interaction, first obtaining permission from the students to tape them. These tapes can then be listened to or viewed. While doing this, depending on the action research focus, a number of things can be done. For example, sketches can be made of seating arrangements, the teacher's use of classroom space, or students' facial expressions. The teacher as action researcher can also plan to tally certain behaviors, such as the number and kinds of questions asked, the number of seconds the teacher waits for students to answer questions, or the number of times different kinds of praise behaviors are used. Short transcriptions of such behaviors can also be made. These transcriptions can be studied on their own. They could also be coded with an observation system such as FOCUS (Fanselow 1977a, 1987), COLT (Allen, Fröhlich, & Spada 1984; Spada 1990), or TALOS (Ullmann & Geva 1982). The idea is for the teacher to consider ways to describe and analyze behaviors that can be used to better understand what goes on in the classroom relative to the area of action research interest. (For a more detailed discussion of describing and analyzing teaching behaviors, see Chapter 3.)[2]

To return to the example: the EFL high school teacher in Japan planned to have a friend videotape her class (in exchange for her videotaping her friend's class). She planned to make short transcriptions and analyze the English used in the instructions she gives, and, just as important, to study the consequences these English-language instructions seem to have on the students, including their nonverbal behaviors. (Do the students start the task right away? Look and act puzzled? Ask each other in Japanese what they are to do?) She also planned to tally the amount of time she speaks Japanese in class and to view the tape and jot down short transcriptions of interaction and notes and draw sketches illustrating what happens during times she asks students questions in English.

Of course, the research methodology part of a plan can also include techniques used to learn more about a problem or concern (discussed earlier). For example, interviews, questionnaires, or journal correspondence can be used to find out what students think about what happened. The EFL teacher could have used one of these ways to learn about what the students thought

2 Also see Day (1990), Fanselow (1988), Good and Brophy (1987), Nunan (1990), Wajnryb (1992), who offer a variety of instruments and ways to collect and analyze descriptions of teaching.

and felt about listening to the instructions in English and answering questions posed in English. By asking the students for feedback, the teacher would not only be learning about how well the action worked, but also letting the students know that she cares about their opinions, attitudes, and feelings about what goes on in the classroom.

Acting on the plan

With a research plan in mind, the teacher is now ready for action! Teachers can benefit from being "deliberate" (Kemmis & McTaggart 1982: 8). Of course, as experienced teachers know, no teaching plan can be completely controlled. Things happen that are unpredictable, and plans need to be changed. Teachers also need to bear in mind that bringing in a new action is inherently risky. Although predictions can be made about how students will react, things could unfold in unexpected ways. For example, the EFL teacher deliberately used English to give instructions and ask questions, and she realized the possibility that her students might not cooperate with her plan or not clearly understand what she was doing or why.

Teachers also need to implement a way to collect descriptions of teaching, and this can be problematic. Well-intentioned teachers have left tape recorders unplugged, discovered that video camera batteries are dead, or found that students are more amused with the video camera than the lesson. (If a camera is used, I recommend that the teacher tape the class several times, including the class to be studied, so that students get used to being recorded.)

Observing the action

It is impossible – or at the least very difficult – to observe ourselves while teaching. That is why, if the teacher is a participant in the action, I recommend audiotaping or videotaping. This provides a record of what went on that can be studied.

In addition, we need to focus attention on things pertinent to the research emphasis. As Kemmis and McTaggart point out, when observing, we need to observe "the action process, the effects of action, the circumstances of and constraints on action, the way circumstances and constraints limit or channel the planned action and its effects, and other issues that arise" (ibid., 9).

To illustrate this observation process, let us return to the EFL teacher in Japan. She had a videotape made of her class. Then, as planned, she made short transcripts of her instructions in English, studied students' reactions to them, and viewed and took notes on, and drew sketches of, her interactions with students when she asked them questions in English. She discovered that most of the students appeared to be following the instructions, but most could not start the task (to silently read a passage in their text and prepare answers to three questions) without first confirming the instructions in Japanese. Moreover, when she asked questions in English that were not in the text, most students, as she predicted, avoided eye contact with her and did not volunteer to answer.

There were also several surprises. She was surprised that it took much more time than she had anticipated for the question–answer session. She only had time to ask half the questions she had prepared to ask. She was also surprised that two students who were usually quiet volunteered to answer questions, and did so in fairly fluent English.

In regard to how constraints limit or channel the planned action and its effects, she saw that the number of students (more than forty) and the room itself and the way students were sitting (in rows) limited the kind of question–answer communication she was hoping to have with them. She noticed, for instance, that she stood in the front of the room and most interaction took place with students sitting in the front left side of the room.

The EFL teacher's observation was limited to the analysis of a videotape. Although this tape was quite useful in that she could closely observe her own and students' behavior, she really had to guess about what students thought and felt about the experience. The teacher pointed out that she might have learned more if she had had the students complete a short questionnaire or had held short interviews with some of them. Then, she could compare the student data with her own observations and interpretations of what she saw on the tape.

Reflecting on the observation

As mentioned earlier, a plan is *pro*spective. In contrast, reflection can be "retrospective – it recalls action as it has been recorded in observation. It seeks to make sense of processes, problems, issues and constraints" (Kemmis & McTaggart 1982: 9).[3] Reflecting on what happened in the class is aided by asking questions: What do I know now that I did not know before? Am I closer to solving the problem? Do I need to pose the problem or concern in a different way? Is there a larger issue that needs to be resolved? It

---

3 There are different approaches to understand reflection. Schön (1983, 1987), for example, discusses *reflection-in-action* (dealing with on-the-spot professional problems as they occur) and contrasts this type of reflection with *reflection-on-action* (analyzing action after the event). Others who discuss reflection include Bartlett (1990), Farrell (1996), Schulman (1987), van Manen (1977), and Wallace (1996).

is beneficial to explore these kinds of questions during group meetings. Others who have followed the action research project will sometimes provide useful answers to, or at least hunches about, such questions. Others can act as listeners, as well, giving opportunities to each teacher, through talk, to process observations and classroom experience into something more meaningful. (See Chapter 8 for an example of this. See also Edge [1992] for procedures aimed at fostering such listening and talk.)

The EFL teacher searched for answers to such questions and asked classmates in her M.A. TESOL program practicum seminar for their ideas. She believed that she gained much more awareness of how much Japanese is actually used in her English classes; she also felt a stronger commitment to using more English. In addition, she realized that giving instructions and asking a few questions (not in the text) in English is only the beginning. She knew that she would have to take the students gradually through a process of switching from Japanese to using English and that this would not be easy.

One reason for this, she thought, was of the limitations placed on her and the students because of conservative, traditional beliefs within the Japanese educational system. In this regard, this teacher, and her practicum classmates, said they felt discouraged about the prospect of successfully getting students to use English as a medium of communication in the class. They felt powerless to bring about change in a system that treats learning English like an academic subject, encourages teachers to teach English in ways that prepare students for college entrance exams, and provides required textbooks and curriculum, leaving little room for teachers to bring in their own materials and lessons. However, several members of the practicum, having read the work of Fanselow (1987), pointed out that change is still possible, that even small changes in classroom interaction can have big consequences for the students. This finding was encouraging as they continued to discuss and grapple with their common concern.

Setting the next goal

By now, the teacher has identified and searched for knowledge about a problem, planned an action or intervention that aims at solving the problem or concern, and implemented, observed, and reflected on this planned action. The cycle has come full circle. The next step is for the teacher to reidentify and further posture the problem or concern, although he or she should feel free to identify and pose a new one. The cycle then continues through planning, acting, observing, and reflecting.

Remembering the advice that small changes can have big consequences, the EFL teacher decided that she would continue to explore ways to get students to use English to communicate their ideas and feelings. To begin, she wanted to explore ways to make her instructions in English more comprehensible to the students. Based on conversations with other teachers in the practicum, she decided to use an overhead projector to show her instructions, but she would make this a cloze activity (by leaving out every fifth word). Students could read as they listened to her instructions and fill in the missing words.

Gradually, based on observation and reflection, she would add other ways to make English a part of classroom life. She would continue to ask questions in English. She would also give students chances to ask her questions. To initiate this, she would give them time to write down their questions about a topic in the text. Students could then take turns asking her and classmates their questions. Gradually, she also hoped to make use of published activities she had studied, adapting them to her class based on topics and grammar in the required text. Her awareness of what started out as a roughly articulated concern had expanded and deepened with each of the steps identified above.

Reporting

An important part of doing action research is that of reporting. I have seen teachers report their action research process and findings in a variety of settings, including at group meetings with other teachers who have also worked on projects, at local, regional, and national conferences, and through publications. In Chapter 10, for example, Zubeyde Tezel reports on a project she worked on at a language institute. Her first report on this project was at an institute meeting with her support group. She later reported on her research at a regional TESOL conference, and eventually reported on it at the annual TESOL convention.

I see reporting as an important part of doing action research because it offers teachers chances to think through their goals, plans, actions, observations, and reflections in an explicit way. It can lead to changes in both the goals and the process of action research, as well as provide a feeling of accomplishment and pride.

A few remarks on the action research process

Before providing examples of action research, I want to conclude this section by pointing out a few things that I like about it. One is that it is rarely short-term. As van Lier (1993) observes, action research "is a way of working in which every answer raises new questions, and one can thus never quite say, 'I've finished'" (p. 6). Also, I like the idea that I can pose a problem or concern connected to my teaching and work toward resolving it without feeling that I have failed if it is not resolved. In the spirit of exploration, I can simply restate my goal and redesign my plan using my acquired knowledge and experience to continue in my efforts to resolve the problem.

I also like the fact that we are not limited to working through an action research problem alone. In fact, I find the collaborative nature of action research to be thought-provoking and stress-reducing.

In addition, I like the fact that we do not have to limit our research to just the classroom. As should be clear from some of the examples given in this chapter, problems are often identified in the classroom. However, "things that happen in the classroom are inevitably linked to things that happen outside the classroom" (van Lier, personal communication).

Finally, I like the way action can be used to explore our teaching beliefs and practices. Like the high school teacher in Japan, we can look beyond solving the problem or addressing the concern by focusing attention on exploring our own teaching as it relates to the problem or concern. We can seek knowledge about our own beliefs and teaching behaviors as we work toward solving the problem or addressing our concern.

What are examples of action research?

So far, we have brought two action research projects into our discussion. The first was done by an ESL teacher in an intensive language institute. The teacher, Agnes, was concerned that some students consistently cut class. She raised questions: "Why are students cutting class? Does this behavior reflect what we do in class?" and she took action to solve the problem. The second action research project was done by an EFL high school teacher in Japan. Because one of her goals was to offer chances for students to express themselves in English, she was concerned about the extent to which Japanese was being used in class by both her and the students. After investigating the times English and Japanese were used, she took action to increase the use of English as the medium of communication between her and the students.

These examples illustrate that action research is based on problems and concerns that are very real for teachers and seen as relevant to student learning. In this section, I would like to consider other action research projects that teachers have worked on.

Here are some of the action research projects teachers have worked on.[4]

Research problems	*Corresponding Questions*
Students don't talk very much in class. They seem reserved and reluctant to express themselves in English.	How much do students talk? How much do I talk? Does my talking block students from talking? What kinds of activities promote student talk? Which ones possibly block it? Does not talking mean not learning?
Some students are disruptive. They talk with each other in their native languages during group work and take classmates off task.	When do these students talk loudly? What possibly triggers this behavior? What exactly happens when these disruptive students are in a group? Are these students disruptive only when they are with certain students? What happens if I keep them apart? What other ways are these students disruptive?
After I give instructions for students to do a group work activity, they don't seem to know what to do.	How do I give instructions? What do students do and say just after I give these instructions? Do they ask each other what they are supposed to do? Ask me? Talk about other things? Begin the task? If students don't understand what to do, how can I change the way I give instructions so that they can more fully comprehend them?
I bet most of my students would enjoy learning songs and experiencing other authentic listening materials.	What songs and other authentic materials should I use? Are there any authentic songs published for ESL students? How can I use these materials so they are comprehensible to the students?

4 Keep in mind that this is a sample list of action research projects, taken out of context. You might also be interested in the research topics in Nunan (1989, 1990) Richards and Lockhart (1994), and Wallace (1998).

I'm confused about whether or not to treat students' spoken language errors. When I treat their errors, I feel like I'm interfering with communication, and I'm not sure it actually makes a difference. But, students tell me that they want me to correct their errors.

What happens when I don't correct students' spoken language errors? What happens when I do? At present, when do I correct errors? What errors do I correct? How do I correct the errors? Do students know when I correct their errors?

The kinds of activities and exercises in the assigned textbook don't match the goals of the course objectives set by the curriculum committee. The text is grammar exercise- and explanation-based. The goals of the course are to teach students to communicate.

What exactly happens when we follow the text? Is there any "real" communication? What are the patterns of interaction in the classroom when we follow the text? How can I adapt communication activities to the text? If I (and others who use the text) decide that the present text does not meet the needs of the students or course goals, can we change texts? How can we convince the curriculum committee to allow us to select our own texts?

Many of the students at this language institute seem bored. They don't really seem interested in learning the language.

What do the students feel about their language-learning experiences in my class? In other language classes? Are they bored? If so, why? If they are bored, how can I motivate them to take interest? What can the school do to motivate them?

Task Break

Study the list of issues, problems, or concerns in the left-hand column along with the corresponding questions. Select one. Consider how you might go about finding answers to the questions connected to the problem. How might you collect and analyze data to help you answer the questions?

How much research skill is needed
to do action research?

Some teachers say, "But, I don't know very much about doing research. How can I possibly do an adequate job?" These teachers have a legitimate concern. I used to feel this way myself. I carried an attitude that only those in elite academic circles can do research.

The emphasis of action research, however, is for teachers to address what goes on in classrooms and schools by discovering, posing, and possibly solving problems. This does not require that we have highly sophisticated empirical research skills. This is in line with Wallace (1996), who suggests that teachers "should be encouraged to pursue a mode of inquiry which more closely complements the normal professional activity of classroom teachers" (p. 293). This is why I recommend that we use informal interviewing, observe, take photos, and correspond through letters, E-mail, and dialogue journals.

It is also possible for us to study inquiry skills that we can apply to our own way of doing action research. Thorne and Wang (1996), for example, provided chances for novice teachers to develop inquiry skills as a part of learning to do action research at Beijing Normal University. Their action research project took place over a 2-semester period, during which time the "trainee teachers" team-taught to Science and Humanities undergraduates at the university 5 hours each week.

During the first semester, the goal was to give the novice teachers an orientation to action research. For instance, they studied ways to collect and analyze data through case studies, learner diaries, observation sheets, and questionnaires. They also had lessons on the use of video to gain awareness of teaching concerns. They viewed tapes of former trainees – which was thought to be more convincing than showing tapes of Western teachers – and studied their projects. They also studied how peers from the previous year used questionnaires as a part of their inquiry. At the end of the first semester, each pair worked on planning a research project by identifying a problem with their teaching based on studying and reflecting on their teacher diaries and student learner diaries. Project areas included more effective management of group work, increasing oral interaction, and teaching grammar points.[5] During the second semester, the novice teachers carried out their projects.

5 Also see Nunan (1990), who shows teachers how to develop their inquiry skills by taking them through five stages of developing an action research plan, each with useful sets of activities for teachers to experience.

An excellent source for teachers who like to do action research is Michael Wallace's (1998) *Action Research for Language Teachers*. Wallace not only sees action research as something that teachers can accomplish, but clearly explains and illustrates how we can go about doing it by keeping field notes, logs, journal, diaries, or personal accounts, collecting verbal reports, observing, conducting interviews, and doing case studies.

I agree with Wallace and with Thorne and Wang that teachers can learn the skills needed to do action research. I even think it is fun. In fact, my own experience with action research has led me to study qualitative research methodologies and techniques, especially those used by anthropologists. I have been able to adapt what I have learned to my research in my classroom, university, and larger community. For example, I closely studied a book titled *The Professional Stranger: An Informal Introduction to Ethnography* by Michael Agar (1980) and was able to apply Agar's principles to my research activities. One concept I like very much is that of the *one-down position*. Instead of treating the participants in the research as subjects who supply needed information, the researcher approaches them as people who can teach the researcher about what it means to be a participant in a particular context, such as what it means to be a student in an ESL class.

I also read about interviewing in qualitative research. Two books stand out: *Qualitative Interviewing: The Art of Hearing Data* by Herbert Rubin and Irene Rubin (1995) and *The Ethnographic Interview* by James Spradely (1979). I have been able to adapt their interviewing principles to my way of doing action research. Two useful ideas include continually paraphrasing to check understanding and reminding the person that I am interested in his or her point of view, not what the person believes I want to hear. I also follow Spradely's question types and process. He begins an interview with descriptive questions. I especially like his grand-tour questions. These questions aim at getting the person being interviewed to describe things from his or her perspective from a fairly general and wide perspective. For example, when trying to understand why a student was not paying attention or doing his homework, I asked, "What are all the ways you use English in your life?" and "Take me through a typical weekday in your life." After thinking about his answers, I later ask what Spradely calls mini-tour questions: "You said that you have a job some evenings to earn extra money. Tell me about your job."

It was amazing how much I learned from this student about how his choices and obligations seemed to interfere with his studies. I was able to use my new knowledge to work with him to reach my goal of getting him to engage himself more fully in the class.

The point here is not what I learned about research techniques but that an interest in and an effort to learn about them can prove to be useful to the action researcher.

Task Break

Get together with two or three other teachers. Together, do the following:

1. Reread and discuss the procedures for doing action research.
2. Identify a teaching problem. If all of you are teaching, each person should identify and pose a real problem. If you have trouble, try talking about your class with other members of the group. If you are not teaching, act as a supporting member of the group.
3. Consider ways to learn more about the problem.
4. Learn more about the problem.
5. Discuss what you learned about the problem.
6. Create a plan to solve the problem.
7. Act on the plan.
8. Observe what happened.
9. Reflect on what happened.

If you are involved in an in-service or preservice teacher-education program, write up an informal report that communicates the process you used, including (1) what the problem was, (2) how you learned more about the problem and what you learned, (3) your plan to solve the problem, (4) how you implemented your plan and what you learned, (5) your reflections, and (6) what you are considering doing next.

Concluding remarks

As I pointed out at the beginning of this chapter, action research has grown in popularity and is considered by some teachers and teacher educators to be an important part of our professional lives. Many teachers like action research because of the emphasis on problem solving. It is useful and they can see the relevance of doing it. However, although doing action research can raise our teaching awareness, it can also limit us from gaining awareness because it focuses so narrowly on solving problems.

As we point out throughout this book, exploration of teaching is much more than solving problems. We can explore simply to enjoy exploring, for example, by doing the opposite of what we normally do or trying out teaching ideas simply to see what happens. We can also explore by contrasting what we believe we do in the class with what we actually do, as well as contrast what we believe about teaching and learning with what we have students do in the classroom.

I encourage you to problem-solve through action research. I also encourage you to go beyond problem solving by exploring through other avenues to awareness discussed in this book.

5 Reflecting through a teaching journal

Jerry G. Gebhard

> In reworking, rethinking, and interpreting the diary entries, teachers can gain powerful insights into their own classroom behavior and motivation.
> —K. M. Bailey (1990: 225)

I lived in Thailand for a number of years, and I spent my first 2 years in the northeast. For some of this time I kept what I call a travel/learning journal. I wrote about my experiences living with Thai village families, traveling with Buddhist monks, and discovering new foods. Some of these foods I never imagined I would eat, such as red ant eggs, which instantly became a delicacy for me (and have been every since). I also kept a record of the Thai language I was learning and how I used it. I used the journal as a way to plan, for example, how I would bargain for food at the market, explain symptoms to a doctor, and follow correct protocol at a Thai wedding. I then wrote about the experiences themselves by describing what happened. This descriptive knowledge helped me to plan my next cultural encounter – for example, to negotiate differently at the market.

I later found myself living and teaching English in Bangkok. I continued to write in my journal. I still wrote about my adventures, people I met, and language I learned. But, I also wrote about my teaching ideas and plans, thoughts on teaching and learning, and what went on in the lessons I taught. (See the examples of journal entries in the Appendix to this chapter.) Although I admit I had no clear conceptualization about how exploration could lead to awareness, I was still doing things such as planning lessons based on feedback from students, tape-recording a few classes, listening to the tapes and analyzing what went on, and sharing lesson plans and teaching materials and ideas with other teachers.[1]

---

1 I first started using tapes of my teaching as a means to explore quite by accident. I taped a class to study students' language errors. I wanted to play the tape back,

Since these initial journaling experiences in Thailand, I have studied, adapted, and tried out different ways to keep a teaching journal. I have asked the student teachers I supervise to do the same. Over the years, I have developed an exploratory approach to keeping a teaching journal. With this in mind, the point of this chapter is to explain and illustrate the use of a teaching journal to explore teaching with the aim of gaining awareness of our teaching practices and beliefs. I do this by answering the following:

- What is a teaching journal?
- What do teachers write about? What could they be writing about?
- What types of responses to journal entries are possible?

What is a teaching journal?

As it is defined in the literature, the usual teaching journal is a first person account of a series of teaching experiences.[2] The idea is to write about teaching experiences as regularly as possible over a period of time, then to analyze these entries for patterns and conspicuous events. A teaching journal can also function as a place to celebrate discoveries, successes, and "golden moments" (Fanselow 1987), as well as to "criticize, doubt, express frustration, and raise questions" (Bailey 1990: 218). In addition, it can create an opportunity to confront the affective aspects of being a teacher, including what annoys, disconcerts, frustrates, encourages, influences, motivates, and inspires us.

As I emphasize throughout this chapter, teaching journals can be a place for us to explore our teaching beliefs and practices. We can use the journal not only to plan and analyze our lessons, but also to plan and carry out our own exploration projects. In addition, journals can be a place for us to collaborate on projects, with other teachers and teacher educators, as well as to focus attention on the assumptions underlying exploration itself. For

write some of the students' language on the board, and have the class analyze it for errors and correctness. But, I also ended up listening to myself and the students, and I found myself listening to my own use of exaggerated language. I wondered what would happen if I spoke naturally in the class, without exaggerating my English. I tried it, and decided to tape-record the class to see how I changed my use of language and how the students reacted to my natural use of English.

2 There are a number of publications by those who write about the use of second language teaching journals. These include Bailey (1990), Brinton and Holten (1989), Brinton, Holten, and Goodwin (1993), Brock, Yu, and Wong (1992), Farrell (1996), Fattah (1993), Gebhard and Duncan (1992), Holten and Brinton (1995), Jarvis (1992), and McDonough (1994).

example, it is possible to discuss the difference between prescription and description, the value of nonjudgment, how we can take on responsibility for our own teaching, how we can pay attention to our use of language to talk about teaching, and different avenues we can use to explore teaching. (See Chapter 1 for an overview of these assumptions.)

There is no one way to keep a teaching journal. The approach varies, as with any creative endeavor to better understand ourselves and our behavior. Here, I provide two directions a teaching journal can take: intrapersonal and dialogical. I encourage you to be open to these ideas, but also to consider other possible ways to process a journal based on particular contexts and needs.

An intrapersonal journal

As *intrapersonal* journalists, we are both the writers and the audience of our own journals. Teacher educators generally encourage us to focus our journal entries on what we perceive to have gone on in our classrooms. Some also see value, however, in writing about our beliefs about teaching and learning, the students in our classes, our own language learning experiences and how that relates to teaching, and anything related to teaching.

One way teachers write in journals is through a kind of "stream-of-consciousness" writing. The intrapersonal journalist sees no particular need to worry about grammar, style, or organization, because the emphasis is on obtaining a record of teaching and feelings and thoughts about it. I encourage this type of writing because writing freely about whatever comes into our minds is a form of exploration that can generate lots of ideas and awareness about ourselves as teachers and our teaching.

I also see value, however, in writing down plans, observations, thoughts, and feelings in an organized way. For example, through stream-of-consciousness writing, an interest in the way I was giving students directions to classroom activities surfaced. I decided to explore what would happen if I gave students directions to a small-group activity on an overhead, rather than giving them orally, my usual way. As I wrote in my journal, my way of writing changed. As I planned the details of the lesson, I wrote slowly and neatly. As I wrote, I stopped to imagine myself not talking at all as the students arrived, turning on the overhead, gesturing for the students to read and follow the instructions. I also methodically wrote about my predictions about how individual students would react to my unusual way of introducing an activity and starting the class.

I tape-recorded the beginning of the class. Later, as I listened to the tape, I described what went on, including details about my behavior (e.g., how long

I was silent and when), wrote down comments students made when they saw the instructions projected on an overhead projector screen (e.g., some became silent and started copying the instructions into their notebooks). I also reflected and wrote on whether or not my predictions about individual students' reactions came true (they did not) and whether or not the way I actually gave the instructions matched how I had planned to give them. (I discovered that they did not always match. For example, I had planned to be completely silent, but I talked with several students as they entered the classroom.) I also thought about and mindfully wrote down alternative ways that I could give instructions (e.g., by giving them as a dictation or on a handout that they would read, but probably not start copying down).

The idea here is that stream-of-consciousness writing, in which we write about anything seemingly relevant that comes into our heads, is one way to write in an intrapersonal journal. But, we can also write methodically. Both types of entries can be combined.

As Bailey (1990) recommends, after a period of time and a number of entries, a logical step is to review journal entries, analyze teaching and record prominent events, and look for patterns in teaching behaviors. I add that we can also try to understand our feelings related to what went on in the classroom. I agree with Bailey that this analysis of the journal entries is critically important, and I suggest reading entries more than once, jotting down thoughts as we read.

In addition, I suggest that teachers give interpretations to the patterns and events in their teaching. As discussed in Chapter 3 and illustrated in Chapter 9, interpretations can be made through a wide variety of criteria, including knowledge based on classroom-centered research, learning theory, classroom experience, and more. As also discussed in Chapter 3, it seems appropriate here to follow Fanselow's (1988) advice to add outlandish, even opposite, interpretations to your normal ones to remind you that for any one interpretation, there are many others.

Task Break

Have you every kept a personal journal or diary?
What was the experience like for you?

A dialogue journal

Keeping an intrapersonal journal is difficult for some of us because we are writing for and to ourselves. There is no outside audience for the journal, something that many of us find to be a motivating force behind our writing. Outside audiences for our writing also provide a source of feedback, as well as a way to share teaching ideas, and explore practices and beliefs. As a result, some of us prefer to work with a dialogue journal because it creates both an audience for our writing and a relationship with someone who is sensitive to our teaching explorations.

The process of keeping a dialogue journal begins with the teacher. As with the intrapersonal teaching journal, the teacher is responsible for writing in the journal – recording descriptions, thoughts, and feelings about teaching, as well as analyzing journal entries for salient events and patterns. A dialogue journal differs from an intrapersonal journal in several ways. Unlike an intrapersonal journal, in which the emphasis is on introspection through communication with oneself, the purpose of a dialogue journal is to gain awareness through interaction with others. The objective is for the teachers to connect with a teacher educator or other teachers, to establish rapport through which they can ask each other questions, respond to these questions, react to comments, and basically communicate ideas about teaching beliefs and practices.

Brinton, Holten, and Goodwin (1993) point out that a dialogue journal shares many of the characteristics of personal letter writing. As they emphasize, the process of writing back and forth should deepen and personalize the relationship between the journal writers in a positive, trusting way. If the process is working, the teacher should "find the dialogue journal a safe place to write questions, concerns, failures and successes" (p. 16). As Roderick (1986) puts it, both teachers and teacher educators become "co-constructors of the educational experience" (p. 308).

A dialogue journal also differs from an intrapersonal journal in that we may be more cautious about what to include in it. For example, in an intrapersonal type of journal, we might sometimes find ourselves going off on tangents, some very personal in nature. We do not usually worry about it, however, because we know that no one will be purposefully reading these entries. In a dialogue journal, that is not the case, for another person will indeed be reading and commenting on what is written.

Admittedly, keeping a dialogue journal can be threatening to some teachers. One reason is that we are sometimes asked to face ourselves and to learn things about ourselves that we have trouble understanding or accepting and are perhaps not ready to disclose to others. As Jarvis (1992) puts it, it can be like writing "confessions or bearing the soul."

Bailey (1990) offers a suggestion that aims at avoiding a possibly disconcerting situation while at the same time allowing teachers to write freely in their journals. She recommends that before giving the journal to the teacher educator, supervisor, or another teacher, the teacher as journalist revise the entries to create a public version of the journal. Teachers I have worked with in a variety of teacher-education programs have reacted very favorably to this part of the journaling process, although some have said that the process of rewriting parts of their journal created more work than they had expected. They added, however, that by creating a public version of their journal, they gained an additional chance to critically reflect on their teaching beliefs and practices, a positive experience for most of them.

As Brinton, Holten, and Goodwin (1993) point out, another difference between an intrapersonal and dialogue journal, when the journaling dialogue is between a teacher and teacher educator or supervisor, is the vital role that the teacher educator can play in transforming the teacher's isolated thoughts and ideas into a meaningful whole through the types of responses given to the questions and comments posed by teachers in their journals. It is important for teachers and teacher educators to be aware of the kinds of responses that are possible in a journal and that can promote meaningful interaction and worthwhile reflection, as well as create opportunities for teachers to synthesize their experience. (See the section, titled "What types of responses to journal entries are possible?") I also believe that teacher educators are not the only ones who can provide meaningful interaction through their responses to teachers' questions. Teachers who communicate with other teachers through a journal can also do this, especially when they realize that a teacher educator is, in reality, simply an experienced teacher with a title and "some" power, and that teachers can empower themselves to carry out in-depth inquiry into teaching and learning.

A group of teachers at City Polytechnic of Hong Kong, Mark Brock, Bartholomew Yu, and Matilda Wong (1992), have illustrated that teacher educators are not always needed to have meaningful dialogue and that teachers can collaboratively network on their own to create an ongoing dialogue. They explored teaching by passing a journal back and forth, adding descriptive observations of their own teaching, asking each other questions and for advice, and commenting on remarks made. They also met weekly to talk about their entries, as well as to analyze their collaborative journal, synthesize recurring issues and concerns, and create a public version.

A collaborative dialogue journal also offers the opportunity for us to cooperate with each other on teaching projects. For example, through journal interaction, a few of us might decide to see what happens in our writing classes when we do the same activity. We could create the lesson plan together through joint journal entries, then describe what happened in each of our classes during the activity, read essays written by the students in our respective classes, and so on.

Likewise, a collaborative dialogue journal offers chances for us to support each other's efforts to explore our teaching. We can each write about what we want to explore. For example, I might be interested in gaining awareness of the way students and I read in class, whereas you might be interested in how you set up and carry out group-work activities, use the blackboard, give directions, or take roll. We could then share descriptions about how we do these things. For example, I might describe how we do oral reading, each student taking a turn to read out loud. And, we could share our plans to explore, giving each other ideas. For example, you might suggest I do the opposite by having students read silently at their seats while listening to soft music. We could then share what happens as a result of exploring. For example, I might report that the students said they enjoyed reading silently while listening to music and that 80% of the students answered all the comprehension questions correctly.

It is easy to see the possible benefits of teachers interacting through a collaborative dialogue journal, and I believe that such collaborative efforts can provide chances for teachers to take on responsibility for learning about teaching from each other, and this process can indeed provide many benefits to teachers. For example, Brock, Yu, and Wong state, "Through diary writing and sharing experience, we gained new suggestions and ideas from one another and discovered new options for approaching particular teaching tasks" (1992: 304). They point out that "the sharing of feelings and opinions through responding to one another and discussing experiences provided encouragement and support" (ibid., 304).

I have had mixed reactions to the use of collaborative journals in a pre-service teacher-education program, however. Not all the teachers liked or wanted to participate with peers in a collaborative journaling experience, and many of the novice teachers claimed that they did not know enough about teaching to give much more than what they considered to be trivial comments and responses to questions. These same teachers also pointed out, however, that they gained knowledge from the more experienced teachers in relation to answers they got to their questions. Experienced teachers in the program likewise indicated that answering novice teachers' questions gave them much to think about.

What do teachers write about?
What could they be writing about?

Let's begin this section with a task.

Task Break

- Study the list of questions below. Put a check next to any question you think matches your concerns as a teacher at present.

  1. What are different group-work activities?
  2. How can I use visual materials in my teaching?
  3. How can I get over being so nervous in class?
  4. Why do I feel so good about my teaching one day and so bad the next?
  5. How can I give clearer instructions?
  6. What language errors should I correct? How should I correct them?
  7. How do other teachers get students to do their homework?
  8. What can I do when I have 5 extra minutes at the end of class?
  9. How can I make more effective use of students' time?
  10. The students know more grammar than me! What can I do?
  11. How do I find enough time to prepare my lessons?
  12. How can I get students to take on responsibility for their own learning?
  13. What can I do in class tomorrow?
  14. How can I identify the learning strategies students use?
  15. Can students master new learning strategies?
  16. What culture should I teach? My own? Or should I teach them to adapt to any culture while using English?
  17. How can I get the administration to change its textbook and other policies?
  18. What is the best way to teach?

- Study the questions you put a check next to. Select three questions that you believe to be the most relevant for you right now in your teaching.
- If you are studying with other teachers, compare your choices.

(Continued)

> • Read the rest of this section on what teachers write about, especially with regard to the questions they ask. Consider your questions in relation to how long you have been teaching. For example, if you are new to teaching, you possibly ask questions related to survival (questions 3, 4, 6, 8, 10, 11, 13, 18). If you have much experience, you possibly ask questions related to issues and learning (questions 9, 12, 14, 16, 17).

Through an informal analysis of teaching journals, I have discovered that teachers write about many different topics and raise a variety of questions related to these topics. However, the nature of the topics and related questions seem to vary according to the degree of experience they have. Consider, for example, the sample list of questions that novice and experienced teachers raised in their journals.

My informal exploration of inexperienced teachers' questions as they relate to topics discussed in their journals is in line with research done on content teaching by Berliner (1986), Fuller (1969), and Fuller and Brown (1975), as well as with more recent research in second language teacher development by Holten and Brinton (1995), Numrich (1996), and Richards and Ho (1998). Novice teachers tend to limit their questions to those about teaching techniques, ways to solve teaching problems, and survival concerns. They want to know how to teach, and many are looking for advice on the best way to teach, for example, how they should correct students' language errors, give clear instructions, teach a reading lesson, grade compositions, use the chalkboard, and so on. Inexperienced teachers also tend to raise more questions and address topics that focus attention on themselves, in particular their feelings about their teaching. Closely connected, Richards and Ho (1998) discovered that only about 20% of the questions that thirty-two preservice teachers in a Hong Kong M.A. TESL program asked in their journals could be considered to be reflective.

Inexperienced teachers	*Experienced Teachers*
• How can I get over being so nervous in class?	• How can I make more effective use of students' time?
• Why do I feel so good about my teaching one day and so bad the next?	• How can I get students to take on more responsibility for their own learning?

- What can I do in class tomorrow?
- How can I give clearer instructions?
- What language errors should I correct? How should I correct them?
- What can I do when I have 5 extra minutes at the end of class?

- How can I identify the learning strategies students use?
- Can students master new strategies?
- What culture should I teach? My own? Or should I teach them to adapt to any culture while using English?

Does experience as a teacher lead to asking more types of questions and becoming more reflective? I am tempted to say that this is true. Experienced teachers seem to raise questions that transcend concern with "What can I do tomorrow in class?" and "What is the best way to teach?" Instead, these questions indicate concern with student learning and teaching issues.[3] But there is little research on this topic, so I hesitate to speculate too much.

I do believe, however, that teaching teachers how to explore, no matter how much or how little classroom experience they have, can provide opportunities for them to raise a great variety of questions and to reflect on teaching. This is because exploration leads to new knowledge and new questions. With this in mind, I end this section with some journal-writing activities that we can use to explore teaching. In other words, these are topics we could be writing about in our journals.

One activity is to write about your own experience as a language learner. By writing about your own experience, you can consider how your language-learning experiences have possibly influenced the way you teach. Have you had a favorite teacher who made an impression on you or who influenced your beliefs about second language teaching and learning? Have you had negative experiences that have had an impact on your beliefs and practices?[4]

---

3 Freeman (1991) was able to identify a number of concerns of foreign language teachers over an 18-month period. He discovered, for example, that experienced teachers in his study had a quandary over balancing spontaneous communication with keeping control through discipline, and the use of real-world language as opposed to artificial classroom language. Farrell (1996) studied the journals of three experienced EFL teachers in Korea. He discovered that two of the teachers were reflective in their orientation to teaching, and raised critical issues about their teaching.

4 Bailey (1990), Bailey et al. (1996), and Johnson (1999) also recommend that teachers reflect on how their language-learning experience may have influenced their teaching beliefs and practices. This idea stems from Lortie's (1975) concept of the *apprenticeship of observation*, that we spend much time as students observing teaching and this experience influences how we teach and our beliefs about teaching and learning.

You can also use journals to plan what you will do in the classroom. You can work through lesson plans, including jotting down activities and step-by-step procedures for carrying them out, sketching out seating arrangements, noting time constraints and predicting how much time each step in an activity might take, and so on. Along with these lesson plans, you can consider the kinds of behaviors you want to explore in your teaching. You can ask questions and narrow them. For example: What aspects of your teaching are you genuinely interested in learning more about? Questioning behaviors? Then, what specifically about questioning? The content of your questions? The content of the students' questions? The source and targets of questions in the class? The difference between the kinds of questions you ask inside and outside the classroom? Or, are you interested in language error treatment? When do you treat errors? How do you treat errors? What kinds of errors do you treat? Should errors be corrected at all? (See Chapters 3 and 4 for other ideas.)

You can also explore by following the avenues of exploration that Robert Oprandy and I wrote about in Chapter 1. For example, as you plan, you can consider asking yourself such questions as these: Will I try to identify a teaching behavior I use over and over again, then try the opposite to see what happens? Will I explore to see if how I believe I teach (for example, giving students chances to talk a lot in class) is congruent with how I actually teach? Will I explore to gain awareness of my beliefs about teaching (for example, believing in student-centered activities) and the way I teach (for example, drilling students on points of grammar)? Or do I want to explore a problem or concern in my teaching?

Planning is only part of exploration. You can also observe and write about what happens when you implement the plan. For example, after tape-recording, analyzing, and writing about the use of questions in the classroom where you teach, you could try to understand how people use questions in contexts outside classrooms, as well as make use of this knowledge in your teaching. Or, if your interest includes how you treat learners' oral errors, you might tape-record your lessons, listen to the tapes while jotting down examples in your journals of when you treat errors, and write about the patterns in your error treatment, alternative ways you might try out to treat errors differently, and how your way of treating errors matches or fails to match your beliefs about error treatment and language learning.

You can also explore simply to explore without any planning at all! Then you can write about what happened. For example, I sometimes tape-record interaction in class, randomly select 5 minutes of the class to listen to, and, as I listen to this segment, describe what is going on in the class. Sometimes I hear something that makes me curious and I listen more selectively, for example, to the way I consistently interrupt a particular student, not letting him finish his sentences. While I am listening, I might jot down ideas about alternative ways to teach – for instance, by doing the opposite and being silent, purposely letting the student finish his sentences. I do not do this necessarily because I think it is better; I do it because I want to see what happens. The same is true for many of my explorations. I explore out of pure curiosity and, as much as possible, without preconceived ideas about what it is that I should be doing as a teacher.

It is also possible to explore by observing and writing about what goes on in other teachers' classrooms. I have made it a point to observe other teachers' classrooms since the late 1970s. Even when I am very busy, I find the time. Why? Because I usually take away from the observation experience a lot of teaching ideas. As I discussed in Chapter 3, following Fanselow's (1988) ideas, by visiting classrooms I am able to see my own teaching in the teaching of others.

You can also write about exploration itself. I see great value in teachers writing about what exploration is and some of the issues related to exploration. As Robert Oprandy and I discussed in Chapter 1, to explore we need to take on responsibility for our own teaching. Yet, in many teaching contexts, teachers are not given opportunities to explore. Rather, we are expected to imitate and follow the prescriptions of others. You can also write about the complexity of exploration. In Chapter 1, we discussed the necessity of letting go of judgments and our preconceived notions about good or bad teaching. In reality, though, it is not easy to do so. It is one thing to say that we want to free ourselves by simply seeing teaching as clearly as possible and to make decisions based on our observations and reflections rather than on blind acceptance of others' ideas about how we should teach. It is another thing to put this belief into practice. Such issues are well worth writing about in our journals, perhaps even more so in a dialogue journal, where we can have an ongoing discussion.

Task Break

Study my journal entries in the Appendix at the end of this chapter. What did I write about in entries 18, 19, and 20? How was I exploring? What other ways could I use my journal to explore teaching?

What types of responses to journal entries are possible?

Teachers and teacher educators or supervisors can respond to journal entries in a variety of ways. Based on the investigation of Brinton, Holten, and Goodwin (1993) and my own exploration, I characterize and illustrate seven response types.

Response types and their possible benefits

Affective and personalizing comments
- Can give journals their letter-like quality.
- Can provide a personal tone.
- Can contribute to establishing rapport.
- Can help to build confidence.

Procedural comments
- Can remind teachers of established rules and procedures.
- Can provide a means to negotiate procedures.
- Can communicate expectations of the teacher educator, supervisor, or peer teacher.
- Can furnish information about assignments or agreed-on explorations.

Direct responses to questions
- Can provide knowledge directly related to the journalist's inquiry agenda.
- Can promote knowledge that can be used for more extensive commenting.

Understanding responses
- Can function as a mirror for the teacher to see his or her ideas, practices, feelings, or attitudes more clearly.
- Can act as a catalyst for new lines of inquiry.

Exploratory suggestions
- Can provide ways for teachers to explore teaching.
- Can furnish a means for teachers to gain awareness of teaching beliefs and practices.

Synthesis comments and questions
- Can provide a link between comments given earlier and comments just given.
- Can raise issues for teachers.
- Can provide an opportunity to pull together pieces of knowledge to form new concepts.

Unsolicited comments and questions
- Can draw journalist's attention to aspects of teaching.
- Can raise new issues and lines of inquiry.

Affective and personalizing comments

Here are some examples of affective and personalizing comments: "I really enjoyed your story about meeting your student in the street," and "What an interesting question!" Like Brinton, Holten, and Goodwin, I think of these as affective and personalizing comments because they are meant to reduce anxiety for the teacher, build a sense of rapport, and establish an informal relationship similar to one between two people writing personal letters back and forth.

Procedural comments

As Brinton, Holtin, and Goodwin (1993) mention, in teacher education settings procedural comments are often used as reminders of when assignments are due and to review established rules. Here are a few examples of such comments: "I notice you write in your journal only twice each week. I thought we said we would write in it three times," and "Do you want to meet to talk about journal topics? It might help if we meet to talk about things."

Direct responses to questions

Consider this direct response to a teacher's question that I wrote in the margin of her journal:

You asked, "How can I make language comprehensible to students?" Well, there is no easy answer. I remember that Long (1987) points out several possibilities. He suggests language is made more comprehensible when speakers use extra-linguistic fillers (gestures, special facial expressions, drawings and pictures), use confirmation and comprehension checks, and keep conversations in the "here and now." I personally like to slow down my speech, keeping normal intonation going, as well as use slightly exaggerated nonverbal behavior (for instance, by scratching my slightly tilted head, and making my face look puzzled, lip slightly curled to the side of my face, when I say, "That's a tough question").

Some teachers seem to appreciate direct responses to their questions. Brinton, Holten, and Goodwin point out that such direct responses are important because they not only allow the teacher to set the topical agenda and initiate dialogue, but also affirm for the teacher that the topic is sound, even insightful enough to act as "a springboard for commenting more extensively on the topic raised, perhaps discussing relevant research findings, mentioning teaching strategies for handling a given situation, and citing relevant literature" (1993: 17).

Understanding responses

I can appreciate straightforward responses. However, I also believe that teachers can benefit from searching for answers to their own questions, if for no other reason than that they will discover many additional incidental things in the process. The next response type enables the teacher educator to show an understanding of the problems the teacher writes about in the journal without telling how to solve the problem.

Here is an example of an understanding response:

You state that you don't want to treat students' errors in your conversation class because this can interfere with the natural flow of interaction. You also say that you are frustrated because students ask for feedback. You also seem to be searching for ways to give them feedback on their language use in more indirect ways, such as jotting down their errors and giving them to students later to correct. Am I correct in my understanding?

Curran (1976, 1978) and Rardin, Tranel, Green, and Tirone (1988) tell of the value of closely listening to what others are saying, as well as in giving a recognized understanding of what was said. As in the example above, as a teacher educator, rather than giving my opinion or suggestions, I sometimes paraphrase what teachers have written in their journals to provide a "mirror" image of their ideas and feelings. Although not all teachers like to be faced with their own ideas and statements of attitudes and feelings, some teachers have told me that such understanding responses have provided an opportunity for them to clarify or discern their ideas, attitudes, and feelings. Such awareness frees them to search for answers to their own questions. It sometimes leaves them invigorated and in control of their own learning, rather than feeling as if they are constantly being helped to find answers to the questions they have.

Exploratory suggestions

As explained in Chapter 1, there are at least four different avenues to awareness, which suggest different ways to explore our teaching. These include exploration through (1) problem solving, (2) seeing what happens by trying the opposite or adapting random teaching behaviors, (3) seeing what is by contrasting what we do with what we think we do or by considering what we believe in light of what we do, and (4) clarifying our feelings. As we read other teachers' journals, we can respond by offering suggestions about how to explore their teaching through one or more of these ways.

Synthesis comments and questions

It is also possible to offer what I call synthesis comments and questions. Here is an example:

You made the point many times earlier in your journal that students do not always seem receptive to what is going on in class. Your last few entries have been about how receptive these same students are to recent classes. What do you think is different? Why are these same students acting so differently?

Some teachers are too close to their teaching to see what might be obvious to an outside reader. One advantage of synthesis responses is that they provide a means for teachers to see patterns in their teaching, bring issues to light, and generally let teachers make connections between comments they make in their journals.

Unsolicited comments and suggestions

A final response type involves the use of unsolicited comments and suggestions. As Brinton, Holten, and Goodwin point out, it is possible for teacher educators (and, I would add, teachers reading each other's journals) to "respond to issues raised between the lines" (1993: 16). Here is an example of a comment I recently heard a teacher educator make: "I notice you rarely discuss classroom management in your journal, although you have verbally expressed interest in a variety of management topics, for example, how to set up group work and how to use time efficiently. I would be interested in your ideas on management."

Some teachers value unsolicited comments and suggestions. However, some prefer to generate their own lines of inquiry and do not appreciate a lot of comments or suggestions. When I am writing in a journal, and I find myself offering too many ideas too often, I like to remember something Fanselow (1997) points out: being given information perpetually could imply that the person is incapable of discovering that information by herself or himself.

Task Break

1. Study the response types discussed above. As a teacher or teacher educator, which response types do you favor?
2. Read the sample pages from the teaching journal located in the Appendix to this chapter. Imagine that you have been asked to respond to the journal entries. Using the response types given in this chapter, respond to the entries. If possible, read other teachers' responses to the same journal entries.

Some concluding remarks and a special task

I encourage you to keep a journal at least once in your life for an extended period of time. If you accept the challenge of keeping a journal, take the task seriously. Keeping a journal can be a waste of time if it is done in a rote kind of way, but it can be a very rewarding experience if accepted with interest and a genuine desire to explore. With this in mind, I offer one final task, one that differs from other tasks in that I ask you to do it for an extended period of time.

Task Break

Here is a chance to keep a journal. If you are teaching, write about this experience. If you are presently not teaching, keep a journal anyway. Write about your experiences as a student of teaching. If you are a supervisor, you may prefer to write about your work with teachers.

- Select one of the journaling processes discussed in this chapter. Base your decision on your context and interest. Keep this journal for at least a month (preferably longer), following the suggestions given in this chapter.
- After a month, read your entries. If you are keeping an intrapersonal journal, write a private summary of what you have learned. If you are keeping a dialogue journal, create a public version that includes a synthesis of what you learned. Then, meet with those who have agreed to read and respond to your entries.
- At the end of this experience, consider the value of keeping a journal.

Appendix

A Teaching Journal   Thammasat University, Bangkok

Entry 18

I thought that this would be a good time to think through the lesson I will do tomorrow in the listening-speaking class. I told the students that we would do an activity of reporting verbs. They want to practice using them. I guess I had better be prepared!

Let s see, I plan to begin the class by collecting their homework. I hope that most of the students did the workbook activity on reporting verbs. They seem to have trouble with using the pronoun with the verb to tell, as in He told me he was happy or She told us to do our homework. I noticed that a few of the students write and say things like, He told he was happy. Maybe these students are confused with the reporting verb said, as in He said he was happy. Anyway, I think I will tape-record the class. I can listen to it to analyze what kinds of problems these students have with reporting verbs.

OK! Onward with the lesson plan! I think I will open the lesson by reviewing the grammatical rules for reporting verbs. I can review the handout I gave them in class yesterday. Then, I will demonstrate what I want them to do in small groups. I will show them the postcards that I brought from different countries. It s lucky I kept these cards from friends and family! They not only decorated my wall at home for a while, but are now proving to be a very useful teaching material! It is true what they say. Almost anything can be used as teaching material! I will demonstrate, reading the message on the back of the card silently. Then, I will ask Natapon to ask me, Who s the card from? and What s she/he say? Then, I will report. I ll use reporting verbs   something like this: The card s from my friend Joel. He s now living in Japan. He says he is visiting Osaka, and he tells me that he will come to visit me in Thailand in January.

Hmmm . . . I notice that his handwriting isn t very easy to read. I wonder if the students will be able to figure it out. I better look carefully at the writing on the other cards, perhaps not use ones that are just too difficult to comprehend for one reason or another. Oh! I have an idea. I ll use some of the cards from friends. I can also use the blank cards I have from my travels. I can write things on them that the students can understand, maybe even some things the students might find funny. It certainly is lucky I buy cards when I travel and then forget to write to my friends! I must have 20 or so postcards somewhere in my desk.

OK! Onward with the lesson plan. I will point out that we use the present tense when reporting from something we read. I ll also emphasize that they need to use the pronoun with tells   He tells me. . . After the demonstration, I ll put students into small groups. I think I ll try something I saw Wilson do the other day when I sat in on his class. I ll divide students into groups of five students by handing out different kinds of candy. The students with the lemon drops will form one group, students with cherry flavor will form another group. Hmmm . . . I wonder what kind of interesting candy I can find. I had better head for the market this afternoon.

I ll designate in the room where each group is located, and once students are in groups, I ll give each student two postcards. I ll also give each group a list of questions they can ask (for example, *Who s the card from?* and *What s she say?*). I better write this up next. I will designate one student in each group to be the reader. The other students can then ask him or her questions, and the reader can answer their questions by reporting. As students finish with cards, I ll collect them and pass them on to other groups. They will get lots of practice reading authentic English and reporting.

OK! This seems like a doable lesson. I think I ll head for the market to see what kind of candy I can buy.

Entry 19

Well, today s lesson didn t go exactly like I planned! To begin, I left the candy on my desk. So, I just grouped students who were sitting near each other. When I demonstrated the reporting verb activity, students seemed to catch on right away. I m glad about that.

I m also glad that I tape-recorded the lesson. Let s see. I think I will listen to the tape now. I ll listen to the beginning. Then, since I kept the tape recorder with a couple of the groups for a period of time, I think I ll listen in on one or two of the groups to see if they use reporting verbs and if they still have problems. I can write as I listen. Hmmm . . . there certainly is a lot of noise as the students enter. They are talking in Thai. I wonder how I could get them to use English from the time they enter the door. I think I ll talk with them about this. I read about a teacher who established an English community of learners. She had them establish their own rules for language use in the classroom. This might be an idea. I wonder where I read that. Oh, yeah, it was in English Teaching Forum, I think a couple issues back.

OK, how about the students use of reporting verbs? Let s see, the students in on the tape, at least in this group, shows me that they are doing what I expected them to do. They are asking the reader questions about what s on the postcard. But, they seem to be reading from the handout I gave them. It seems fairly rote. The reader is reporting.

Nittiya: *Who is the card from? (reading)*
Shoopan: *It's from Jerry.*
Nittiya: *Where is he? (reading)*
Shoopan: *Japan.*
Natapon: *What he say? (not reading)*
Shoopan: *He says he has a good time in Japan. He says the weather is good.*
Nittiya: *Does he ask you any questions? (reading)*
Shoopan: *He ask me if I want to go to Japan.*

OK, this example seems fairly typical of the way students are doing this activity. They are reading questions from the handout. Well, I suppose this is one way. Actually, this is a fairly predictable thing for them to do. I wonder what I can do so that students don't just read the questions.

I also notice that most of the students do use the pronoun when they use ask. But, as I search for examples of students' use of tell + pronoun, I discover that students aren't using this reporting verb at all. I wonder why?

Wow! What am I hearing? I just fast-forwarded the tape and stopped to listen. I hear a lot of Thai. What are they talking about? If I'm not mistaken, I think they are talking about soccer. Yes, the world football matches! Goodness! Their voices are soft. I wonder how long they speak Thai. Amazing! I just timed it. Over 4 minutes. Why didn't I hear this? Are other groups speaking Thai, too? Yes, they are. Here's another example. Oh! I got it! When I'm with groups on one side of the room, and the students finish with the postcards (which doesn't seem to take them long to do), they start up conversations in Thai. Interesting discovery.

So, what to do about this? The problem seems to be with the activity. I could give them tasks that take longer and engage them more. What else could I do? I wonder. I think I'll do the opposite just to see what happens. I'll have them spend 10 minutes of class time speaking in Thai. They won't be allowed to speak any English. I wonder what will happen? Will this get the point across that they are there to learn English?

Entry 20

Today I observed Michael's class. He's doing an activity in which groups of students are writing and putting on their own skits. Each group has a set designer, a director, and a team of actors. I wonder who the writers were? Everyone in the group? Anyway, today they were practicing. They are planning to invite guests. I suppose classmates and other teachers. They will also film each skit.

As I watched what was going on, I saw how engaged the students were. They were using English most of the time, and two students asked the teacher for help with language: What's this thing called in English? Is this sentence correct? That never happens in my class. Another thing I noticed was that students asked each other questions, real questions, in English. They were communicating in English. Very little Thai. I will have to talk with Michael about how he gets students to use so much English. Today was a real eye-opener!

Wish I had more time to write! Oh, well! Got to go.

6 *Exploring with a supervisor*

Robert Oprandy

> Supervision can no longer be viewed as a one-way phenomenon,
> an imposition of supervisory control on a docile teacher. . . .
> Both parties have resources on which they may draw – neither
> is defenseless and both are responsible for the environment,
> the context, they coconstruct.
>
> —D. Waite (1993: 697)

We have emphasized how we can raise our awareness of teaching through engaging in any of a number of exploratory activities. The more we do so, the greater the likelihood we can consider the core questions of who we are as teachers, the roles we wish to assume, and whether/how to change classroom behaviors to align more closely with our beliefs about teaching and learning. Beginning to articulate those beliefs, however tentatively, and then striving to make our behaviors and those of our students increasingly congruent with those beliefs, is at the heart of the process of teacher exploration. As we have argued elsewhere, observation, action research, journaling, and learning through talk with teachers (including supervising teachers) are invaluable means by which we can approximate how we visualize ourselves as teachers. Each of these activities can be seen as spokes within the wheel of the exploring teacher's journey of awareness.

In Chapter 8 we emphasize the importance of talk among teachers in what is often described as a "lonely profession." That chapter contains a vivid example of how *collaborative conversations* with other teachers can help us overcome the isolation endemic to the teaching profession (Greene 1973; Lortie 1975; Waller 1967). Although we encourage the establishment of increased opportunities for teachers to talk with each other, we fully realize that most schools and the schedules, curricula, and tests that tend to drive them are not structured to afford many, if any, such opportunities for teacher-to-teacher shop talk. Instead, the hierarchical structures we have inherited usually mandate administrators or supervisors to observe and comment on our work. The usual expectation is that a short chat or more formal discussion of the observed class will follow, and may also precede, such observations. These discussions, then, are the prescribed settings in which we tend to talk about our work. As such, they can provide another avenue – in some cases, the only one besides self-reflection – for considering the core concerns regarding our identity as teachers, the roles we (may) play, the beliefs we have about teaching and learning and the behaviors we try out as we work with learners.

As egalitarian as many of us pretend to be in such teacher–supervisor conferences, a hierarchy is nevertheless present and necessarily affects the kind of talk that marks such discussions (Arcario 1994; McFaul & Cooper 1984; Tirone 1990; Waite 1993). Chances for a teacher's advancement or even rehiring may be influenced, to some extent, by those who observe and then direct these discussions. Without minimizing how powerful a position supervisors can have regarding a teacher's livelihood, I prefer to focus in this chapter on the following questions:

- What is the nature of talk that teachers usually engage in with supervisors, and what roles are congruent with such talk?
- How can teachers assume more responsibility for the kinds of talk they have with supervisors, and what can supervisors do to share such responsibility?
- What contexts promote talk between teachers and supervisors?

My responses to these questions call for teachers to assume more responsibility for what transpires in the teacher–supervisor relationship. Supervisors and language program administrators reading this book are, in turn, encouraged to think about how to allow teachers more initiative in and responsibility for directing the nature of the talk they (the teachers) have with those observing and evaluating their work. Shifting the responsibility, as well as increasing attention to how we use language and structure our conversations, are reflective of the exploratory approach laid out in the Preface and Chapter 1.

We will look at the questions first from the teacher's perspective and then from the supervisor's point of view. From each perspective will emerge practical suggestions for weaving webs between the often discomforting hierarchical, informational, and relational gaps that can separate supervisors and the teachers with whom they work. The ultimate goal is to level the playing field to the extent we can, to promote the kind of collegial coaching and cooperative exploration other teacher educators are also promoting (Dantonio 1995; Edge 1992; Showers 1985).

What is the nature of talk that teachers engage in with supervisors, and what roles are congruent with such talk?

Research on supervision shows that supervisors usually dictate the nature of talk in post-observation conferences with teachers (Lacey 1977). These conferences are the most common forum in which teacher–supervisor talk occurs. Waite (1993) confirmed that supervisors enjoy a privileged position in such conferences, generating the "data," initiating conferences and topics for discussion, and determining what teacher responses are sufficient and redirecting the talk when a teacher's response is considered insufficient.

Waite also identified three roles that teachers assumed in the supervisory sessions he studied. He found that some teachers assume a "passive conference role," in which the teacher listens to the supervisor, often says "uh-huh," and occasionally agrees by saying something like "Yeah, that would be a good idea." Such behavior encourages supervisors to talk more. Meanwhile, the passive teacher is generally "unable or unwilling to forcefully counter the supervisor's direct and indirect criticisms" (Waite, 1993: 696). This role would seem to complement nicely the privileged position that supervisors tend to enjoy during such conferences.

Waite found other teachers enacting "collaborative conference roles," characterized by active listening and by timing and phrasing their utterances in ways that would not appear confrontational. Such teachers seem to have a great deal of communicative competence as well as an ability to advance their agendas. It is this kind of role that I promote and provide strategies for in this chapter.

Waite found a third kind of teacher role in conferences with supervisors, which he called the "adversarial role." He gives examples of talk in which a teacher competed for the floor and was reluctant to accept her supervisor's comments or even the supervisor's role as her evaluator. The adversarial supervisee may be rare given Arcario's (1994) finding of not a single instance (in eleven post-observation discussions in three different schools) where a request by a supervisor to identify problems was met with resistance. His study, though, was of preservice teachers fulfilling a practice teaching requirement of their M.A. degree programs. In such cases, of course, failing such an important requirement would seem not worth the risk of being adversarial.

Closely scrutinizing post-observation conferences between ESL student teachers and supervisors in New York City, Arcario (1994) found a persistent pattern in the way such talk was structured. In what he calls "the canonical conversation of post-observation conferences," Arcario found that the talk consisted of three phases: an opening evaluative move, an evaluative sequence (evaluation-justification-prescription), and a closing.

Task Break

1. List advantages and disadvantages of assuming each of the three roles Waite identified – the passive, the collaborative, and the adversarial. If doing this with a partner, compare and discuss the items on your lists.

2. If you can do so, tape-record a conference you have with a supervisor (or with a teacher if you are a supervisor). Tally how many times during the conference the teacher seems to be playing each of the three roles. Transcribe a short exchange or two where the teacher could have assumed a role other than the one you tallied. What might have transpired to make the teacher assume that other role?

3. *If you are a teacher,* which of the three roles do you think you play or would play in conferences with supervisors and list three or four reasons why? Which would you prefer to play? Why? *If you are a supervisor,* consider the role(s) played by one of the teachers with whom you have conferences. Does your behavior influence the(se) role(s)? If so, how? Which of the three roles do you prefer teachers to play? Why? What can you do to try to arrange for teachers to assume that role?

The opening evaluative move was always accomplished by the supervisor either making a direct evaluative comment, such as "I liked your lesson," or inviting the teacher to give an evaluation of the lesson (e.g., "How did you feel about it?"). In either case, the supervisor serves the ball. Most of what follows this move "is an extended evaluation or critique sequence, or series of evaluation sequences" (p. 56), in which the teacher's performance is evaluated both by the supervisor and by the student teacher. This phase ends with prescriptions of "what the teacher should/could have done in the observed lesson, or what the teacher should/could do the next time" (pp. 57–58).

Interestingly, the powerful role that supervisors assume in structuring such meetings and in eliciting information from teachers parallels the roles that teachers take on in their classes (Bellack, Kliebard, Hyman, & Smith

1966), that is, supervisor : teacher : : teacher : student. If the evaluation of teachers that occurs in post-observation conferences follows a structure similar to how teachers work with learners in the classroom, it appears that both teachers and their supervisors arrange for the usual transmission model of education to dictate how they work together. Having established such a structure, they usually lock themselves into the concomitant roles that support the structure of such talk. This works against more collaborative conversations such as those demonstrated by the teachers in Chapter 8. Even when collaborative exploration supersedes evaluation as the purpose of teacher-to-teacher talk, the lure of following the established structure is still strong, making it difficult for us to break away from that structure.

Playing the usual supervisor–teacher game makes for an uneven playing field tilted to the supervisor's advantage. This presents problems for both participants. Teachers feel vulnerable, trying to guess what the observer wants to see, often tailoring their lessons to show that they can do what the supervisor is looking for or what the official observation form dictates. Teachers who do not agree with the learning assumptions of their supervisors or those implied by the observation form – and who do not exhibit classroom arrangements and behaviors congruent with such assumptions – could be assigned a diminished number of teaching hours in the next hiring cycle. Or worse, they might even put their jobs in jeopardy.

Supervisors may also feel uncomfortable playing the supervisory (or "snoopervisory") game. I become anxious, even after years of experience working with teachers, and especially when visiting newly hired teachers, who often assume a defensive stance in trying to please me. I cannot count the number of times I have seen teachers arrange to do lessons on comparatives and/or superlatives, on giving directions, or on the present continuous tense. Such lessons lend themselves to the use of concrete visual referents that are easy to get language learners to understand and practice. To this day, I cringe a bit when I realize that I will be observing yet another variation on one of these three much too familiar themes.

If one believes that communication is a dynamic co-construction of meaning, then the roles incumbent on supervisors and teachers in the traditional evaluation-oriented post-observation conferences would seem limited. Such roles fit with the transmission model of communication, which presumes a one-way, linear conveyance of messages from one with supposedly superior knowledge (the supervisor in this case) to one with presumably less knowledge (the teacher). The transmission model does not support the qualities of communication in the dynamic model. Nor does it allow for communication to be a truly two-way (or more) interplay of ideas, feelings, and reactions that reflect the creative co-constructions of the moment. The transmission model, akin to the *training* model of teacher education mentioned in the Preface, also does not fit into the exploratory approach we encourage.

Given the nature of talk called for in the dynamic model of communication, I suggest a new set of roles for supervisors and teachers that may result not only in a wider range of structures in teacher–supervisor conferences than Waite (1993) and Arcario (1994) found. It will also demand a range of (1) possible contexts in which the talk can occur, (2) topics to talk about, and (3) activities to promote such talk. With such a range to choose from, teachers may be more likely to find a match for their preferences. This may, in turn, open up the talk in a way that allows for more give-and-take and for more freedom from the usual constraints of post-observation conferences than the aforementioned studies uncovered. On the other hand, the deeply ingrained individual and institutional expectations of what should occur during such conferences make it very difficult to veer sharply away from the usual structure of such talk.

Task Break

Draw a sketch, either realistic or symbolic, of the typical context in which you (as a teacher or supervisor) have engaged in a post-observation conference. If you are new to teaching, make your sketch according to how you would visualize such future conferences.

1. Under the sketch, list the kinds of topics you recall talking about. (If you are a novice teacher who has yet to have such a discussion, what topics do you expect to come up when you do meet with a supervisor for the first time?) Put a line through those topics you felt were not (or will not be) very helpful to you in your development as a teacher (or to the teachers you worked with if you are a supervisor).
2. Add to the list other topics that might have been (or might be) incorporated into such discussions.
3. How closely did (or would) such discussions parallel the structure of "the canonical conversation of post-observation conferences" that Arcario found in his study?

/_____ /_____ /
Very different   Somewhat similar   The same
                  but also different

If you put an X on the left side of the line, characterize the differences. If you put an X on the right side,
what activities could have promoted noncanonical
talk during such discussions?

How can teachers assume more responsibility for the kinds of talk they have with supervisors, and what can supervisors do to share such responsibility?

In responding to both parts of this question, in each section below I will
consider the teacher's and the supervisor's perspectives. Numerous concrete
options open to each person will be mentioned, but before such options can
materialize, both parties may have to consider the stances they take in considering what to talk about and how to accomplish such talk.

Assuming a doubting or believing stance

You may be asking, "If post-observation conferences are so prescribed, no
matter how many contextual or topical possibilities I think of and no matter
how many different ideas of activities for promoting talk with supervisors
I conjure up, how can the essential nature of such talk change?" With good
reason, you may be questioning how much control you have over such talk,
or how you can take the initiative to change it. After all, school contexts,
especially those in urban settings, house themes of fragmentation and isolation, stratification, standardization, and reactionism (McFaul & Cooper
1984). It would be easy to give in to a homeostatic inertia far from the life
force that may have led you into teaching in the first place.

Such a fatalistic outlook assumes a doubting stance, which usually takes
one of two forms among the several hundred teachers and teacher educators
I have worked with in my quarter of a century in education. ("They" in what
follows refers to a class of students or of teachers-in-training. "I" refers to
either a teacher or a supervisor taking such a stance.)

1. I/They can't do that.   ⎫
                                   ⎬   Doubting stances
2. But how can I/they do that?   ⎭

Neither position 1 nor 2 holds much promise for accomplishing the doing to which the speaker (teacher or supervisor) refers. There is, however, a glimmer of possibility in the questioning of the second position.

Borrowing Elbow's (1973) *doubting game* and *believing game* metaphors, the movement from the second doubting stance to the third stance (a believing position) requires a simple substitution of one conjunction ("and") for another ("but"):

2. But how can I/they do that?
   ⇓
3. And how can I/they do that?

What results is a dramatic shift in perception of oneself as a teacher (or supervisor) and the trust one places in others to create new possibilities. The more we co-construct contexts, topics, and activities for talk that are congruent with the third stance, the easier it will be to attain the confidence and realize our competence in being able to achieve the fourth stance.

3. And how can I/they do that? ⎫
                                ⎬   Believing stances
4. And how! I/They can do that. ⎭

Of course, a mere change in tone of voice and in the ordering of words will not promise a *believing game* conviction in one's own and others' abilities. A significant shift in stance results from moving further into a "believing game" conviction. I believe that great athletes and sports coaches, actors and directors, teachers, supervisors, and teacher educators, or successful people in any walk of life, assume the third and fourth stances much of the time. In doing so, they bring to life the clichés I so often hear attributed to the great athletes: "They make those around them better" and "They raise their teammates (and their competitors) up to their own high level of performance." That is why Marva Collins (1992) and Jaime Escalante (portrayed in the movie *Stand and Deliver*) were able to do exemplary teaching despite the challenging circumstances they faced in the inner-city schools of Chicago and Los Angeles, respectively. The security they felt in themselves and in their beliefs about teaching and learning – and about their students' capabilities – opened up the kind of trusting relationship and effective performance that made it increasingly easier for everyone (teacher and students first, administrators, parents, and the public later) to play the believing game.

So having assumed a believing game stance that is focused on creating possibilities rooted in an exploratory spirit, we need not maintain a homeostatic, ritualistic kind of conversation with our counterpart. Nor do we need to continue to play the roles others have assumed before us. Teachers and supervisors willing to take risks and responsibility for a more dynamic way of relating to one another might wish to consider numerous new arrangements in which to converse.

Task Break

1. Assume a *believing game* stance and list what you would like to talk about with your supervisor both prior to and after a class she or he will observe. If you are a supervisor, consider how you can provide the teachers you observe with more choice in how you will use the time you spend together prior to and after the lessons you observe.
2. As a teacher being observed (or as a supervisor visiting teachers' classes), what are some *doubting game* beliefs that you or others in your position have thought about or expressed regarding observations? Write each belief in a *doubting game* column and change it into a *believing game* statement as in the following example:

Doubting game statement	*Believing game statement*
The supervisor wants only to evaluate my teaching performance.	I can take the initiative so that the supervisor will view the observation as a learning experience for both of us.

The believing game stance can be played out in many ways by teachers in relationship to their supervisors and vice versa. What follows is a set of ideas (adapted slightly from Roth [1984]) for how teachers can take more initiative and control over the nature of the conferences they will have with supervisors and colleagues. The ideas, if taken from a supervisor's perspective, offer many opportunities to allow teachers choices. With each choice, there will necessarily emerge different contexts, topics, and activities that will further define the relationship and talk between the conversants.

Such a relationship need not be marked by the anxiety both teachers and supervisors usually experience as they enter into the emotion-laden cycle of pre- and post-observation conferences. Such talk can be ripe for possibilities for professional exploration and awareness raising by both parties, as we will see in Chapters 8 and 9. These opportunities need not be usurped by the evaluative bureaucratic goals for which they were originally designed.

Taking responsibility for the nature of the talk

In interviews with eight supervisors and upon reflecting on his own work as a supervisor of in-service teachers in New York City, James Roth came up with suggestions for teachers facing evaluations. Aimed at what he titled "Replacing Trauma with Growth" and at finding what he called "a better way (than alcohol or valium) to deal with evaluations," Roth's list (below, with some adaptations) gives plenty of guidelines for you as teacher or supervisor to take more responsibility for determining the kinds of conversations you might have preceding and following observed lessons. He also suggests ways to reduce potential trauma during the observations.

Suggestions for teachers facing evaluation
  I. Before the Lesson
    A. Getting to know the supervisor
      1. Drop in to discuss specific lessons or teaching in general.
      2. Ask whether you can observe the supervisor or whether she or he can suggest another teacher you could observe.
      3. Invite the supervisor to come in for an informal observation before the formal one.
      4. Ask others in the school about the supervisor's reputation as teacher and supervisor, that is, what characterizes her or his teaching and what she or he tends to look for when observing others.
    B. Questions to ask far in advance
      1. How many official observations are required each term or school year?
      2. Can the observations be either unscheduled or scheduled?
      3. Can an audiotape or videotape be substituted for an observer's visit?
      4. Can you (if you are new to the school) see a copy of the official evaluation form and discuss any ambiguous parts with your supervisor?
      5. Can you be observed again if the first time goes poorly? (Roth suggests asking this of someone besides your supervisor or administrator.)

C. Working on your teaching to prepare for the observation
   1. Have other teachers observe and discuss your lessons. Tape one or more lessons and fill out copies of the official evaluation forms for them.
   2. Have students evaluate the class either formally or informally; then consider ways to work on their suggestions.
   3. Work on a specific aspect of your teaching so that when you are observed it is something you have been developing, not something totally new. (This can also be a topic of discussion with the supervisor before and after the observed lesson.)
D. Preparing for a pre-observation conference
   1. Set the date for the conference at least a few days before the observation, if possible. (If you cannot meet, at least arrange a phone call or E-mail exchange.)
   2. Write up a lesson plan, if possible, including objectives (for the students and for you), materials to be used, the chronology of activities, ways of assessing learning, follow-up, questions you have about the plan or areas needing special attention.
   3. Provide a term-long context for the lesson. This could include theories you have tried to incorporate, particular aspects of teaching you are working on, reactions to the course and any particular students, what you have learned about teaching/learning in the class, long-range aims of the course, and so on.
   4. Look over the evaluation sheet you will be judged by.
   5. Take note of students' evaluations of your class, if any have been done.
   6. Consider whether to design a tally/observation sheet for your supervisor to record descriptive data about your class, perhaps at particular points during the lesson. (This will be discussed later in this chapter.)
   7. Decide whether you want a scheduled or unscheduled observation if the choice exists.
E. The pre-observation conference: you could ask
   1. how long the supervisor plans to stay;
   2. when she or he will come in (or you may be asked your preference);
   3. what parts of the evaluation form to pay particular attention to;
   4. how your teaching will be evaluated (if there is no form);
   5. what teaching philosophy the institution subscribes to;
   6. what teaching principles the supervisor considers important;

7. if you will have time in the post-observation discussion to reflect on your lesson;
8. when you can expect the post-observation discussion to occur or if you can both schedule a time for that now;
9. if the supervisor prefers to be introduced to the class;
10. if the supervisor has any pet peeves, for example, certain types of lessons she or he has seen too many of;
11. if the supervisor has particular expertise you can draw on.
F. The pre-observation conference: you could mention
1. any feelings you have about the upcoming lesson/observation;
2. risks you plan to take or aspects of your teaching you are working on;
3. students that require special attention and how you deal with them;
4. where you prefer the supervisor to sit in the room, if this concerns you;
5. when you prefer that the supervisor come into the room;
6. the plan for the lesson and aims for the course;
7. anything you want the supervisor to pay particular attention to in your lesson or about your teaching;
8. any plan(s) you might have for involving the supervisor in the lesson (but ask if that would be all right).
G. Just before the lesson
1. Get all handouts and an updated plan to the supervisor as soon as possible.
2. Decide whether to tell the students about the observation, and if so, that YOU will be observed, not them.
II. During the lesson
A. Audiotape or videotape the lesson.
B. Follow up on promises made prior to the lesson (see I E. 9 and 10 and F. 4 and 8).
C. Concentrate on what you and the students are doing, not on the supervisor.
D. Reconfirm (sometime that day) when the post-observation discussion will take place.
III. After the lesson
A. Prior to the post-observation discussion, you might want to
1. jot down as many reactions as you can (immediately following the lesson and/or while attending to the tape of the class);
2. think about: surprises and expectations that were met; your feelings about specific/general occurrences; what you would have done differently; any follow-up you can foresee; what you learned about teaching/learning; questions for the supervisor;

3. if there is time, fill out the evaluation form your supervisor is using or any observation/tally sheets you designed for the supervisor to use while observing the class.

B. During the post-observation discussion

1. Try to state some of your reactions before the supervisor states her or his and some alternatives you have thought of since the observed lesson.

2. Have some written reactions to the lesson ready to give to the supervisor at the beginning or end of the conference.

3. Be open to the supervisor's comments without being unduly self-critical.

4. State nondefensively and nonconfrontationally any disagreements you have with the supervisor's evaluation.

5. Have questions ready and ask for suggestions.

6. Be appreciative of helpful suggestions.

7. Take notes on salient remarks made by the supervisor.

8. At the end of the discussion, try to summarize a few major points you learned from it.

9. Invite the supervisor, if you wish, to observe you again informally before the next formal observation will take place.

10. Tape your conference if the supervisor is open to it and you want to learn more from it.

11. Ask for another observation if it is clear that your supervisor is dissatisfied with your lesson.

C. After the discussion

1. Write your reactions to the discussion, including what you felt you learned from it and the class, and file it.

2. If you receive and are expected to sign an observation report, read it carefully before signing it.

3. Write a reaction to any statements on the report you strongly disagree with (and perhaps with those you do agree with). If a form is available for this purpose, use it.

4. If you were satisfied with the discussion and the report, a thank-you note is not a bad idea.

Task Break

1. *If you are a teacher*, put a check next to each of the items above that you would like to consider the next time you are to be observed. Then, put into action as many of the checked items (and others

you would like to add to the list) as you can the next time you are observed. Afterward reflect on what you would do differently in taking such initiative subsequently.

2. *If you are a supervisor*, consider how to rewrite the above list in a way that can provide options for the teachers with whom you will work. Offer them these options the next time you schedule observations. Afterward, reflect on how you would change the options for subsequent observations.

Roth's meticulous chronology from before to after being observed is one commonsense approach to exploring how you can take responsibility for the nature of the talk you have with a supervisor (or, in the case of supervisors, of providing opportunities for teachers to do so). Many practical alternatives emerge from this chronological approach, as was experienced by doing the Task Break above. Another approach offering additional alternatives for teachers and supervisors is the 5 Ws and H that all journalism students learn about as they practice writing lead sentences for news stories. The WHO, WHAT, WHEN, WHERE, HOW, and WHY of the talk between teachers and supervisors provide other options in which responsibility for the nature of their talk can be framed. These questions will help us address my third major question.

What contexts promote talk between teachers and supervisors?

By varying the 5 Ws and H, supervisors and teachers necessarily change the contexts in which such talk occurs. In language teaching, we have relearned in the past few decades how important it is to extend the contexts in which students use the target language in purposeful ways.[1] Formalistic notions of the transmission of knowledge *about* language from teachers (and from

1 We have *relearned* what activist language teachers such as John Amos Comenius and Johann Bernhard Basedow demonstrated centuries ago. In 1776, Basedow invited language educators from throughout Europe to see his school and the interactive nature of his approach to language instruction. His students put on plays, sang songs, and conversed with one another in German. For a historical sketch of the activist-formalist distinction in language teaching, see Oprandy (1988).

reference books and textbooks) to students – without a great deal of interaction requiring students to use the language as a means to achieving more
meaningful goals in a variety of contexts – have been considered a dead end
if used exclusively. I believe that the same is true for teachers interested in
heightening their awareness of teaching. Breaking the pattern of pre- and
post-observation discussions aimed at serving merely evaluative institutional
goals might create a wider range of talk more in tune with both teachers'
and supervisors' developmental needs and wishes.

WHO will talk?

The teacher who takes the initiative might ask to be observed not only by the
person usually responsible for doing so (though this may be unavoidable),
but also by someone (or some people) other than the usual supervisor – for
example, by

- a teaching colleague (or colleagues);
- yourself, if videotaped or audiotaped, with or without the presence of a
  supervisor (or even with students from the taped or other classes);
- another observer from within or outside of the institution.

More than one of these options might be used during the school year. Pre-
and/or post-observations with a variety of observers – or written (or audiotaped) reflections if you observe yourself – extend and diversify the nature
of talk about teaching; each person's perspective casts different shades of
gray on the composite of sketches making up the gallery of perspectives on
what occurs in your classes.

These options are also available to the supervisor who is open to trying
something different. Such a supervisor might wish to offer teachers, when
feasible or allowable within the institution, to choose from among these options or others she or he comes up with in consultation with teachers. If the
supervisor must be one of the observers, that does not preclude other options from being used as well.

WHAT will be talked about?

A note on observation forms.   Although a prescribed observation form
may need to be used by the supervisors at your school, you might be able
to suggest which sections of the form are of most interest to you. Alterna-
tively, you might adapt or add to the form in some way that would allow the
supervisor to tune in to aspects of your teaching to which you would like
her or him to pay particular attention when visiting your classes. If use of a

particular form is not mandatory, you might want to develop an observation form of your own, consulting with your supervisor and/or administrator about what is in it.

Your own observation form, or one designed by a committee of your colleagues, could be particularly useful if you are teaching a class emphasizing a particular skill area or content area (e.g., English for International Business or Vocational English) for which a generic observation form may be inadequate. Taking such initiative would put your agenda up front. This can supplement what the supervisor usually looks for or what the more generic institutional form may dictate that she or he consider in writing up an evaluation of your teaching. The supervisor might be grateful for being able to use a form much more congruent with the nature of what happens in such specialized courses.

If you are engaged in doing an action research project, or considering one (see Chapter 4), the observer could be asked to tune in to some aspect of the class, for at least part of the time, that would help inform that research. In the process, the supervisor might have insights that could prove useful to you in conceptualizing or carrying out the project. In addition, the supervisor's entering into the topic will open, perhaps, an ongoing avenue of professional communication between the two of you.

Consider, for example, the simple observation form that follows. I ask student teachers in my practicum courses to use it for two representative 10-minute time periods when observing each other in order to get a better idea of who is communicating with whom. The form was designed with Fanselow's (1987) *source* and *target* of communication in mind. (See Chapter 3 for an overview of Fanselow's FOCUS.) A teacher concerned about how much he or she talks in class and whom he or she addresses might wish to have an observer use the form for certain agreed-upon periods of time during the lesson. Later, they can explore what came out of the observations in an effort to raise awareness about this specific aspect of classroom interaction.

Perhaps a list of topics that correspond to such simple but telling observation forms could be made available, and teachers could choose which of these they would like the supervisor (or whoever else observes them) to use at least part of the time that they observe a class. In addition to the *source* and *target* of communication example shown on the next page, topics and accompanying observation forms might include question (or task) types, distribution of talk, and wait time, among others. See Appendixes A and B for samples you might want to try out. Also, in Chapter 3, you might wish to peruse the plethora of possibilities that can provide your supervisor with lenses to bring to your class while observing it.

Form: Source and targets of communication
KEY:
T = Teacher   S = Student   G = Specified group   C = Entire class
Ss = 2 or more students   O = Other (e.g., passage, object, slide, drawing)

DATA

T → C	→	→	→	→	→
S → T	→	→	→	→	→
T → S	→	→	→	→	→
→	→	→	→	→	→

(*Note:* Each of these columns would be much longer to capture many more of the source–target combinations being observed in, say, two 10-minute samplings.)

TOTALS

T → C _____	S → T _____	O → C _____
T → S _____	Ss → T _____	O → S _____
T → G _____	S → C _____	O → G _____
T → O _____	S → S _____	S → O _____
C → T _____	S → Ss _____	G → O _____

   Other combinations?

Alternatives to observation forms and to talk about observations.   Because observation forms have often provided parameters for what is discussed in post-observation discussions and because it is in observation-related discussions that teachers most often talk shop in a formal way at school, this chapter has so far focused on talk about observations. Observation-related discussions can, of course, be done in a number of ways that are useful to both teachers and supervisors. If they are the only formal means by which teachers and supervisors talk shop, however, they can also limit the WHAT of their talk. Consider what else they can talk about.

Task Break

1. List a few other topics, besides what will or did happen in an observed class, that teachers and supervisors can talk about. Then compare your list with others' and compile a lengthier list.

2. Which items on your list would it be possible for you to discuss with a supervisor (or with a teacher, if you are a supervisor) in the context of your school and given the time constraints you and your discussant may have? Add *observation-related discussions* to your list. Next, rank the list in order of preference, that is, what topics you are most to least interested in discussing with your supervisor (or with a particular teacher, if you are a supervisor).
3. What is keeping you from discussing the items you ranked high on the list if, in fact, you do not discuss them? What can you do to facilitate your having such discussions?

Having tried this Task Break with teachers and supervisors I work with, we came up with the list below of alternatives to *prescribed observation-related discussions* that can provide contexts for teacher–supervisor talk. The list is of stimuli to which the discussants would attend and which would be catalysts for their talk. The stimuli may relate to the teacher's or the supervisor's teaching, or someone else's (e.g., the first item on the list). The idea is to level the playing field and open up the talk from the constraints inherent in the usual post-observation discussions. In so doing, the spirit of exploration that we promote throughout this book may be achieved.

- one of a file of videotaped lessons requested of a wide range of teachers from within and outside of the institution
- a jointly viewed lesson that a colleague taught
- the teacher's and/or supervisor's (if also teaching) long-range plan for a course being taught that term
- a lesson plan for an upcoming or a particularly memorable class
- a transcribed portion of a lesson
- a sample (or samples) from files of ideas for teaching grammar points, functions, learner strategies, nonlanguage-specific themes (e.g., civil rights, dinosaurs), pronunciation, vocabulary, songs, and so on
- data or findings from an action research project, perhaps a coinvestigation the two of you are doing
- notes from a session attended at a professional conference
- points highlighted on a journal article that seemed particularly relevant to your own teaching
- an instructional material that one of you has used or was thinking of using
- a plan for or follow-up to a presentation at a conference or at a professional development day at your school

- a draft/outline of an article or book review for possible publication or of an abstract for a presentation that one of you hopes to give at a conference
- an advocacy issue having to do with a particular student or with a broader sociopolitical issue in the school, community, or profession

The supervisor's perspective on WHAT.   The supervisor's perspective on the question of what to talk about can also take into consideration the above-mentioned possibilities. The options discussed so far are aimed mostly at the needs of the teacher, whose developing awareness one would expect to be paramount in discussions with supervisors. Nevertheless, the complex character of dynamic communication means that the supervisor's needs in such discussions can also be considered. The flip side of all the suggestions for teachers is that they can be transformed into options that supervisors can encourage teachers to choose from so that the teachers, too, can take on some of the responsibility for the nature of the talk that will, to some extent, define their relationship. To level the playing field even more, supervisors can choose to work on one of the items on the list and be prepared to discuss with teachers her or his reflections on that work.

The supervisor's needs have traditionally been of an administratively obligatory nature, part of the job description that requires one with supposedly more knowledge and/or experience to judge those with less. What about the supervisor's needs as a learner, as one who might want to get something for herself or himself out of discussions with teachers? Perhaps the supervisor is particularly interested in some aspect of the teaching-learning dynamic or is doing research on classroom interaction. What benefits might the supervisor be able to reap from doing an observation? Perhaps the supervisor has a long-range plan for a class the teacher has recently taught and would like to benefit from the teacher's thinking about such a course. Might those benefits help to open up a more genuine interchange between the supervisor and the teacher?

The communicative orthodoxy that has taken hold in language pedagogy has led most practitioners to believe that the more genuine the conversations and the more closely attuned they are to the needs and interests of the conversants, the more deeply internalized will be the language necessary to carry on such conversations. The same may be true of talk between supervisors and teachers who have *integrative*, not just *instrumental*, purposes for discussing teaching and learning (Gardner & Lambert 1972); that is, they talk to deepen their awareness of teaching, not just to go through administrative motions. Creative use of their time together will make them more positively disposed to future discussions, both formal and informal. The effect of this on morale, not to mention the desire to explore more of the teaching terrain, cannot be overestimated.

HOW *will the talk be structured?*

The HOW of observation discussions.   While taking initiative on the WHAT, you might want to negotiate the HOW of the talk preceding or following an observation. Before considering how the talk might be structured, the following questions might arise concerning how teachers are observed:

- Do I want the observer to sit along the side of the room, behind the class, in front of the students, or among them?
- Do I want to introduce the observer, have the observer introduce herself or himself, or not call attention to the observer at all?
- Do I want to have the class audiotaped or videotaped during the visit? if so, by whom?
- Do I want the observer to capture as many verbatim exchanges as possible, especially as they might relate to a particular aspect of my teaching on which I would like feedback?
- Would I like to make use of the supervisor (if she or he is willing) during small-group work, perhaps to be a participant observer during such segments of the class?

These and any number of other questions concerning how the observation is conducted may have an impact, if only slight, on what is subsequently observed. More pertinent to this discussion, though, is how the talk between the observer and the observed will be conducted.

The structure of the talk.   As mentioned earlier, there appears to be a canonical structure to the talk between teachers and their supervisors. Arcario (1994) found that such conversations move through three stages, with evaluation at center stage. As Chapter 8 illustrates, talk can be quite different from that of the canon if the roles and purposes of the observed and observers are changed and if the talk is structured differently to be in accord with such roles and purposes. As the collaborating teachers in Chapter 8 discovered, however, it is difficult to break entirely from the virtually preordained nature of such conversations. The lure of the canon is quite strong.

WHERE *and* WHEN *will the talk take place?*

In my experience, most teachers feel more secure knowing where and when they will be observed. By setting up a schedule early in the term or school year, you can consider which class and during what part of your long-range plan you would most like an observer to see you. This decision may be based on a need not to flaunt your particular skills but to get feedback on some aspect of your teaching that you are focusing on or are concerned about. Your purposes for choosing the place and time of the observation can be made public in advance, thus clarifying that the purpose of the visit is as much for you and your goals as it is for the administration and its needs. Of course, the supervisor's constraints may have a bearing on the where and when of the observations, though tape recorders can help overcome such constraints. In any case, getting a jump on other teachers by setting up the where and when early on in a term or school year can be to your advantage.

Another reason for taking initiative might be to state your preference *not* to know where and when you will be observed. Perhaps a random visit (or visits), in which it will be impossible to obsess about the impending observation, is more to your liking. This option might also be preferable for a supervisor trying to squeeze such visits into a packed schedule: the added flexibility might be a welcome relief. The only major disadvantage of random visits might be that the teacher may have planned a test or a lengthy writing activity on a day that the supervisor pops into class. A procedure for signaling such classes could, of course, be devised.

Another time consideration is whether to be observed for one full class session or for a few periodic visits of shorter duration. Instead of the observer coming for an entire 2-hour class, you might have three half-hour visits followed by one or more post-observation discussions. This option is obviously more complicated to arrange, but not necessarily for the teacher who stated a preference for random visits.

This leads us again to consideration of the supervisor's perspective on the question being addressed. It seems that the gesture of giving some leeway to teachers on the WHERE and WHEN of observations would make them feel a bit more secure, perhaps generating a bit less anxiety than is necessary.

The where and when of the observation itself is one pair of questions. The where and when of the pre- and post-observation discussions raises a separate pair of questions. If you feel more comfortable in a café, in your living room, or in a video viewing room, and if you prefer to have something to snack on or drink while discussing your classes, you might suggest your preferred setting, if it will not unduly inconvenience the supervisor. Supervisors might want to suggest a choice of places, if time pressures afford it, leaving an open-ended "or wherever else you would like to discuss your class" as a final choice.

The ultimate question: WHY talk?

There may be any number of reasons why one person will supervise another in their workplace. The most obvious is to maintain a standard of performance. Unfortunately, in my view, this most often presumes a privileged position for the supervisor, who is considered the fount of wisdom. Believe it or not, this position may make supervisors uncomfortable. By discussing ahead of time the whys of such visits, you can open up a relational and professional space more fruitful than that engendered by having both parties (or more than two, as suggested above under the WHO options) hide behind the unspoken assumptions of what supervision usually entails.

What might some of the whys be? Consider these:

1. Evaluation of a teacher's performance: The reasons behind this can include the need to cut back the size of the teaching staff, to provide supporting documentation for granting/denying a promotion, to do what has always been done (i.e., performance of a ritual act), or to see what is going on in the program. Can you think of others?
2. Establishing collegiality among workmates: Talking shop allows for workers to learn about and thus avail themselves of the human resources their workplace has invested in. The teacher may demonstrate just the kind of technique the supervisor has been looking for and hoping to implement in her or his own classes. The supervisor might, for example, upon seeing a teacher use a video segment in class, share the video digest available through the international TESOL organization that the program just happened to receive in the mail that week. The loneliness of teaching can be minimized the more we share what we do with colleagues.
3. Exploring the teaching-learning dynamic: Learning more about the intricate interplay of factors at play in classrooms is fascinating. Going beyond what we filter through our own perceptions is so necessary in developing awareness, as we discuss throughout this book.

Task Break

From your perspective as a teacher or supervisor, or both, list a few more WHYS. Compare your list with that of a colleague. Teachers and their supervisors are urged to do this exercise together.

Armed with a host of alternatives suggested thus far, we can imagine how each choice we make will not only influence the nature of the conversations we have as the one being observed or as the observer, but also affect the contexts in which we talk, the topics we discuss, and the activities that precede, accompany, or follow our discussions.

My hunch is that those who explore some of these possibilities will also be the same teachers and supervisors willing to play the *believing game* referred to earlier. That stance lends itself more readily to exploring new options and to taking the kinds of initiatives suggested here.

Appendix A: Understanding or not understanding

Observe instances when students clearly seem to be understanding and others when they seem to be having difficulty understanding either their teacher or a classmate. Explain each situation before answering the appropriate question(s).

Understanding
1. What is present that might be helping the student(s) understand?
2. What is absent from the situation that might have helped the student(s) understand?

Not understanding
1. What is happening that could be making it difficult for the student(s) to understand?
2. What is absent that, if it had been present, might have helped the student(s) understand?

Appendix B: Observing from one student's perspective

1. Follow a lesson for two 10-minute segments from the perspective of a single student; that is, observe what the student seems to be doing and keep a running record of what you see. For example:
   - Listens to teacher's directions to open book to p. 23
   - Opens book to p. 23
   - Chats to neighboring student in Spanish
   - Looks at picture on p. 23, points to stylishly dressed woman in picture, says "Fancy!" etc.
2. Write some reflections on what you observed. Were your observations of those 10-minute segments of the lesson affected by what you saw that single student doing?

7 *Making personal connections to teaching*

Robert Oprandy

> . . . self understanding requires something quite different from the methods, study plans, and skills of a "know-how" sort that are usually emphasized in education. Methods and techniques, group work, role playing, and other devices are useful at certain points. But these educational techniques are not what is primarily needed. They can be used merely as a kind of external manipulation. . . . What is needed is a more personal kind of searching, which will enable the teacher to identify his own concerns and to share the concerns of his students.
> —A. T. Jersild (1955: 3)

As the interlocking circles of Figure 7.1 show, there is a connection between who we are as teachers and who we are as people. The closer we are in the classroom to who/how we are outside of it, the more genuine we can be in the presence of our students. Also, the more self-actualized we are as people, the more we have to draw on during classes, as well as in life in general. Exploring oneself and relating life experience to teaching (the subject here and in Chapter 11) round out our approach to language-teaching awareness.

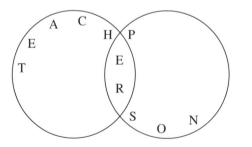

Figure 7.1

The connection shown in Figure 7.1 has raised several questions I explore while teaching English as a foreign or second language. Here are some of the *connecting questions* addressed in the pages that follow:

1. Do I play the *believing game* both in and out of the classroom?[1]
2. Do I reflect on teaching and learning in and out of the classroom?
3. Am I developing myself personally and professionally?
4. Am I learning a language (or languages) and skills or subjects not directly related to language teaching?
5. Am I *real* in and out of school?
6. How does language teaching fit into my vision of who I am (becoming) and how I'd like the world to be?

The personal nature of these questions necessitates a switch in this chapter to a first person singular perspective. After all, these are *my* connecting questions; yours might be quite different. If you journey along with me on how my personal collection of questions connects with who I am (attempting to become) as a teacher, my hope is that it will help you articulate your own connecting questions. Along the way, if some of my questions seem important enough for you to consider, then you will be that much further along the road of linking who you are as teacher with who you are outside of school.

All of the activities detailed in the preceding chapters are suggestive of ways to heighten our awareness of teaching and/or to help colleagues or trainees do so. It seems, however, that such activities will ring hollow unless you also come to grips with your own connecting questions, that is, those that link your teaching and nonteaching selves. In reflecting on the ideas in this chapter and in taking breaks to do the accompanying tasks, you will, in a sense, simulate the experience of language learners who attempt to link their foreign/second language selves with their native language selves. Just as they try to find themselves in their target language/culture, we as teachers need to do the same. After all, teaching has its own language and culture to which we need to accommodate ourselves if we are to thrive or survive in this demanding profession. By exploring how our personal and professional development intersect, we assume that we can hasten this accommodation process.

As we grow, both professionally and personally, our questions change; your list, and mine, will necessarily be modified over time. Some questions will loom larger at some points, diminish in importance at other times, and disappear altogether, perhaps to reappear in the future. The questions, I address in the sections that follow have lingered long in my consciousness as

---

1 The *believing game* and *doubting game* perspectives are borrowed from the Appendix of Peter Elbow's classic book *Writing without Teachers* (1973).

I plan and implement courses and lessons. I expect them to stay with me for the duration of my teaching career. By having you enter into my thinking and feelings about the interconnections between my personal and professional lives, I hope that, by the end of this chapter, you will be spurred to articulate more of your own connecting questions than those you jot down in the following Task Break.

Task Break

Jot down a few of what you consider to be your own *connecting questions*. Don't be concerned that you do not yet know much about what is meant by such questions. Share your questions with one or more partners who have done the same thing. Discuss how the questions relate who you are (becoming) as teachers to who you are outside of school.

Do I play the "believing game" both in and out of the classroom?

As discussed in Chapter 6, teachers and their supervisors will at times assume *believing game*, and, at other times, *doubting game*, stances vis-à-vis the students or teachers they work with. We looked at how such stances can affect the nature of the talk teachers and supervisors enter into as they discuss their craft. In this section I will discuss the importance, both in and out of school, of playing the believing game.

In the personal realm, I need to notice the extent to which I play both the doubting and the believing games in my life outside of school. The habits I develop there carry over into my classes and into my relationships with those I work with at school. The extent to which I believe in people's potential in general presumably affects how much I believe in my students' abilities. The rich research on teachers' expectations of their students lends substantial support for how our predispositions toward others can affect not only how they perform, but also their self-esteem. Herbert Kohl (1984: 58) also argues for playing, primarily, the believing game:

We don't know what people (ourselves included) could become, and any limit on expectations will become a limit on learning. That is why I choose to think of energy instead of potential. The model is fluid – energy flows, it can be expended or renewed, latent or active, it can be transformed from one form or manifestation to another. It exists in all areas of life, the emotional and physical as well as the intellectual and artistic. All youngsters have this energy, and a substantial part of the craft of teaching consists of knowing how to tap into children's energy sources or removing impediments to their flow.

There is a well-established line of research backing up Kohl's belief in the power of teachers' expectations of students. Brophy and Evertson (1981) studied twenty-seven teachers in a variety of elementary schools, noting how they interacted with pupils. First, the teachers ranked the students according to thirteen attributes, including "calmness," "maturity," "creativity," and "probable achievement." Then the researchers observed the teachers using a coding system with seventy-three dimensions of teacher behavior, which were then compared with the teachers' ratings of the students. They found, for example, that teachers kept "rejected" students (that is, students they had ranked low on the thirteen attributes) under close scrutiny, often reminding them of their responsibilities, treating them impatiently, refusing their personal requests, and even holding them up as bad examples to their classmates.

Other experimental studies suggest that teachers' judgments of and behavior toward students are linked to various features of the learners. Braun's review of literature on teacher expectancies (1976) identified that a learner's sex, ethnicity, and attractiveness were among the features affecting how teachers view and act toward students. Kornblau (1982) found that teachers have predetermined profiles for "teachable" or model pupils. They then respond to individual students according to how well they match these profiles. Rosenthal and Jacobson's seminal study (1968) in this area suggested that individual students will achieve at higher levels if teachers expect high levels of achievement from them. All of these studies suggest how powerfully our expectations of students can influence how we work with them.

I will never forget one session with a teacher who realized just how telling her expectations of a particular student were and how similar those expectations were to those she had had of her daughter during her daughter's adolescence. We were viewing a videotape of her teaching ESL to adult immigrants, and I observed a fleeting pained facial expression she made upon asking a student a question. I stopped and rewound the tape and asked her to watch again. I asked her to consider which of Eric Berne's ego states (in *Games People Play*) she had assumed and which she had attributed to the student to whom she directed the question and the facial expression. Was she relating to the student in an adult-to-adult manner, or was it child-to-child, critical parent-to-child, or nurturing parent-to-child? Upon focusing on the fleeting grimace, which she had not noticed the first time, she became teary-eyed. She realized that she was playing critical parent and was addressing the adult student as she would a child or teenager. Her expectation was that the student would not answer the question correctly and she was already pained by the incorrect response she expected to get. Moreover, she revealed that that was the same way that she had treated her daughter for much of her adolescence; she connected such treatment to the fact that their relationship was still strained some 10 years later.

She asked me to observe her class later that week and to view it with Berne's ego states in mind. We were both amazed by how differently she addressed her students and by how much more of an adult-to-adult relationship she had succeeded in implementing. Her tone of voice no longer could be characterized as parent-to-child. She felt so relieved and discussed over the rest of the semester how much that moment of video viewing had meant to her in terms of developing more positive expectations of and more of an adult relationship toward her students – who, after all, *were* adults.

Task Break

1. What are the attributes of learners you feel you would respond to most favorably? Least favorably? How do you think such attributions would affect your students' learning process?
2. Consider the following quotation. Do you think McDonald's assessment is true of most, if not all, teachers? Can you think of a particular teacher or two who had a strong belief in you? What were some other traits of that/those teacher(s)?

   In even the most courageous and reflective teaching, believing takes precedence over doubting in the sense that the teacher tempers his or her believing with doubt, not the other way around. Of course, the reflective teacher faces up to failure every time he or she reads a set of student papers, or thinks rigorously about what Carmen and Eric have actually learned, or dares to subject bright plans to critical light. But then, at least in the best circumstances, he or she returns wholeheartedly to believing in the papers' signs of progress, in Carmen's and Eric's potential to pull through, and in the efficacy of the plans. In the end, belief predominates. (McDonald 1992: 18)

3. Consider a time you were not believed in as a student. How did that affect you in that learning experience?

One of my goals is to become increasingly like the kind of reflective, believing teacher described by McDonald in the preceding Task Break. We are all prone to use labels in thinking about individual students; but such labels ("slow," "bright," "challenged," "attentive," "tuned out"), as well as those used to characterize classes of students ("good/bad chemistry," "accelerated," "at risk"), get in the way of truly attending to what those students or classes are doing. As cognizant as I am of the literature on teacher expectations, I still find myself at times labeling students or conjuring up images of them – negative, positive, or neutral – that block me from seeing more accurately what they are contributing to the class and what they are doing in their own learning process. At such times, teaching from the beginner's mind stance discussed in Chapter 1 would seem to be in order. Checking myself when the tendency to label arises is challenging. In the spirit of exploration, trying on a different label than the one that first pops to mind can be insightful.

Consider what happened one day when I observed a practice teacher in a central California elementary pullout ESL class. Warned in advance that a particular student was being considered for the designation "learning-disabled" and that he might have an adverse effect on the class, I sat back and watched. The boy in question seemed to me to have unbridled energy that he was anxious to use in creative ways. He also seemed bored at times by the prearranged activities that awaited him and his group mates in the three stations they visited and worked in. At one station, he concocted a creative twist on the given activity, transforming it into a more engaging game for him and his group mates.

After the class, I suggested that the boy could be viewed as "exceptional" rather than "learning-disabled." This seemed to surprise the observed teacher, who also seemed encouraged by the possibilities surrounding this new label. The discussion she and I had about some of the boy's specific behaviors that led me to my characterization, as well as to the cooperating teacher's "learning-disabled" label, helped us both explore what these terms mean to us and how our use of them, if only among ourselves, might influence the child so labeled.

Playing the believing game outside of school so as to increase the likelihood of assuming such a stance inside the classroom is another of the goals I have set for myself. I am not proposing here that we allow our critical skills to atrophy or that they do not play an important role in our (teaching) lives. What I have found, however, is that those who are willing to suspend disbelief long enough to consider other (and others') perspectives have more to draw on in deciding what to incorporate into their repertoire of possibilities in and out of classroom. Those who are not so inclined and tend to let the doubting game mentality rule them also limit their possibilities and those of the students they teach.

I am reminded of how differently language teachers reacted to the teaching innovations of Caleb Gattegno (1976) and Charles Curran (1976) when they and their associates, respectively, led their Silent Way and Counseling-Learning workshops in the 1970s and 1980s.[2] Those who yielded to these innovative educational philosophies to see what might be useful in them, especially those who went beyond the initial introductory workshops, developed transformative insights into the power of silence and empathetic understanding. They gained experiential knowledge of the "subordination of teaching to learning" that to this day influences how many of them view their work with students. Those who were quick to put down these avant-garde approaches (including some writers of methods texts who had never had firsthand experiences of the approaches) perhaps never allowed themselves the chance to experience or practice alternatives that they may have grown to appreciate and learn from in time.

In nonclassroom contexts, I am constantly reminded of the doubting and believing game mentalities. Watching parents with their children, for example, we can see how constrained some children are and how free others are to explore their worlds. As a Peace Corps volunteer in Thailand, I was struck by the godlike treatment of young children there. Mothers would follow them around with spoons or chopsticks of food, which the children would eat when *they* were ready to do so. This contrasts sharply with the treatment of toddlers in the United States, who are often sat down, strapped into a constraining high chair, and practically forced to eat on command, with their parents coaxing, cajoling, or even forcing them to get food into their mouths. In Thailand, the parents seemed to believe that the children knew when they were ready for food. In the United States, perhaps many parents doubt that their children will eat unless they intercede. The connection between different child-rearing practices and the way we teach and how students behave in schools would be a fascinating research topic.

The health arena is another fertile field for contrasting the believing and

2 Such workshops are still available at Educational Solutions, Inc., and through the Counseling-Learning Institutes. However, when the approaches were new to the profession of language teaching was when I was most struck by the range of doubting to believing game reactions there were to Gattegno's and Curran's theories and practices.

doubting games. Satisfied with a Western, scientific approach to medicine, many doctors in the West have snubbed serious alternatives to health care that they are, finally, often grudgingly, recognizing. When I lived in Ghana, European medical researchers were finally attempting to tap the vast knowledge of the herbalists who were healing many tropical diseases that the more "modern" doctors were frequently at a loss to deal with. Although a healthy questioning of others' perspectives serves a real purpose, especially when considering issues of life and death, blatant disregard for potentially useful alternatives seems shortsighted.

The more I reflect on the nature of learning (and teaching) that I see in nonclassroom settings, the easier it is for me to see how the belief we have in learners, wherever they are learning, can affect their willingness to throw themselves into whatever tasks they are tackling. The ways in which people make sense of puzzling moments and seek, either individually or with others, to make or co-construct meaning seem to vary enormously (see Phenix 1964 and Gardner 1991). Careful attention to these varying responses seems to me to be a major part of our work. When we pay such attention, we are much more likely to meet one of Phenix's chief conditions for imaginative teaching:

an unconditional faith in the possibility of realizing meaning through awakened imagination in any and every student, no matter what appearances may indicate to the contrary. This faith is not to be confused with a blind optimism in the goodness and indefinite perfectibility of every person. It is rather a working conviction about the essential nature of persons and of the highest human good by which persons are ultimately constrained, namely, the fulfillment of meaning. (1964: 351)

The boundaries of a classroom or of a school are much too limited for doing the work of attending to the ways people make meaning. One way to overcome that limitation is to reflect on teaching-learning moments wherever and whenever they occur, both in and out of the classroom.

Do I reflect on teaching and learning in and out of the classroom?

This book presents a multitude of ideas on how teachers can reflect on the teaching-learning dynamic in the classroom. One of the aims of this Chapter is to extend such reflection beyond the boundaries of the school, connecting our work with what we observe in nonschool settings.[3] One way to

3 I almost decided to call these *nonteaching* settings, but are there really any places where teaching and learning are not occurring? Is there ever a communicator who is not playing the role of teacher or learner?

keep the language teacher cap on my head wherever I am is in the search for authentic language teaching materials. While straphanging in a New York City subway car one day, I was struck by a description on an advertisement of a new degree being offered by Adelphi University. It was a business degree designed for commuters traveling to and from the city at least an hour and a half each way on the Long Island Railroad. They could take courses in a specially designated car on the commuter train. Figuring that this would be great material for use in my ESL class, I pulled fifteen of the flyers off the pad on the subway car wall and incorporated the advertisement into the reading class I myself was commuting to that morning.

Observant, resourceful teachers are always on the lookout for material that will enliven their classes. They keep blank videotapes in their VCRs and cassettes in their radio/audiotape recorders, ready for snippets of particularly timely or timeless authentic material. For example, one January on Martin Luther King Day, I kept feeding cassettes into a radio/tape recorder set on a station running a daylong King retrospective. Into the third or fourth hour of taping, I heard the perfect snippet. It was a very clear, slow 2–3-minute reading by the civil-rights leader of a particularly powerful section of King's "Letter from Birmingham Jail." Using that excerpt, I developed two consecutive lessons (in Oprandy 1993–1994) that dealt with the issue of racial discrimination in the United States, lessons I pulled out ever since when teaching students with a high-enough English-language proficiency.

The search for compelling authentic material is an obvious, perhaps more surface-level, way we reflect on the art and craft of teaching beyond the bounds of the school. Another, perhaps less obvious, way to reflect on the connections between learning in nonschool and in classroom contexts is to notice moments when people interact with one another or in some other way involve themselves in doing naturally the things we have students work on in class. Fanselow (1991) mentions, for example, how much he learns from observing people read. Rather than relying solely on ideas from methods books and teachers' manuals, he has garnered many techniques from observing people using or attending to language wherever he goes. Watching readers on trains, for instance, he is reminded that, except for those studying, people usually read a text that they have chosen. In classrooms, however, teachers tend to select the material students read. He also notes that we often have to read signs that are reflected in windowpanes, requiring that we read print backward. Both of these observations suggest possible alternatives that we can bring into classrooms – allowing students to choose their own reading material and asking them at times to read reflected text.

At a Puccini opera, Fanselow considered ideas for doing classroom role plays:

The first thing that struck me, as it strikes almost anyone who does not understand the language in which an opera is sung, is that much meaning is conveyed through the setting, the costumes, the props and the facial expressions and gestures of the performers. Like many of our realizations, this one is obvious! Yet, it rarely seems to be taken into account when we ask our students to perform dialogues during role-playing activities. (1992b: 15)

Watching parents with their children in parks provides more grist for the teaching mill about either promising practices or those better avoided. I have been curious to notice the differences in freedom that parents allow their toddlers. Some allow their children to explore on their own, whereas others pull in the reins tightly. It is clear which toddlers are used to such freedom: their confidence and curiosity seem stronger than those waiting to be chided by overprotective parents.

Then there is the way parents react, verbally and nonverbally, to their children's explorations. Here again, the expectations we have regarding others' abilities come into play:

as children we learned how to walk before we learned how to talk, so that no parent or teacher could put ideas in our minds about the right and wrong styles, or make us aware of our progress relative to others. Consequently, we didn't experience self-condemnation or take credit for doing well. We were not concerned with our self-image, and so our energy went into growing and learning instead of trying to live up to the expectations of others. Gallwey (1976: 11)

In searching for materials that can enliven my classes or in finding connections between teaching-learning in out-of-class settings, I am striving to become more like the exceptional teachers Perrone (1991: 117) wrote about: "They see connecting points everywhere. It is not possible to take a walk with them without noting that they are almost always seeing around them possibilities for their students. They make particular note of books, insist on 'checking out' libraries and museums, write down addresses of people and places." An example of this happened when I attended an art exhibit of "Cornerworks" in which the painter placed his vertical paintings in the corners of the gallery rooms. I was struck by the effect that placement of the paintings had on pulling my eyes along the walls toward each cornerwork. Because I often use slides in my teaching, I decided to incorporate the cornerwork idea into my next slide show. Instead of using a screen or flat wall, I projected the slides into a corner of the classroom. The effect was similar to what happened to me at the museum. Several students mentioned how much depth the corners of the room gave to the slides.

Through broadening and deepening my out-of-school interests, I can touch base more readily with the ideas, interests, and needs of learners. I often sit in cafés ripping out newspaper articles about my ESL students' countries or on topics in which they have expressed or demonstrated interest. It just so happens that world geography and planetary current events are of great interest to me. When I hand relevant articles to students for their own reading pleasure and to read at their own convenience, it connects us in a personal, individual way that makes them realize that I wish to include them in the club of English users. I love chatting with them before and after classes about their takes on the events described or opinions given in the articles. This creates a role reversal in which they become teachers and I am their student encouraging them to share their expertise with me.

Because I am only one source of ideas and of language input for our students, it seems incumbent on me to vary the sources of input as much as possible (see Oprandy 1994a for many ideas on how to do this). The contacts I make outside of school are important in that regard. By acquainting myself with a diversity of people with a range of backgrounds and experiences, I can tap them as potential resources to bring into school, if not live, then via audiotape or videotape. Social-service workers, artists, musicians, writers, dancers, farmers, construction workers, and politicians have a variety of specialized abilities and experiences that can enliven a classroom.

Am I developing myself personally and professionally?

I get a kick out of presenting and publishing my ideas, but I most often take care of my professional sustenance by reading journals and professional books, attending workshops and conferences, and helping out with projects that the local, state, national, and international professional teaching organizations are involved with. Most often, I work at my craft by developing materials and activities for the students I work with and discussing these with other teachers predisposed to "talking shop" (such as the elementary school ESL teacher in Chapter 8). No matter how one continues to explore teaching-learning, such exploration is facilitated by communicating with others what we learn from doing such activities. Time for professional development is usually extremely limited in schools. While administering ESL programs in New York City, my assistant director, Helen Truax, and I distributed the list below of suggestions for our large part-time faculty to work on their craft despite their limited time. If they wished to put the results of their explorations in the file in the teachers' room for others to see, they were invited to do so.

1. Write a statement of a professional goal or goals you'd like to work on this cycle with a running log of how you attempted to meet the goal(s) through a diary of reflections, transcripts of segments from lessons, or descriptions of classroom activities.
2. Write a memo to faculty informing them of an article you've read, or of a text you've reviewed, which gave you practical insights that could be implemented in the classroom. Attach to the memo a copy of the article or sections of the text.
3. Observe another teacher and write a nonjudgmental description of several of the activities to be shared with the teacher observed and, if she or he doesn't mind, with the faculty at large.
4. Attend a professional development seminar and report on anything of particular interest that you learned. Attach any handouts to your report that will be of interest to faculty colleagues.
5. Videotape one of your lessons and observe that lesson by using one of the observation instruments available in the Observation Tasks folder in the faculty room or by using an instrument you develop.
6. (One of your own.)

If I were administering that program today, I would add activity choices to the list that would encourage dissemination of the teachers' ideas/practices to the language-teaching profession as a whole. Such activities would encourage teachers to develop materials for potential publication, to write abstracts in order to present their ideas at conferences, and to do (collaborative) research projects to write up in professional newsletters or journals. In addition, I would encourage journaling and many of the other activities detailed in this book.

Task Break

1. From the list of professional development activities above, put a checkmark next to those you have done. If you are new to teaching, which two or three would you prefer to do and why?
2. Of the activities you did not check, which would you consider doing in the future? What are some other activities you would add to the list?
3. How do you feel about doing personal development without being paid to do so?

Of course, part-time faculty should not be obliged to do such professional development activities without being paid. Nor should there be any negative repercussions in rehiring decisions about those who prefer not to take part in such activities (unless, of course, their contracts demand involvement in such activities). We found, however, that almost all the teachers in our center chose to work on one of the activities. Although it was not contractually compulsory for our faculty to do more than their assigned instruction, most expended the time, energy, and professional pride necessary to share with their colleagues what they were exploring in their teaching. Teaching is a lonely profession, one in which no other professional usually watches or discusses our work once we are sequestered behind the closed door of the classroom. Many caring, proud teachers want to break the silence, as those in Chapters 8 and 9 demonstrate.

Going beyond day-to-day teaching concerns, we might want to consider joining or renewing our membership in professional organizations. We might inquire about and make plans to attend upcoming conferences and to volunteer to work at them for an hour or two. With some experience under our belts, we might choose to submit an abstract presenting our current thinking, practices, or research at a future conference – or at least discuss such ideas with colleagues and friends. Those who engage in the above-mentioned kinds of activities tend to push their boundaries to the edge of their competence, unsatisfied with getting by with their usual ways of doing things. They renew themselves each year with new projects and fresh ideas. Besides augmenting their self-respect, they also gain the respect of their colleagues and others in the profession. All of this contributes to their sense of feeling what Frank Smith (1988) calls membership in the club, in this case membership in the profession of teaching.

Our sense of who we are as teachers is also fostered by our general sense of self, which, in turn, is fostered by the extent to which we work on our personal development. Recently I took an oil-painting class, picking up an artist's paintbrush for the first time since elementary school. My classmates and I learned to make the medium, to stretch and treat canvases, to paint ten shades of gray between white and black, to see objects and their colors with much more heightened attention, and to be in a creative process, much like what our language students go through as they try to express and explore meanings together in a foreign tongue. Learning all these things and putting myself in the position of learner was incredibly instructive. It made me reflect a great deal on how I was being taught and on how uniquely my classmates and I were reacting to our lessons.

I was struck, for example, by how the lessons were structured. At the beginning of each class, there was minimal input from the teacher. This was followed by lots of individual practice/play with the teacher's ideas. During these playful practice parts of the lesson, we all had enough space to do our own thing and to take our own breaks to look at what our classmates were doing at their easels. This allowed me to pick up ideas from here and there and to look anew at my own canvas and the forms, brush strokes, and color choices I was making. I noticed that some students were using the whole studio in the way I was; others stayed primarily at their own easels, intent mostly on what they themselves were doing. What seemed important was that the choice was ours. The teacher would come around and make one or two comments here and there, but for the most part she would attend to student solicitations for her help. The class would usually close with a quick summary point or two from the teacher.

As pleased as I was by the way the lessons were structured, I felt that it would also have been useful for us as a group to gather for 10 to 15 minutes each week to share what we were noticing, struggling with, and excited about in our painting. This would have allowed us to reflect a bit more on our process as painters, to "talk shop" as painters, however new we were to creating works of art, and to learn from one another's insights and feelings. Feeling membership in the club of painters might have been accelerated by such discussions.

My experience as an art student contained many lessons for me as a language teacher. I have begun to think more about how to make the language classroom into a studio where students can come to work on their language skills. I am reminded here of outstanding learning centers attached to English-language programs at Riverside Church in New York City and in Phanat Nikhom, Thailand (during the time of the influx of Laotian and Cambodian refugees there). The directors of both centers provided substantial orientation to the students who chose to use the centers during nonclass hours. They also managed to create a multitude of tasks, both structured and open-ended, for users of their centers to choose from.

Carefully chosen articles and books were available along with audiotaped readings of them, as were songs with transcribed lyrics. Videos and taped television programs provided further sources of input. Tape recorders with blank tapes were available for pairs or small groups of students to tape conversations, which they could later listen to and discuss the ways they expressed or could have better communicated their ideas. Picture files provided stimuli for conversations when conversants ran out of things to talk about, which seemed rare. Well-marked folders contained a plethora of grammar, listening, and vocabulary exercises. Reading kits, timely authentic reading materials, as well as student essays and poems were found in reading areas. Games of all kinds could also be checked out and played.

The buzz of activity in these learning centers with minimal input from the people running them is most memorable. People came to use the center for their own purposes, which seemed to heighten the engagement they had with the tasks they chose for themselves on a given day.

The idea of applying models of other learning contexts to language programs already resides in such learning centers. How to bring that idea into our classes, not just into centers attached to language programs, is a worthwhile challenge. It is one that particularly struck me as a result of being in my art studio class. Finding connections between all types of personal development activities and the craft of language teaching may expand our repertoire as teachers. At the same time, it makes our professional consciousness and creativity come alive wherever we go as we take more notice of whatever we do.

Task Break

1. Consider one area of personal development that you have been working on (or have worked on in the past). List several specific memories of that experience. Are there any implications for teaching language?
2. What are some areas of personal development that you have hoped to work on but have not been able to up to now? In what ways do you expect such development to connect with your professional development as a teacher?

The ways I develop myself personally bring my teacher self to the fore in so many activities I engage in outside of school. Perhaps I am overly fixated on thinking so often about teaching and learning, but I find that that is part of the joy of being a teacher. It stimulates me to discover new wrinkles in my craft, just as Jerry Gebhard will demonstrate in Chapter 11, where he narrates some of his experiences learning yoga.

As instructive as personal exploration is in deriving lessons for our teaching, it seems that the closest simulation we can have of what our students go through is to be language students ourselves.

Am I learning a language (or languages) and skills or subjects not directly related to language teaching?

Can we truly keep tabs on what it means to acquire/learn a language without being in the process of doing it ourselves? As I struggle with the Thai I learned as a Peace Corps volunteer many years ago or find myself listening to and watching news on a local Spanish TV station, my sensitivity for what my language students go through is strengthened. My avoidance strategies, such as circumlocution, winding around the vocabulary word or expression that would best get to the point I am trying to express in Thai, remind me of strategies my students employ. It also highlights the fact that a more direct approach ("What *is* the word for . . . ?") will improve the likelihood of retrieving that more precise word or expression the next time I need it, thereby eliminating the need to talk around it. Being a language learner can have an obvious impact on how I teach. Continuing to learn a foreign language – or at least more about the language we teach – helps foster continual reflection on what it means to work actively on acquiring/learning languages.

The connections between being a language learner and a language teacher are quite apparent. What is less evident are the connections we can make between being a learner of skills/subjects other than languages and the insights we can glean for a deepened awareness of teaching. I will exemplify such connections by referring to the skills I acquired as a pizza maker. The number of details I was forced to attend to and get the feel for when stretching balls of dough into pizza pies reminds me of the range of syntactic, semantic, and phonological information a language learner must keep in mind or get a sense of while stretching strings of sounds, words, and phrases into meaningful statements and questions. It also reminds me of the sense I acquired as a teacher for when it was time to move on from one activity to the next in my lesson plan. How much to stretch an activity, like dough, without weakening it, and how much support to give students, like the dusting of flour on the marble table beneath the dough, are important decisions. I had to get the feel for flattening each piece of dough evenly and fingering the edge to make a raised rim that would later hold back the sauce once the pie was in the oven. I had to use an appropriate dusting of flour between the dough and the marble-topped table on which I stretched it – enough to keep the semistretched piece of dough moving in a circular motion under my hands, but not so much that the pie would later be caked with flour underneath it, spoiling the flavor that a clean, crispy crust has.

While attending to the pie dough, I had to expand my consciousness of the kinds of toppings people asked for, who had ordered what, and in what order they were to be served. We found all this easier to do from memory than to write up receipts because our time was so limited. We just did it, and the more we did it, the easier it became, even on those Friday nights when we made more than 230 pies. Perhaps that level of intense concentration contributed to my later confidence as a teacher in being able to learn all my students' names in the first hour or two of a course – even in classes of forty or more students! I have often credited my pizza-making skills with helping me to develop as a language teacher.

Task Break

1. What is a skill or subject you have learned that may influence how you teach?
2. List some of the specifics of the above-mentioned skill or subject that demand careful attention. Then consider the parallels between those details and the teaching and/or learning of languages.

Details of skill/subject   Connections to teaching-learning

By developing skills in painting and pizza making, and through my experiences as a continuing learner of Thai and Spanish, I have made numerous connections to the teaching and learning of languages. All these experiences have helped me feel more confident as a communicator, leader, facilitator, provider of feedback, and so many other roles I have had to assume as a teacher. The more consciously I connect my own processes as a learner to those of my students, the easier it is for me to understand what they are grappling with and how they are attempting to progress in the language they are studying or acquiring.

McDonald (1992), in trying to discover his teacher's voice, mentions the importance of stepping outside the classroom and learning "to hold my worklife at a distance . . . and to search for perspective on the events inside" (p. 11). This kind of stepping outside into our personal spheres and searching for perspective on what we do in our work seems as important an activity as any of the avenues of exploration promoted in this book.

Personal exploration – whether through active learning of languages and other subjects/skills, through yoga (as my coauthor relates in Chapter 11), through psychoanalysis, or whatever other means – can bring more liveliness to our work and to the students with whom we relate. If "cultivation of the life of imagination is the distinctive office and ultimate aim of general education," as Phenix claims (1964), then we teachers must "exemplify an imaginative quality of mind" (p. 350):

> [The teacher's] own imagination must also be alive in respect to his own existence. If it is, he communicates a quality of authentic life – of having been grasped at the core of his personality by the power of meaning – and the students apprehend this quality of reality even if they do not share in the articular meanings that the teacher experiences. (ibid., 351)

Through continual connections we make between the personal and professional realms of our lives, we can more readily and convincingly communicate the quality of authentic life that Phenix urges us to cultivate. Authenticity is also at the heart of my next connecting question.

Am I *real* in and out of school?

Genuineness or "realness" was considered by Carl Rogers (1983) to be the most basic of the attitudes that facilitate learning:

> When the facilitator is a real person, being what she is, entering into a relationship with the learner without presenting a front or a facade, she is much more likely to be effective. This means that the feelings that she is experiencing are available to her, available to her awareness, that she is able to live these feelings, be them, and able to communicate them if appropriate. It means that she comes into a direct personal encounter with the learner, meeting her on a person-to-person basis. It means that she is *being* herself, not denying herself. . . . Thus, she is a person to her students, not a faceless embodiment of a curricular requirement nor a sterile tube through which knowledge is passed from one generation to the next. (pp. 121–122)

Such genuineness Rogers found in a sixth grade teacher, Barbara Shiel, who was able to share not only her positive feelings but also those of anger and frustration. Because she arranged for art materials to be readily available, her room was often messy, but the messiness rubbed agonizingly against her orderly nature:

> Finally, one day I told the children . . . that the mess was driving me to distraction. Did they have a solution? It was suggested that there were some volunteers who could clean up. . . . I said it didn't seem fair to me to have the same people clean up all the time for others – but it would solve it for me. "Well, some people like to clean," they replied. So that's the way it is. (p. 123)

By clearly communicating her feelings, Shiel states the limits of her comfort zone. The youngsters, in turn, respect her feelings and account for them in their proposed solution. Their teacher relates, "I used to get upset and feel guilty when I became angry. I finally realized the children could accept *my* feelings too. And it is important for them to know when they've 'pushed me.' I have my limits, too" (ibid., 123).

This reminds me of a time at Eastern Michigan University when I was teaching a summer ESL class whose students had grown lax late in the course in coming to class with completed homework assignments. To express my frustration, I jumped out of the second-floor window on to a ledge that jutted out several feet below, the existence of which some students seemed to be unaware. After momentarily disappearing from view as I crouched on the ledge, I stood up and peered at them through an open window. From that position, and after the excited screams subsided, I had their full attention for the short speech that followed.

I told them how much our work in class depended on theirs at home and that I could not teach them without working from what they did. My lesson plans, I added, usually were crafted with the assumption that some of the time would be spent as follow-up to what they had done at home. If they had not fulfilled their responsibility, I could not meet mine. It was their class, not mine. They were the ones who had traveled from all over the globe to study in the United States. I told them I would leave the class for 5 minutes for them to discuss my thoughts and feelings. I came back; they apologized and told me they would turn things around. The problem, with some minor exceptions by a couple of students, never resurfaced. As with Shiel, my clear and dramatic indication of how much I needed the students to understand my feelings, communicated to them in a genuine way, had been heard.

In my experience both as a teacher and as a teacher educator, being real is not easily accomplished. In viewing thousands of hours of teaching, I agree with Rogers's contention that "It is quite customary for teachers rather consciously to put on the mask, the role, the facade of being a teacher and to wear this facade all day, removing it only when they have left the school at night" (ibid., 122).

Having said this, I am quite aware that the issue of authenticity is slippery because what is authentic in classrooms does, in fact, differ markedly from what is authentic elsewhere. van Lier (1996: 124) exemplifies this nicely in the following exchange:

A Open your mouth wide, please. Hold still for a moment, if you can.
B (mumbling through multiple gadgets) Ish ick gowa 'ur'?

Making the point that the type of language is obviously connected to the setting, which most readers will easily identify as occurring in a dentist's office, van Lier suggests that in that setting "no one complains about the artificiality of the language . . . , yet in the case of the classroom such complaints are common" (ibid., 124). van Lier devotes an extremely informative chapter to the various meanings of "authenticity" as it relates to language teaching, which can propel you much further into this topic than I do here.

I prefer to focus on what I have found helpful in terms of being a more genuine person/teacher. I have found that the kinds of communication that tend to increase trust contribute to a sense of security among classroom participants, students and teacher alike. Such security, in turn, leads to an environment conducive to learning rather than to defending oneself. What kind of communication tends to increase trust? According to Giffin (in Stevick 1976: 96), it is communication in which the speaker.

is describing what he sees, rather than passing judgment on it . . . is interested in solving a problem, rather than in controlling [someone] . . . seems to be stating tentative rather that final conclusions . . . [is seen by the other as being] spontaneous and sincere, not motivated by some concealed purpose . . . is personally involved in the exchange, and not just an aloof observer. [Brackets are mine.]

There is a quality of trustworthiness that comes from being less judgmental, by not having to control another person, by not having to be infallible, by being sincere and spontaneous, and by truly engaging oneself with others. At the core of this kind of communication is the skill of active listening (not in a mechanical, manipulative way) in an effort to truly understand the other person.

Active listening requires a kind of nondirective understanding elaborated upon by Curran (1970, 1978) and given more recent treatment by Rardin et al. (1988), Rardin and Oprandy (1985), and Edge (1992). Curran characterized this kind of understanding as follows:

There is a rhythm that people have towards one another, almost like the diastolic and systolic action of the heart, or like breathing. This is the rhythm of life . . . a kind of breathing rhythm when, at the right moment, the listener knows that he is the listener and the speaker knows that he will be delicately, sensitively and artistically listened to. (1970: 15)

How interesting, as my colleague Peter Shaw discovered in an ESL class one day, that the Chinese character for "listen" contains three parts. One is for "ear," another for "heart," and the third for "open." Hearing with an open heart is one of the main ways to pave the road to a trusting relationship and to establish an atmosphere in which learners, and the teacher, feel more secure. By modeling this the best we can as teachers, we also open up the possibility for students to listen well to one another (Rardin & Oprandy 1985).

The kind of communication that fosters trust can, of course, be practiced outside of class and become part of who we are in the personal realm of our lives. I have been fortunate to have people in my life whom I can rely on to get this kind of understanding at critical junctures as well as in the normal flow of my life. When I reciprocate, I get to practice the skills of active listening, which have now become part and parcel of how I communicate with people. These skills transfer to the classroom and to the one-to-one chats I have with students outside of the classroom.

To summarize my quest regarding to what extent I am being real: I strive to establish a relationship with my students that is trustful and open and not one in which useless power games are played. In such a class, I want to be able to state, as Barbara Shiel did with her sixth graders, the limits beyond which I cannot go in order for all of us to accomplish what we come to class to do. Most of all, I want my students to feel understood and to know that I will make every attempt to understand the meanings we are constructing together. All of this does not mean abrogating my responsibility to be the leader of the classes I teach. To be authoritative is quite different from being authoritarian. These are responsibilities I get paid for. I find, though, that such leadership comes more easily the more genuine or real I feel in the presence of others, including those outside as well as inside of school.

How does language teaching fit into my vision of who I am (becoming) and how I'd like the world to be?

As a Peace Corps trainer in Thailand, I encountered several confused trainees. I will never forget one who came up to me one late afternoon after a grueling day of Thai lessons some time during the second week of the 12-week intensive training program. She burst into tears and proceeded to relate what was upsetting her. She felt like a dummy in her Thai class; everyone except her was more or less understanding what was being discussed and practiced. The level of frustration and the feeling that she was falling more and more behind her classmates with each class were crushing her spirit, especially given that she had always been a successful learner. I listened in an active way, crystallizing what she was saying and feeling.

What eventually came out was that she had not really decided whether to complete the training and stay in Thailand for the subsequent 2 years.

Upon unearthing that crucial revelation, she then began to grapple with the feelings around whether to stay or return to the States. About half an hour later it was clear to her that, in fact, she truly wanted to be a Peace Corps volunteer and to accomplish what she had traveled some fifteen thousand miles to do.

With that realization and the clarity that accompanied it, she dug in that night and into the wee hours of the morning to review all her notes, the teacher's handouts, and the textbook lessons she had been exposed to since the beginning of the training program. Within a couple of days, she felt a part of the class and was able to participate as she had not been able to earlier. Her commitment to being a Thai-language student and to staying in Thailand to teach English was all she needed to get beyond what was blocking her. Her identity as a Peace Corps volunteer was forming. Interestingly, she wound up extending her service an additional year beyond the usual 2-year stint.

This volunteer's decision reminds me of how idiosyncratically we all come to our decisions about whether to teach, and, if so, how much to give of ourselves to our chosen profession. In addition, there is the consideration of what is in it for us. What is the yield for our incredible investment of time, energy, and, in most cases, money spent on educating ourselves about teaching?

For me, it was about the final three words in the song "Procession" by the Moody Blues, which was composed of a string of words ending in "-tion" and beginning with "creation." The song was about human evolution and ended with "Communication, Compassion, Solution." Although I worry to some extent about linguistic imperialism as English spreads around the globe, at the same time, I would rather see the world's people have some common means of communicating their fears, excitement, needs, and goals. If English is the principal means to do that, so be it. Who can stop the human need to communicate, in any case? Only through genuine, person-to-person communication can we begin to have the kind of compassion that will enable us to solve so many of the problems that have plagued humanity throughout history. It is my hope that we can move beyond nationalism to internationalism in the twenty-first century. That is one of my major reasons for being a language teacher. Teaching at a college where every student must be competent in at least one second language and where half the students are from outside the United States, I am constantly struck by the way language brings such diversity together. One of my great joys in life is to play a part in mixing such diversity.

Having spent 5 years of my life in the Peace Corps and having taught and/or trained teachers on five continents, I consider myself a global citizen, one who keeps in touch with so much of the world through my contacts with its people. My first ESL class in New York City was composed of eighteen students from fifteen different countries. The classroom, in Long Island City, Queens, faced the East River. One day, I glanced across the river and pointed, asking "Do you know what building that is over there?" I was not sure if many of the recent immigrant students in class knew. A few said, "UN." Acknowledging their answer, I said, "But this [I made a circling gesture at the class] is the real UN," at which many of them nodded in agreement that accompanied the excited twinkling of my eyes.

Task Break

1. How does language teaching fit into your vision of who you are (becoming) and how you would like the world to be?
2. Go back to the connecting questions you listed while doing the first Task Break in this chapter. What other questions do you want to add to your list? How do you expect to explore one or more of your questions?

A final note

By exploring my own connecting questions, that is, those that link my professional and personal selves, I have tried to demonstrate a reflective process that has the potential of making teaching come alive for me wherever I go and in most things I do. This is similar to being on the lookout everywhere for material I can make use of in class, things that will help concretize the content of what my students are working on. At a deeper level, I actively consider who I am (becoming) as a teacher through the everyday experiences I encounter. Dewey (1938: 48) captured the connectivity of our experiences well when he wrote:

As an individual passes from one situation to another, his world, his environment, expands or contracts. He does not find himself living in another world but in a different part or aspect of one and the same world. What he has learned in the way of knowledge and skill in one situation becomes an instrument of understanding and dealing effectively with the situations which follow. The process goes on as long as life and learning continue.

As my grandmother used to say, "The more things you put in your basket the better, because you never know when you will need to pull one out."

In the quotation at the beginning of this chapter, Jersild suggests that there is much more to developing awareness as a teacher than learning the latest techniques and methods. The personal searching one must do may be, in the final analysis, more central to our work. The nontransferable goods in the form of the values and beliefs we bring to and model in class may well be those that outlast in our students' memories any of the official content of our courses. The more we connect the personal and professional parts of our selves, the more such goods we carry into the classroom.

PART III:
EXAMPLES OF
TEACHERS' EXPLORATIONS

In Part II we focused on how and why teachers, including teacher educators, can explore their teaching. We turn in Part III to the explorations of pre- and in-service teachers, at times in collaboration with others, who explored the kinds of processes described in the first two parts of the book. The examples provided in Part III fill in the details of the broader contours laid out in Chapters 1–7. The awareness that emerges from, as well as the challenges in carrying out, explorations of teaching become quite transparent as you read the four examples described in the following pages.

8 Teachers talking about teaching
Collaborative conversations about an elementary ESL class

Robert Oprandy
with Laura Golden and Kayoko Shiomi

> A "truly collaborative approach" [is] one that operates on prin-
> ciples of open professionality; where the aims of teacher and
> researcher are fused into one; where decision-making and
> products are jointly owned, where power is shared and both
> are "empowered" by the activity.
>
> —P. Woods (1995: 124)

Observation, action research, and talk with other teachers (including supervisors), as discussed in Chapters 3, 4, and 6, are three major processes of
exploration discussed in Part II. What follows is a report on a project that
brought together aspects of all three of these processes. The report shows
the convergence of three teachers' perspectives on what occurred in an ESL
class taught by Laura Golden in a New York City elementary school. Teachers talking with each other about teaching would seem the most feasible and
obvious activity for reflecting on teaching and learning. The literature on
teaching, however, indicates that this is not usually the case. Teachers seldom have or make time to discuss what they do. Of particular interest, then,
is how the collaborative conversations among the three of us broke the silent
barrier that so often separates the worlds of teachers, who, for any number
of reasons, find limited opportunities to talk shop with each other.

Several questions emerge as we describe and consider the implications
of our conversations. These were not questions we set out to answer as we
began our collaboration but ones that took on interest as we reflected on
and analyzed our conversations. Who we are and what we accomplished
will become clear as we address the four following questions:

- What advantages derive from exploring teaching-learning collaboratively?
- What was the context for doing our collaborative inquiry and how did we get started?
- What was the nature of our talk, and how was it similar to and different from usual teacher–supervisor conferences?
- What did our conversations achieve?

What advantages derive from exploring teaching-learning collaboratively?

The loneliness of teachers is legendary. Given the tight structure of a teacher's school day and the limited time set aside for professional development activities, teachers are generally left alone with their inner speech regarding the hundreds of decisions they need to make daily, as Jackson (1968) observed. Addressing such feelings with colleagues is rare. "You can be in a school for years and never see an advisor," report May and Sigsworth (1987: 259). "There's no outside person ever coming to give you that bit of a lift really."

This sense of isolation can be especially true for ESL teachers. Often one is the only ESL professional in a school, perhaps in an entire school district. We have read several "Please help!" messages on a K–12 ESL teachers' E-mail network from isolated English teachers in school districts throughout the world. Teachers need an outlet for all the emotions connected to their professional sense of well-being. Working on collaborative projects, particularly with trusted peers or mentors, at the same school or at a nearby school or teachers college, affords us such an option.

Laura, the ESL teacher in this project, admitted that she was "not very interested in personal conversation" with her colleagues at school. By this she meant the kind of chit chat and gossip that seldom touched on the professional concerns she had. Instead, she continued,

I am interested in dialoguing about kids and . . . things that I notice in my teaching and their learning . . . and I found it very, very hard to find people that I could talk to about that. You know, to me . . . there are so many things that are depressing about the public schools that to sit around and talk about it just gets me more depressed. So, you know, unless I'm talking about a specific incident or a specific kid or, you know, an idea that I am thinking about in my head, I don't really want to, like, sit around and chat.

Although the loneliness of the classroom teacher has been well documented, that of teacher educators has not. They may suffer similarly, though for different reasons. Many long to be back in the kinds of classrooms for which they themselves were trained, if only to "teach" vicariously through doing classroom-based research. Others want to discuss their own teaching practices and the theories of teaching and learning that drive those practices (Richardson 1994). Still others would like to work in a collaborative way on classroom-oriented research with those closest to the action, that is, with classroom teachers. Folding such research into their work with teacher-learners at their college or university brings it alive and lends more credence to the points being made in the higher education courses they teach and the practica whose seminars they lead. It would seem, then, that collaboration of the kind described below would be a powerful antidote for such longing among teacher educators as well as lonely classroom teachers.

Besides reducing the isolation of teaching, there are several other advantages of collaborative exploration of teaching. It can exclude the evaluative component of observation characteristic of the usual top-down, hierarchical, supervisory model, in which "professional development is seen as something that is evaluated with little attention paid to ways teachers evolve expertise in the practice of teaching" (Dantonio 1995: 31). In such a hierarchical model, teachers may perceive their development as externally directed by those with authority. "Teachers are treated as if administrative supervision is necessary to ensure proper behavior. . . . Within this type of evaluation, teachers are viewed as deficient, and their personal knowledge is ignored" (Gitlin & Price 1992: 63). Dantonio (1995: 31) argues:

This hierarchical construct is limiting, and it may damage teachers' self-esteem. It stifles avenues for teachers to reflect on instructional practices and to make sense of teaching and learning. In such a context, any kind of development activity can be a demeaning experience, because teachers have little, if any, impact on their own professional growth, and administrators may be at odds with teachers about what their professional development should entail.

Another advantage of collaborative exploration is that it can provide camaraderie among teachers while building a community of teacher-learners (Neubert & Stover 1994). "Active collaboration," according to Richardson (1994: 7), "leads to shared or mutual reconstruction that is agreed upon by both practitioner and researcher," and although it "is not conducted for purposes of developing general laws related to educational practice, . . . the results are suggestive of new ways of looking at the [practitioner's] context . . . and/or possibilities for changes in practice." Such "new ways of looking" are at the heart of the exploratory approach promoted in this book. Collaborative exploration can also encourage a sense of professionalism that may not have existed prior to working together, fostering incentive for jointly doing classroom research, conference presentations, and even publications (as evidenced by this chapter and the one that follows).

What follows is a report in one setting of the types of discussions that practicing teachers and teacher educators can have if they are open to doing collaborative classroom inquiry. What we accomplished (e.g., in the range of roles we assumed during our discussions) offers hope to others wishing to break out of the shells of isolation separating teachers from their colleagues as well as from teacher educators.

We fully realize how difficult it might be to pull off the kinds of collaborative conversations we had. After all, we had all been trained in the same TESOL program and shared similar ideas about the importance of nonjudgmental, descriptive observation (see Chapter 1 and references to Fanselow in Chapter 3). Our training certainly eased us into the collaborative nature of our conversations.

What was the context for doing our collaborative project and how did we get started?

The setting for our project was a pullout ESL class in a public elementary school in a multicultural neighborhood of New York City. The collaborators were the teacher (Laura), a TESOL teacher educator (Robert), and a Japanese doctoral student interested in assisting with the project (Kayoko). Laura's school was located in a largely Latino, predominantly Dominican, area of Manhattan. More pertinent to the discussion of the project reported on here, however, are the perceived roles the three of us were considering as we began our collaborative effort.

The collaborators and our perceived roles

What follows are profiles of the three collaborators: Robert, Laura, and Kayoko.

The teacher educator.   There were several reasons for Robert's predisposition to doing a collaborative project at a local public school. First was his belief that the elementary and secondary ESL teachers he had trained at a nearby teachers college should have more ownership of and benefit from classroom inquiry once they were in the field. He also felt that their expertise needed to be folded much more into TESOL training programs. By observing and collaborating with an ESL teacher in a school setting similar to those the program's practice teachers worked in, he hoped to bring data and his collaborator (and other classroom teachers) to his practicum seminars. This would allow his teacher-learners at the teachers college to bounce the data and experiences of in-service teachers off the theories/practices they were studying in methods, materials, and theory courses. In addition, they could contrast the ideas of experienced teachers with those they themselves were accumulating through practice teaching.

The second major benefit he derived from collaborative research is that he, too, is a teacher. As such, he models teaching, both in the courses he teaches and in workshops and demonstrations he conducts. Therefore, he was anxious to deepen his understanding of his own classroom practices. This as much as his writing keeps him alive professionally. Talking shop with other teachers keeps him actively thinking about teaching and learning, particularly as it relates to actual contexts rather than the idealized ones so often conjured up in teacher-education programs (Diaz-Rico 1995). As a recent TESOL graduate turned teacher complained in an interview with Silliman (1995), whose dissertation was part of a self-study of an M.A. TESOL program, "One of the things I hope that the program here will start to look at is really making the graduates more prepared for what public school teaching is like" (p. 185). Another of Silliman's interviewees added, "I think that before [the college] runs around trying to change or better itself, I think [it] really ought to figure out what is going on out there" (p. 187) in the public schools.

Exploring teaching and learning with others helps Robert to see through more than his own perceptual filter. Having several perspectives from which to view and discuss what occurs in a classroom opens him up to multiple interpretations of what is seen and heard. Thus, he keeps from getting stuck in seeing schooling through the filter of his own professional training, personal teaching experiences, and biases. By rubbing up against others' ways of seeing teaching-learning, he can more easily and honestly explore anew the complexities and nuances of schooling.

The classroom ESL teacher.   Laura, in her third year of teaching ESL in the elementary school mentioned earlier, had recently finished her M.A. in TESOL at the same teachers college where Robert taught and where Kayoko studied. Her studies followed a 2-year Peace Corps stint as an EFL teacher in Latin America. She was very pleased to be part of such a collaborative effort for several reasons. She was fond of the numerous opportunities for observing and reflecting on teaching and learning that were embedded in her graduate program and felt fortunate once again to have ongoing conversations about the dynamics of one of her ESL classes. She also hoped that two other sets of eyes and ears on her classes would provide more perspective on the everyday concerns that cropped up in her work. As she said in one of our post-observation discussions, "But . . . to me, just having, you know, the opportunity, that we're sitting around and talking about what you've observed in the classroom and just kind of heightening the awareness or stepping back from it and just discussing it, I think that is *so* important."

Laura was relaxed and welcoming during the observations and post-observation discussions of her classes. Her sense of co-ownership in the project and her realization that our purpose was descriptive, not prescriptive, contributed to her openness.

The doctoral student.　A Japanese doctoral student serving as a project assistant was the third collaborator. Kayoko, with her 7 years of EFL teaching experience and interest in observing classroom interaction, was responsible for videotaping and transcribing the classes we all observed. In addition, she played an equally collaborative role during post-observation discussions, though she contributed less quantity of talk to our joint conversations. She was, in fact, quite surprised when she learned in our second discussion that she could be more than the usual project assistant, especially when we decided to write an abstract to present preliminary findings at a statewide conference later in the year. In a discussion of how each of us saw our role(s) in the research, Kayoko commented: "At first, I was an assistant, so I thought maybe I [would] just help you with videotaping . . . and then you [referring to Robert] said, um, 'We're gonna have a presentation in the fall.' Then I thought, 'Ooh'!"

Kayoko's comparative comments regarding ESL and EFL teaching in the United States and Japan, respectively, and her keen eye for details in Laura's classes continually broadened and clarified the observations and insights that emerged during our discussions.

Getting started

There are numerous ways of doing collaborative inquiry (see, e.g., Dantonio 1995 on *collegial coaching*, Neubert & Stover 1994 on *peer coaching*, and Edge 1992 on *cooperative development*). Our own experience unfolded in a way that followed no clear steps. Robert initiated the project, suggesting participation by his former student, Laura, who was teaching at an elementary school in the vicinity of his college. He then determined that his research assistant, Kayoko, was interested in getting involved with the project. Communicating the idea was the catalyst for our first meeting.

Although there may be infinite ways to set up collaborative conversations about teaching, we report here on how our particular project unfolded. We decided in our initial planning meeting to videotape and audiotape the class approximately once a week over a 10-week period in the spring of 1994. These tapes, their transcriptions, field notes, and classroom artifacts (e.g., handouts the children worked on, copies of students' writing and reading journals) were all collected as material for potential data analysis.

It was what followed the classes, however, that became the corpus of data reported on here. Classes usually were immediately followed by post-observation discussions by the three of us on what we had noticed about the class. The materials listed in the preceding paragraph were often stimuli to which we referred as we talked, though we as often relied on our collective memories of the class just observed/taught. These discussions were audiotaped and later transcribed and analyzed with the help of an additional assistant, Joan Brill, resulting in the data reported on here.

Going into the project, Robert felt that his interest in the development of listening acuity, a topic of particular interest in the previous decade (Oprandy 1994a, 1994b; Rardin & Oprandy 1985), might guide his observations and emerge as a topic worthy of closer scrutiny by the three of us. Given Kayoko's co-authoring of a popular EFL listening textbook (Shiomi & Dalton 1990) in Japan, she and Robert initially felt that their interest in this skill area might intersect with what would be observed in Laura's class.

Meanwhile, Kayoko's studies and a great amount of reading she had done in passing her doctoral certification exam and paper made her predisposed to thinking about interaction analysis. Although she and Robert began with these separate, though somewhat connected, themes of what they might observe, all three of us chose to just look and then discuss whatever seemed of interest after each class. Our hope was that a topic or topics would naturally emerge.

Unlike Kayoko and Robert, Laura had no assumptions regarding what we might examine in her classes; she felt that any insights would be useful to her in seeing more of what was going on there than she otherwise could see. As she mentioned during our second meeting, "I keep waiting to figure out what our project's about!" What she was doing intuitively in terms of watchful waiting is what we all agreed to do in practice.

A procession of questions and emphases emerged from our collaborative efforts. This procession demonstrated that the whats and hows of our work together influenced us as we went along. What remained constant was the common philosophical bent we shared, one etched in the TESOL program from which we had all been graduated, that is, to be as nonjudgmental and as descriptive as possible in observing the dynamics of the classes we discussed. (For fuller discussions of this approach to observing classroom behavior, see Chapters 1 and 3.)

Discovering a focus

The central focus of this report of our project came about during numerous scans of the transcribed post-observation discussions the three of us had. As Robert read Arcario's doctoral thesis (1994) and Waite's analysis of teacher–supervisor talk (1993) during the time of our data collection, he began to realize how rich a source of data post-observation discussions are. Additionally, he noticed qualitative differences and similarities between the structure of post-observation discussions that Arcario found and those he and his collaborators had had.

Arcario's study of eleven post-observation conferences between practice teachers and their supervisors, as was mentioned in Chapter 6, uncovered three phases of what he called the "canonical conversations" of such sessions:

1. an "opening evaluative move" by either party;
2. a protracted "evaluative sequence" made up of evaluations (again by either party), justifications, and prescriptions; and
3. a short "closing phase" to terminate the discussion.

Obviously, one would expect evaluation to serve as the primary purpose of such conversations. The terms "supervisor" and "supervisory conferences" themselves imply that evaluation will characterize the sessions, or at least that someone with superior vision will play a central role in them. The structure of the conferences Arcario examined reflects that characterization.

Waite (1993), in his study of post-observation conferences (also mentioned in Chapter 6), found that supervisors generate the "data" referred to in such meetings and initiate both the discussions and the topics to be discussed. Underscoring the judgmental and prescriptive nature of such talk, he found that supervisors determine what teacher responses are sufficient, and, if insufficient, how to redirect the discussion in an effort to get at the points the supervisor wishes or feels obliged to raise.

Task Break

In your role as teacher, supervisor, teacher educator, or administrator, how would you initiate a collaborative inquiry project?

1. List those to whom you would communicate your idea.
2. What would be your plan for such a project?
3. What rationale would you present to potential collaborators in your proposed project?

Get feedback on your responses to these questions from at least one colleague or professional friend.

What was the nature of our talk, and how was it similar to and different from usual teacher–supervisor conferences?

What we found in analyzing the collaborative discussions the three of us had of Laura's classes appeared at first quite different from Arcario's canonical conversations and distinct in some ways from what Waite found. First, the structure of our discussions had phases that contrasted in significant ways from those Arcario found. Second, the roles we assumed were very different from those of the evaluation-oriented nature found in the canon of post-observation talk. Further analysis of the conversations showed, however, that the lure of the canon remained strong and still managed to have some sway over the structure of our talk.

The structure of our collaborative conversations

The structure of our discussions of Laura's classes followed this three-step progression:

1. an initial move, usually by Robert, in the form of an open-ended question;
2. shop talk about the class or anything else occasioned by something observed or thought about, during which time we all played a variety of roles (detailed later); and
3. a short closure, usually of a procedural nature (e.g., setting a date and time for the next observation, checking on tasks we would do before the next meeting).

The closure phase is self-explanatory. The other two phases require some explanation.

An example of an initial move was "Any things that, you know, really struck anyone today?" A response to Robert's question by any of the collaborators, including himself once, moved us immediately into the second, or talking shop, phase of our meetings. For example, Kayoko's response to Robert's question, "[Two of the students] wanna play the role of teacher," led into her descriptions of two instances to support her insight. This was followed by Laura's thoughts about her relationship to one of the two students and a discussion by all of us of student control and initiative in classroom conversations.

The second phase most often began with a descriptive observation or a hypothesis regarding a pattern of interaction noted during the observed class. This led into one of a number of different directions, including:

a) additional descriptive observations by other collaborators;
b) hypotheses about the learners' processes, styles of learning, or behaviors; and
c) storytelling, almost always by Laura, about the learners.

No matter in which direction we went, each conversation had a life all its own; there was no telling where we would wind up, how we would get there, or what roles we would play along the way. We were now talking shop with some undefined but unfolding collaborative agenda in the background.

Although the structure of our collaborative talk reflects a very different agenda from that found in the usual post-observation conferences, what we did *not* do during our conversations also illuminates a contrast to what Arcario and Waite found. In the initial phase, our talk was not marked by the opening evaluative moves Arcario noted, such as "That was a great class!" or by questions that would garner such moves, such as "How did you feel about your class today?" Instead, Robert would generally begin the discussions of the observed lessons with a question such as "Any things that, you know, struck anyone today?" or "Let's see anything that strikes us, I guess." The nondirective, even tentative quality of such solicits led not to judgments of the class but to exploratory talk (Barnes 1992) of an open-ended, interactive nature. That the teacher educator usually initiated our conversations demonstrates, however, how difficult it was to break totally away from the usual structure of teacher–supervisor conferences.

The second phase of our discussions was not characterized, as Arcario found, by prolonged evaluative sequences consisting largely of justification for why certain behaviors were or were not exhibited. Nor was there a need for prescriptive talk. The contrasts between the structure of our talk and that noted by Arcario point to the way the purposes of talk are tied to its character. If Robert or Kayoko had observed Laura as her supervisor, how much would the expectations of such observations have co-opted the three of us into carrying out our talk in ways more congruent with canonical conversations than with the structure of our collaborative conversations?

Like the supervisors Waite observed, Robert usually initiated the conferences and, at times, new topics to discuss once the conversations were under way. In contrast, however, he did not take responsibility for generating the "data" referred to in our discussions. Nor did he judge – overtly at least – the other teachers' contributions to the talk or redirect the discussions in order to highlight his points. When he did change topics, it was because he felt we had come to closure on the topic being discussed and that it was time to move on to another observation any of us had of the lesson being discussed. He was more like the chair of the meetings than like Waite's supervisors, who waited to force their discussions in directions they had predetermined in fulfilling their evaluative function. Robert's role was more in line with the exploratory approach to teaching awareness discussed throughout this book. Nevertheless, it is interesting to note the role we arranged for him to play as chair of our meetings and the attraction that the canonical structure, or at least aspects of it, had on our conversations.

Waite also found that teachers in post-observation discussions tend to assume one of the three roles discussed in Chapter 6: (1) a passive conference role, (2) a collaborative conference role, or (3) an adversarial role. The first is one in which the teacher listens to the supervisor, often says "uh-huh," and occasionally agrees by saying something like "Yeah, that would be a good idea." The passive teacher is generally "unable or unwilling to forcefully counter the supervisor's direct and indirect criticisms" (Waite 1993: 696). Teachers enacting collaborative conference roles do a lot of active listening, timing, and phrasing of their utterances in ways that avoid any appearance of confrontation. Such teachers have an ability to advance their agendas in post-observation discussions, as was encouraged in Chapter 6. Those who played the adversarial role, however, competed for the floor and were reluctant to accept their supervisors' comments or even their role as evaluators.

Laura played neither role 1 nor role 3. Instead, she was clearly collaborative, but not in the sense of attempting to avoid confrontation, as Waite describes role 2. Whereas the teachers playing the collaborative conference role that Waite observed were oriented toward the control exhibited by the supervisors, Laura assumed a proactive, more empowered stance (described in the next section). Waite paints in broad brush strokes three roles that teachers assume during post-observation conferences where evaluative purposes are primarily being played out. The rich texture of our collaborative conversations calls for finer-pointed brushes to detail the wide variety of roles we played.

Table 8.1   Chief roles assumed by the collaborators
during post-observation conversations

Laura's roles
1. Sharer of her own expertise
    a) by storytelling and giving illustrative examples
    b) by informing of the bigger context
        (1) of school and Board of Education policies
        (2) of students' lives: (*a*) outside school and (*b*) in school but outside of class
    c) by explaining her teaching practices and influences
2. Other roles
    a) sharer of reflections on her teaching and of new insights into her students' behaviors and learning processes
    b) sharer of her struggles
        (1) in teaching and in understanding her students' behaviors and learning processes
        (2) in communicating with other teachers about teaching and learning
        (3) in working with school and Board of Education policies
    c) generator of possible research topics

Roles by both Robert and Kayoko (or by either)
1. Responders to Laura's expertise
    a) by giving "understanding responses"
    b) by asking clarifying questions
    c) by expanding on Laura's stories and observations
    d) by acknowledging Laura's teaching practices
2. Sharers of their own areas of expertise

Just Robert	Just Kayoko
a) as researcher	*a)* as student of SLA research on interaction analysis
(1) of literature on teaching and learning	*b)* as EFL teacher in Japan
(2) of teacher education	*c)* as observer of cross-cultural phenomena
(3) of project methodology	
b) as EFL teacher in Thailand	
c) as cross-cultural trainer and observer	

3. Other roles by both Robert and Kayoko
    a) hypothesizers regarding students' behaviors and learning processes
    b) describers of students' behaviors and learning processes
    c) speculators (i.e., "I wonder why S_1 . . .") about students' behaviors and learning processes
    d) generators of possible research topics

Just Robert	Just Kayoko
e) provider of readings from journals and newspaper	*e)* raiser of concerns regarding recording equipment
f) procedural leader re:	
(1) initiation, closure and changing of topics during post-observation discussions; and	
(2) research-related topics	

The varied roles of the collaborators

In the exactly two hundred transcribed pages of post-observation discussions we had, the structure of our talk described above gives a sense of the form of our discussions. The variety of roles we assumed in our conversations gives detail to fill in those forms. Given that none of us were evaluating what took place, what roles did we arrange for one another to play? The chief roles each of us assumed in our discussions can be categorized as shown in Table 8.1.

We hesitate to share these categories, fearing a decontextualized image that detracts from how our individual contributions played off each other as we jointly constructed meaning about what we observed in Laura's classes. The roles she played (e.g., as storyteller, sharer of new insights, or explainer of her practices) were almost always in response to or initiated the roles that Kayoko and Robert most often assumed – those of clarifying questioners, understanding responders (explained below), and describers of the students' behaviors/learning processes. Our discussions as illustrated in Figure 8.1, demonstrate a pronounced orientation in Laura's direction, either between her and Robert or between her and Kayoko. As might be expected, there were also occasional short exchanges between Kayoko and Robert.

Like a psychologist, Laura was very much into the learning processes of each student, trying to figure out what made them tick, why they behaved the way they did. She told many stories about them and infused her talk with illustrative examples of students' behaviors to give flesh to the skeletons our topics raised. Her collaborators sought out her knowledge of the students and what they did through the understanding responses they gave Laura and through the clarifying questions they asked of her. She truly emerged in one sense as the expert. In the realm of her classroom and in the understanding of her students, she reigned supreme, and neither observer questioned that supremacy. The following excerpt illustrates the isosceles quality of the triangularity of many of our discussions, with Laura at the point atop the triangle.

What follows is a discussion initiated by Kayoko about her interest in tallying the amount of class time Laura's Bengali students spoke in their native language.

L: They seem very conscious of the fact that I'm not understanding what they're talking about, so . . . it seems to me like there's a sense, like, "O.K., let's get back to⌈English."
K: ⌊Yeah!
L: "As soon as we think we kind of figured this out." (Laughter)
R: Uh! Uh-huh. Hmm.⌈Mm.
K: ⌊Mm.

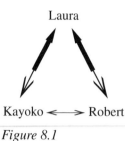

Laura

Kayoko ←——→ Robert

Figure 8.1

L: When [the Haitian girl's] here, it gets a little stickier for me. . . . I kind
    of feel like [she] and I are in the same boat of not understanding them,
    so, you know, it's, uh . . .
R: Sort of an equalizer.
L: Yeah!
R: For the two of you.
R and K: (Laughter)

Following up on Kayoko's observation and idea of tallying the amount
of time Bengali was spoken, Laura demonstrated her expertise vis-à-vis the
students. She mentioned a pattern she had noticed when the Bengalis spoke
their own language. Then she quickly related a story of how she and the
Haitian student sometimes felt when they were excluded from Bengali
exchanges. Kayoko and Robert were oriented toward Laura with nonlinguistic vocalizations ("Mm," "Uh-huh"), with understanding responses
("Sort of an equalizer"), with an exclamation of agreement ("Yeah!"), and
with laughter that overlapped with Laura's. There were many such instances
throughout our discussions of Kayoko's and Robert's arranging for Laura
to tell stories and come up with illustrative examples relating to the topics
we all raised.

The expertise each of us shared ranged well beyond, though it was almost always connected to, the focus on Laura's class that was at the heart
of our conversations. Laura's penchant for relating stories and illustrative
examples at times led to sidebars in which she informed us of the bigger
bureaucratic and sociopolitical context of which her class and students were
a part. Her asides about school and Board of Education policies and about
the students' lives outside of her classroom gave breadth to the narrative to
which we were all contributing. Here are a couple of examples of Laura's
broadening of the context:

• (Regarding standardized tests in reading, math, and science demanded
  periodically by the Board of Education) "I'm not really sure what the test-

ing thing is all about . . . and the thing is those tests are not something to be taken lightly because the score goes on a little sticky [Post-it note], which goes on your record card, which is permanent, that follows you through till twelfth grade. And it affects what middle school you get into and it affects what high school you get into."

- (Concerning one student's experience in school outside of her class and also his life outside of school) "[Student X's] favorite thing he likes to do is to visit his father's store in Queens . . . and he likes to go to Connecticut to visit his uncle, but, you know, immersed in Bengali . . ."
- (Later in the discussion) "This fall, the beginning of this year, I had some real problems with some bullies in [his] class who beat him up during lunchtime. I don't know what that was about. Maybe it's just 'cause he's very bright and they feel threatened, but I'm not sure."

Robert also broadened the context of our discussions from time to time, stepping back to play the professorial role of relating our conversations to scholarly research, to general issues related to teaching and/or learning, and to broader implications of specific observations we discussed.

- (Referring to a scholarly article Robert had photocopied for all of us to read) "He mentioned that interaction, this kind of conversation . . . leads to 'destabilization,' . . . 'destabilization' being something that's essential in learning, providing the impetus to proceed to higher levels. Um, related to Vygotsky's 'Zone of Proximal Development'."[1]
- (Watching a videotape of one of Laura's classes) "I'm always intrigued with how anything that's . . . a common stimulus for students, and, you know, especially where the teacher is kind of out of the way and it's between them and that common stimulus, how much more verbal stuff gets activated by that, I think."
- (Contrasting a study done in Laura's school several years earlier with what appeared to be happening in the school at the time of our project) "It was an ESL reading class. . . . It was really designed just for reading, [and] on the average there was not more than about 3 minutes of reading done in every hour. . . . Whereas here . . . you're doing a lot of reading and writing . . . it seems to be part of their curriculum."

Robert's more than 5 years of teaching outside the United States also embellished our talk, as did other areas of his expertise that are listed in Table 8.1.

---

1 See Vygotsky (1978) for discussion of the "Zone of Proximal Development."

- (After listening to Laura talk about how often teachers are interrupted by public-address announcements) "I'm thinking of a parallel in Thailand. It was during the Vietnam War and the bombing of Laos that was going on by the United States. There was a friend of mine who taught in a school underneath the flight of the . . . planes, the, um, bombers . . . that went so fast and made so much noise . . . that every couple of minutes for about 30 seconds it took for this thing to rip through, make this incredible noise, the walls would shake. . . . So he said there were literally 30 seconds out of every couple of minutes that he had to stop [teaching]."
- (During a discussion of the extended families some of Laura's students live with) "Yeah, in Africa [where Robert had lived] . . . they seemed to have brothers and sisters everywhere. . . . It's kind of comforting, 'cause they could go almost anywhere in the country and find somebody who they consider family, you know?"

Similarly, Kayoko enriched our conversations by virtue of her 7 years as an EFL teacher in Japan; her years of cross-cultural experiences, having lived with a U.S. host family, and having married an American; and her doctoral studies. Here are examples of each of these three areas of expertise that she contributed to our discussions.

- (In a discussion of what might be communicated by a student's silence) "Just being quiet and being silent does not mean that she is not doing anything. . . . She may be doing thinking, and I can relate to that because in Japan when teachers ask you to give her answers to the questions, people are silent. . . . They know the answer but they never raise their hands. . . . They are doing thinking and some of them already know the answers."
- (After Laura mentioned that the Haitian student "can't really warm up to" positive statements by Laura about her good behavior) "It's like [a] compliment. I don't know, but Japanese people are not really used to receiving compliments."
- (When Robert raised the issue of transcription conventions we might use) "I may have [a sheet of such conventions] from my sociolinguistics course . . . but it's more like talking about, um, overruption or interruption. . . . You put like one slash or two slashes."

The dynamic quality of our discussions, as of communication in general, means that it is continuous, circular, not repeatable and irreversible (Forsdale 1981), and that it also has the qualities of a creative, unfolding, co-constructed, and ongoing conversation. Although the varied roles we arranged for each of us to play demonstrate some of the dynamism of our talk, so do the achievements we fulfilled in carrying out those roles.

What did our conversations achieve?

Although the variety of roles we assumed and the dynamic quality those roles lent to our collaborative conversations were instructive of how we worked together, an analysis of what we jointly achieved during our discussions is also illuminating. Two of these achievements are highlighted below, though they in no way account for all that we accomplished through our discussions.

The co-construction of meaning

What three people bring to an interaction, as we often found in our analysis of the children's interaction in Laura's classes, is greater than the sum of its parts. Consider the discovery that unfolded as we discussed the kinds of interaction we observed while reading transcripts of Laura's classes.

After a discussion of instances where students used their prior knowledge and experience in class, Robert stepped back to direct us to a potential area of inquiry.

R: So. OK, so one thing is when student, student as knower or student becomes knower, and . . . it might be very interesting to look at the kind of interaction that happens at those moments. There might be some interesting contrasts there . . . versus when teacher is soliciting, let's say, for certain information . . .

L: . . . Well, for example, in this transcript, like, these questions all here are soliciting answers that are . . . questions that I already know the answer to. But then, like to page 3, when I'm asking them about their writing, it's more asking questions that I don't know the answer to. You know, how do you decide what to put, what order to put the stories in, that sort of thing?

R: Yeah. That's something I did notice as a pattern, I mean that you, you really do ask a lot of solicits, I think, that are . . . geared at trying to understand their process. But, but I think also, at the same time, trying to teach process is my sense. But, but really not knowing, you know, why did they, I mean curious, very curious about why they chose this way . . . rather than another way.

L: Yeah, it's somewhere . . . in between the two [i.e., directed and exploratory talk] because in a sense . . . I'm asking them a question I don't know the answer to, yes, that's true. But it's not the same thing as hav-

ing a conversation because their response is gonna lead me to what I'm
gonna decide what to say to them next. You know.

R: Right.

By reading the transcribed excerpts from the classes and discussing what
we noticed, we all became aware of three kinds of questions and accompanying talk that occurred in Laura's classes. After several more exchanges
in which Laura made increasing sense of the three types of questions she
asked while teaching, Robert again stepped back in an attempt to review
what we had jointly discovered.

R: It looks like, I mean, we've identified, from what I can see, three different areas maybe that, that might be ways of dividing up . . . the types
   of interaction we're looking at. It might be, uh, when student becomes
   knower and then when . . . you do know the answer, and then these more
   exploratory times when you're soliciting, but . . . even though you don't
   know exactly what kind of answer . . . or that there should be any one
   right answer, but you can have a goal in mind that you're sort of moving
   toward . . .

L: Yeah. Yeah, and . . . I think that . . . the role becomes very different because this up here [pointing to one of the three categories, exploratory
   talk, that R had written on the board] to me feels like a conversation, I
   mean, it feels more like the level of speaking to a friend. Where this
   [pointing to a yet unnamed mark in the middle of the continuum] feels
   more like there's a certain authority that comes with being the teacher
   in this setting. You know? Where in this [points to *final draft talk*] that's
   the strongest, I mean, like then you're presenting yourself as the teacher
   who knows the answer, where here [the middle position] it's exploratory, yet the teacher is kind of seen as the one that knows.

R: Uh-huh. So, it's kind of directed exploratory or –

L: Yeah,⌈yeah. Yeah.

K: ⌊Mm.

R: Directed exploratory, yeah. Huh! Directed exploratory.

After Laura and Robert worked hard at delimiting the three categories of
talk, Kayoko, who had typed the transcribed excerpts and thus knew them
better than the others, contributed an example that she felt fit into the exploratory category.

K: When [Student X] asked you about where Jackson Heights was, and you
   didn't know either, so there is a time that students nor teacher don't

know the answer. . . . You're looking at the map but you . . . know where
Jackson Heights is, but you don't know[exactly where 73rd Street is.
L: [Right. Yeah. Yeah.
K: So, maybe that's more like friend-to-friend [exploratory] talk.

Directly after hearing Kayoko's example, Laura further clarified what
she meant by the newly co-constructed directed exploratory type of talk by
referring us to another example.

L: I said, "Go get the map. Let's look at where Carnegie Hall is." So, I
   mean, that's really pretty teacher-directed, as opposed to something
   when they come in and say, "Guess what, Ms. Golden, I went to my father's store this weekend."

Following the discussion of examples and sensing an emerging clarity,
Robert again stepped back, trying to organize the information we had mulled
over. He reiterated that there seemed to be at least three different points on
a continuum–directed, directed exploratory, and exploratory – and then
paraphrased his understanding of what they were.

The excerpts above again illustrate the variety of roles we played in our
discussions. In addition, they show how we co-constructed a meaningful
framework from which to further observe the at least three-part continuum of talk characterizing the interaction between Laura and her students.
Robert's attempts to step back and understand what was being said gave
space for Laura and Kayoko to come up with more examples from which
Laura articulated how their invented term, "directed exploratory," differed
from the other two. The examples, of course, also compelled Robert to step
back again. Something bigger than the actual utterances, that is, the playing out of the perceived roles we had of each other, also had him in the
stepping back, organizing role. Again, one feels the lure of the canonical
conversations in which the higher status of one participant has everyone arranging for that person to play a leadership role.

The variety of roles we assumed during this and all of our discussions shed a patchwork of colors on the classroom interactions we observed.
They also allowed our narrative to unfold as it needed to. We all left
these discussions with a much deeper appreciation for what occurred in
Laura's classes and for the insights into teaching and learning that could
spring from three teachers' use of a common stimulus from which to talk
shop.

What we did with our talk illustrates Bakhtin's (1981) observation that "any concrete discourse (utterance) is entangled, shot through with shared thoughts, points of view. . . . The word, directed toward its object . . . weaves in and out of complex interrelationships, merges with some, recoils from others, intersects with yet a third group: and all this may crucially shape discourse" (p. 276).

The co-construction of meaning is helpful for us to flesh out and clarify what we are thinking about, and, at times, uncover something entirely new, such as the directed exploratory category of talk we saw in Laura's classes. What is perhaps even more exciting is when the building of meanings goes beyond communicative co-construction to purposeful action.

From discussion to action

Taking some of what the three of us had discussed (about Collier's 1987 and 1989 research) into a meeting she had with her principal, Laura reported at one of our later meetings that the principal was able to make use of the information in a plea she was making with the New York State Education Department:

L: We were discussing [in a meeting with the principal] this issue of how long it takes [ESL students to acquire English] and, um, I was talking about, uh, going to Virginia Collier's presentation at the TESOL convention. The principal mentioned that she is, um, writing a . . . letter to Albany to get a waiver so that their, um, LEP [limited English proficient] population doesn't have to take the citywide reading test. Because what happens is there's a contradiction between the research and the practice . . . any student who's been in this country for longer than 2 years has to take the citywide test.

R: Right.

L: And, um, . . . although Virginia Collier will tell you it takes 5 to 7 years to acquire academic language, the city is requiring that the students take the test every 2 years. So, she's writing a letter to Albany to get a waiver so that, apparently [if] you have a special population or something, you can get it waived so the kids don't have to take [the test].

The ripple effect that discussions can have on action cannot be overlooked. Our reading of Collier lent Laura some added expertise that she could share with her principal at an opportune time. That the knowledge Laura shared would find its way into a letter to state officials was an added benefit of our collaborative conversations.

The lure of the canon

Although the nature of the discussions we had varied significantly from the usual post-observation conversations reported on by Arcario and Waite, the *lure of the canon* was also lurking. By virtue of Robert's position as the other collaborators' professor and as the catalyst for the project, he, more than his collaborators, initiated our discussions, changed topics in our conversations, and brought closure to our meetings. He also brought in readings related to our research and at times suggested agendas for our meetings, albeit informally. In all these roles, though, openings were left for Laura and Kayoko to change such agendas, to bring up their own ideas for how we should proceed, and to begin our conversations with their observations of what we had all experienced.

That someone needed to lead and that it turned out to be the teacher educator is not surprising given the power of the hierarchical relationships that were evidently working (Tirone 1990). Also, in U.S. schools, a microcosm of the society as a whole, we usually make of classroom observation an evaluative event that is led by the person seen to be in the superior role or status. Although evaluation was missing from our conversations, we arranged for Robert, given his professorial rank, to chair our discussions.

Conclusions and implications

Despite the lure of the canon, collaborative conversations of teaching such as those reported on here suggest a continuum of possibilities. We need not make of post-observation discussions moments to perform the merely evaluative functions inherent in the gatekeeping demands embedded in U.S. schooling. Doing so implies a relationship between discussants in which one person has power over another, thereby constraining the talk in content, purpose, and roles played. Nor can we reasonably expect those in the usual school formats always to carry out such conversations at the other end of the continuum, where the relationship allows for an equal sharing of power.

Talk in which		Talk in which
one has power	————————————————	conversants share
over another		power equally

Awareness of the nature of more collaborative forms of talk suggests to us many possible positions along the continuum on which we can choose to talk shop. The structure of our talk afforded Robert, the professor and initiator of the project, the opportunity to initiate as well as wind down our discussions, to ask the open-ended questions that got us talking shop, and to be a resource person regarding other research that helped inform ours. In this sense, he took, and was granted, some control over the conversations. For the most part, however, the three of us shared power in the body of our discussions, assuming a variety of roles (mentioned earlier), and inventing our narrative, our questions, and our mode of inquiry as we went along.

Task Break

Think of another field or general life experience, besides education, where the continuum illustrated above (from talk in which one has power over another to talk in which conversants share power equally) comes into play. Consider a context for a point you mark on the continuum, and be ready to explain the context you had in mind for the point you marked.

Of particular interest in our project was the nature of narrative inquiry from three sets of eyes and ears. We found, as Beattie (1995: 54) reports: "Narrative inquiry . . . allows us to acknowledge that educators know their situations in general, social and shared ways and also in unique and personal ways, thus validating the interconnectedness of the past, the present, the future, the personal, and the professional in an educator's life." Connelly and Clandinin (1990: 2) argue:

The main claim for the use of narrative in educational research is that humans are storytelling organisms who, individually and socially, lead storied lives. Thus, the study of narrative is the study of the ways humans experience the world. This general notion translates into the view that education is the construction and re-construction of personal and social stories; teachers and learners are storytellers and characters in their own and others' stories.

In the narrative that unfolded in our discussions of Laura's classes, her story got told. All three collaborators colluded in her giving voice to what was going on in and out of her ESL class in an urban elementary school. We also brought our particular observations, prior experiences, and communicative preferences to bear on the stories we jointly constructed. Robert demonstrated his penchant for giving understanding responses and for stepping back from the particulars to situate our observations in a broader academic context. Kayoko displayed her desire to ask clarifying questions to give laser-like rays of precision to our observations and hypotheses. Laura showed her need to probe deeply into the students' processes and broadly into the factors, personal and bureaucratic, impacting on their work with her. All of our needs were given the space our narrative demanded.

Our joint activity also satiated, for a time at least, the teacher educator's longing to be closer to the action he educates ESL and EFL teachers about. It also afforded him a chance to talk shop about teaching and learning as the teacher he is, as well as to fold a corpus of data around topics he discusses in the practice-teaching seminars he leads. Kayoko returned to Japan with a close-up view of one ESL class she can continue to compare and contrast with EFL classes, which will be invaluable to her in training Japanese teachers of English. In addition, her expertise as an experienced teacher was acknowledged in ways that seldom occurred during her stay in the United States. Laura had a break for 10 weeks from being alone with all she does and thinks and decides about in her hidden hundredfold day-to-day encounters with ESL students.

9 Microteaching and self-observation
Experience in a preservice teacher education program

Jerry G. Gebhard
Mio Hashimoto
Jae-Oke Joe
Hyunhee Lee

Authentic education is to be found in an act of intelligent exploration.

—P. Abbs (1986: 21)

The focus of this chapter is to describe and illustrate how a group of novice and experienced teachers became more aware of their teaching through microteaching and self-observation experiences. Our experiences illustrate and expand upon the processes of awareness raising presented in Chapter 3. The experiences we describe here took place in Observation of Teaching, a course required of all MA TESOL and MATE (Masters in Teaching English) program students. This particular class included ten students from the MA TESOL program, two from the MATE program, and two Ph.D. Rhetoric and Linguistics students. Participants were from Thailand (1), Japan (4), Taiwan (2), Korea (3), Turkey (2), and the United States (3). Four of those who enrolled had teaching experience (4 to 15 years). The others had little or no experience.

We guide our discussion through the following set of questions:

- What was the microteaching and self-observation experience?
- What did we learn from the microteaching and observation experience?
- What examples illustrate the self-observation experience?

What was the microteaching and self-observation experience?

The course began with reading about, discussing, and practicing observation of classroom interaction. For example, we read and discussed the ideas in Day (1990), Fanselow (1988), and a draft of Chapter 3 of this book to better understand the process of describing, analyzing, and interpreting teaching. We also viewed videotapes of teaching in order to practice observing classroom interaction. For example, we categorized and tallied praise behaviors, sources and targets of questions, the content of the teacher's questions, and the times the teacher used English or her native language. We also made short transcriptions of selected segments (e.g., the teacher giving instructions and what happened just after that). After analyzing each type of behavior, we offered our interpretations (e.g., the teacher's instructions were vague; students did not know what to do, leading to a waste of time). Using Fanselow's (1988) advice, we also gave additional, even contrasting, interpretations (e.g., the unclear instructions were great, giving students chances to negotiate meaning in English).

Early in the semester, students agreed to teach two 20-minute lessons to classmates. Each lesson had to teach something real, for example, how to juggle. Each lesson had to be videotaped (by a classmate), and each student teacher had to write a self-observation report, including a description, analysis, and interpretation of the lesson, as well as alternative ways to teach aspects of the same lesson.

Early in the semester, we established four microteaching support groups, each including an experienced teacher who was given the title of "mentor." The mentor was responsible for listening to the teachers, supporting their ideas, and answering questions about lesson planning, materials, and classroom practices. The teacher educator (Gebhard) encouraged mentors to be nonprescriptive, that is, not to tell the inexperienced student teachers how they should teach, but rather to share their teaching experience, indicating to those in the group that these are simply one teacher's teaching practices. Teachers were urged not to accept these ideas as the only or best way to teach, but rather to develop their own teaching practices and consider the beliefs that underlie them. The idea was for the mentors to provide opportunities for the student teachers to design and carry out their own lessons as well as to select aspects of their teaching to observe.

Through their own initiative and with the support of the mentor and others in their group, each student teacher designed and taught two lessons. The second lesson was created after doing the self-observation and writing the report, so the student teachers could make use of the first teaching experience in a systematic way. As a class, the eleven teachers designed and created twenty-two lessons. As the following list shows, these lessons varied in content and purpose. Notice that we use "How to . . ." before each item to emphasize that the point of each lesson was to teach each other how to do something.

Lessons: What the Preservice Teachers Taught
- How to compliment in Malaysian
- How to ask and answer questions in Japanese (Doko ni ikitai? Nani ga tabetai?)
- How to mix primary colors using Play-Doh dough to create colors on a "personality chart"
- How to make Italian dumplings
- How to use basic Korean expressions: Hello, Good-bye, Thank you, Sorry, Nice to meet you.
- How to play "Yut," a traditional Korean game
- How to use Japanese chopsticks
- How to write haiku
- How to order food in a Turkish restaurant
- How to understand humor across cultures
- How to make a good pot of Chinese tea
- How to sing a Japanese song and do hand play
- How to appreciate a popular Japanese fairy tale
- How to make Argentine tea, maté
- How to introduce yourself and greet people in Spanish
- How to read ten Chinese characters
- How to count in Chinese
- How to make origami dolls
- How to make different Japanese dishes with four ingredients
- How to sing "Happy Birthday" in Korean
- How to wear traditional Korean clothes
- How to exercise in an ancient Chinese way

The lessons also varied in the way they were taught, although most of the lessons included some hands-on practice. For example, the lesson on reading Chinese characters included asking classmates to draw pictures of a mountain, a stick-figure person, a door, and other things. Then, the student teacher gave out sheets with characters on them and asked classmates to match the character with the picture. She then made the point that the character for "mountain" looks much like a mountain, the one for a person looks like a person, and so on. Her lesson also included a matching game and a game of "Chinese-character tic-tac-toe." The lesson on making origami dolls took a different hands-on approach. The teacher demonstrated the steps involved in making the doll, then took classmates step by step through the process while each classmate folded paper to create a doll. In the lesson on exercising in an ancient Chinese way, everyone stood up, watched a videotape of the teacher demonstrating each exercise, then followed along. Likewise, the lesson on making Argentine maté included a demonstration, hands-on practice in mixing the tea, and tasting and talking about its flavor.

As noted earlier, every student teacher was required to write up a self-observation report. Making use of the videotape of the class, this report was to include a detailed description (using descriptive techniques studied earlier in the course), an analysis of the teaching based on the collected descriptions, interpretations of the teaching in relation to how the teaching provided (or failed to provide) opportunities for classmates to learn, and alternative ways the student teacher could teach aspects of the lesson. Here is the handout showing the self-observation report requirements:

Self-observation: What to include in your report
- A prose description of what went on in the class. This can include the activities in the class and what the teacher and students did during each of the activities.
- Additions throughout the prose description should be added. These can be based on the use of the observation instruments used to tally behaviors (see Day 1990; Gebhard 1996), as well the addition of transcripts and analysis, sketches of seating arrangements, students' expressions, and activities, as well as on other means to describe. (See Fanselow 1988 and Chapter 3 of this book.)
- Add a section called "Interpretations." In this section, answer the following question: How did the teacher possibly provide or block opportunities for students to learn through the classroom interaction? Offer more than one answer or interpretation. (See Fanselow's 1988 views on interpretations.) Include at least one "outlandish" interpretation.
- Add a section called "Alternatives." In this section, discuss teaching ideas you have. How can different aspects of a lesson be taught? Give this some real thought, and be detailed. It is important to explain the details of your teaching ideas.

Student teachers were encouraged to focus their observations of their teaching on points of interest, as well as to build on the awareness gained from their first teaching and observation experiences. For example, two of the student teachers were interested in learning about the way they give instructions and how students respond to them (first observation). Both were then interested in seeing what happened when they changed the way they give instructions, including the consequences these new ways have on student interaction (second observation). Several were interested in learning more about their questioning behaviors (first observation) and the consequences of changing the way they ask questions, for example, by increasing the use of personal questions (second observation). One student teacher was interested in learning about how much she and her classmates talk (first observation), as well as how she could get classmates to do much of the talking (second observation). It is worth pointing out that not all of the student teachers built on their experience from the first teaching and observation experience in such a systematic or direct way. For example, one student teacher analyzed her voice projection (or lack of it) during her first observation and how students interacted in groups during her second.

To further illustrate what was entailed in the observation reports, at the end of this chapter we include two observation reports based on the second teaching experience. Each report includes a description, analysis, and interpretation of the lesson, as well as a discussion of alternative ways that certain aspects of the lesson could be taught.

Task Break

Imagine that you have been asked to design a short microteaching lesson, teach it while being videotaped, and describe, analyze, and interpret your teaching.

1. What lesson content might you select to teach?
2. How would you go about describing, analyzing, and interpreting your teaching?

What did we learn from the microteaching and observation experience?

At the end of the course, the eleven student teachers and four mentors each wrote a report on what they learned from the microteaching and observation experience. This section opens with a summary of what the student teachers said they learned. Two of the student teachers, Mio Hashimoto and Hyunhee Lee, used the student teachers' reports as a basis for writing this summary. The next section is a summary of what the four mentors reported that they had learned and was written by one of the mentors, Jae-Oke Joe.

The third section is a reflective report on what the teacher educator, Jerry Gebhard, learned from coordinating the microteaching and self-observation experiences and observing the student teachers and mentors as they moved through the process of planning, implementing, and reflecting on micro-lessons.

What student teachers said they learned

The experience of the lesson planning, teaching, and self-observation provided us as prospective teachers with meaningful insight into our future teaching. It gave us an opportunity to go beyond the traditional way of teaching that most of us had in our own language-learning situations and see teaching from different perspectives.

The lesson planning enabled us to create interesting and active lessons that are student-centered, and in which the activities are based on authentic situations. It also helped to guide us through the actual teaching experience by including not only which activities we would do and which procedure we would follow, but also what kind of purpose we would have for each activity. By preparing well for the teaching through a lesson-planning process, we reduced our anxiety, and we did not feel nervous during the actual lessons.

In the actual teaching, many unexpected things occurred. Even though we designed a detailed lesson beforehand, we sometimes needed to stray from it during the lesson. For example, the activities we prepared did not work as well as we had predicted, and the ways of interaction among the teacher and students were not always the same as our expectations. These experiences made us realize that we need to handle the actual situation that we encounter in our lesson in a reflective way so as to build our skills to handle the unexpected. These experiences also taught us that it is to our advantage to have alternative ideas that we can use spontaneously in our teaching.

Furthermore, the self-observation experiences had a great impact on our ways of viewing teaching. By videotaping and then describing our own teaching objectively, we had a chance to view our teaching from different angles and notice what we could not see while teaching. Analysis instruments such as FOCUS and SCORE (see Chapter 3) were especially helpful. They showed us patterns and tendencies in our own teaching that we could not easily see just by watching the video of our teaching. In addition, giving several different interpretations of our teaching enabled us to question our beliefs about teaching and learning, as well as generate fresh teaching ideas. We also found it important to consider behaviors opposite to our commonsense ones so that we could explore different teaching behaviors in the future.

Throughout the experience of lesson planning, teaching, and self-observation, the collaborative work with a mentor and other student teachers proved to be very important. It let us share a variety of ideas with one another and see teaching from others' perspectives. We also learned the importance of being nonjudgmental as we talked about our lessons. However, we also learned that, because of our past tendencies to judge good or bad teaching rather than to withhold such judgments, it is hard to give non-judgmental comments on others' lessons.

The experience in this course taught us how essential self-observation is to teaching. In order to make progress in our teaching, we need to follow three steps: plan (lesson planning), do (teaching), and see (self-observation). Teachers tend to forget the third step, self-observation. However, we found that it is self-observation that lets us reflect on our teaching objectively, find different ways of teaching, and design more contextually relevant lesson plans. We came to realize that teaching is an ongoing process. Self-observation makes teacher exploration possible in a plan–do–see cycle.

What mentors said they learned

Mentors say that it was a "delightful," "exciting," and "important" experience. We learned about the importance of listening, sensitivity, reflection, self-observation, and mentor training.

First, we learned to listen to others. Here are a few mentor comments related to the importance of listening: "If we start the conversation and govern it, we inevitably become the 'authority' who is experienced. Consequently, this makes them [student teachers] limit and confine their creative ideas"; and "Listening to them, I found that they themselves discovered their solutions to some aspects of teaching that they want to change."

Second, we learned to respect our group members' ideas. One mentor commented, "Even though all the members in my group are inexperienced teachers, they always have great ideas on teaching, and they are very creative."

Third, we learned to be reflective in our own teaching. One mentor pointed out, "Mentoring taught me to be sensitive toward students' needs." Another mentor said, "This refreshment of looking back on my own teaching with an open mind gave me a chance to develop myself." Having to look at our own teaching experience as a part of working with other teachers, we also realized that a part of being a mentor is to take a deep reflective look into our teaching.

This mentoring experience was the first time for us to think long about how others can develop their teaching. Although we welcomed the opportunity to mentor, however, we also saw the need to be trained to mentor. For example, emphasizing the need for mentoring training, another participant said, "I have to listen to the others' ideas more than I used to. . . . At the same time, I learned that I myself need to learn more about teaching and teacher education." The implications are that this mentor, along with the rest of us, needed someone to talk with besides the student teachers. We needed a mentor's mentor.

The teacher educator reflects on the experience

During the past 14 weeks, I have had the chance to study student teachers' lesson plans and self-observation reports, consider informal comments that participants made throughout the course, analyze my observations and the student teachers' observations from the many videotaped microteaching sessions, and read written reports on what student teachers and mentors have gained from their microteaching and observation experiences. I also audiotaped some of the classes, listened to the tapes, and did some self-observation of my own based on the interaction captured on these tapes.

My goal was to provide multiple opportunities for the student teachers and mentors to explore their own teaching. I wanted to teach them a process of planning lessons, implementing these lessons, and reflecting on what happened through self-observation. This is what the student teachers categorized as "plan, do, see." The first part of this process, that of planning lessons, was easy to accomplish. We kept it simple by not using readings. We took about an hour to talk about what we thought a lesson plan was and what can be included in a plan. We decided that a plan needs to have a teaching goal or goals (What do I want the students to learn?), procedures for reaching the goal (How will this goal be reached? What activities will be used? What procedures?), materials (What materials will be used to help us reach the goal?), a means to reflect on whether or not the goal was reached (How can I know if the goal was reached?), and a way either to reflect on our teaching behavior and classroom interaction in relation to reaching (or not reaching) the goals, or to simply explore teaching (How can I reflect on my teaching and classroom interaction? How can I explore my teaching beliefs and behaviors?).

In regards, to lesson planning, I noticed that most of the student teachers did include objectives, materials, and procedures. Some included the amount of time they thought each step in the lesson would take. I also noticed that although I encouraged them to include a way to reflect on their teaching and to plan their explorations, most did not include this in their plans. I wonder if this is because most usual plans do not include a plan to explore aspects of our teaching.

The second part of the process, that of teaching, was a collaborative effort. We considered the amount of time we had for student teachers to teach their lessons. We decided that there was enough time for eleven student teachers to teach two 20-minute lessons. We also decided that rather than make believe we were in ESL or EFL classes, student teachers would teach each other something "real." We also decided that the lessons would be "How to . . . ," for example, how to juggle or how to greet in Chinese.

The third part of the process, that of self-observation, was a little more challenging. We took three class periods to study the self-observation process, using three key readings. The first was a draft of Chapter 3 of this book. The second was John Fanselow's 1988 article in *TESOL Quarterly*, "'Let's See': Contrasting Conversations about Teaching." The third was Richard Day's "Teacher Observation in Second Language Teacher Education," from Richards and Nunan's edited book, *Second Language Teacher Education* (1990). We not only read and talked about the chapters, but also tried out the ideas in the readings. For example, while viewing videotapes of classes in a variety of settings, we practiced taking notes, drawing sketches, jotting down dialogues, and tallying behaviors. We also practiced making short transcripts and coding them with FOCUS. In addition, based on our descriptions and analyses, we gave multiple interpretations, including some outlandish ones, to remind us that for any one interpretation, there are many other possible ones (Fanselow 1988). Thus, an exploratory attitude was encouraged.

I asked the student teachers in the class to participate in the decision-making process with me – for example, to decide on how many micro-teaching sessions we would have and the kinds of lessons they would teach – because I wanted to teach them, through my example, that a part of exploration is collaboration. I also tried to provide chances for the student teachers and mentors to collaborate without me. To do this, I had them form four groups, each with one experienced teacher or mentor. (The mentors' experience ranged from 4 to 13 years of teaching.) My purpose was to set up collaborative support groups through which student teachers could talk about their teaching ideas, lesson plans, and observations. Although each group took on its own dynamics and some groups seemed more supportive than others, the plan seemed to work. Three of the groups met a number of times outside of the class, during which time they talked about their plans, teaching, and observations, as well as acted as sources of feedback. It was refreshing to see the reactions of some of the students to their peers' ideas and opinions.

I also wanted to provide chances for the student teachers and mentors to consider their own use of language to talk about teaching. Several times during the course, we stopped to consider whether we shared the same meaning of words such as "enthusiastic," "interesting," and "engaged." We also studied and practiced using low-inference words to describe and talk about teaching, such as language from Fanselow's (1987) FOCUS. For example, I encouraged them to talk about the *sources and targets of communication* (teacher, student, print . . .), the *purposes of communication* (structuring, soliciting, responding, reacting), the *mediums used to communicate content* (linguistic, nonlinguistic, paralinguistic, silence), and more. (See Chapter 3 for more detail on the metalanguage of FOCUS.) We also monitored each other's use of language that shows judgment, for example, when using words such as "good," "bad," "excellent," and "poor" to talk about teaching.

I noticed, however, that when student teachers and mentors talked – especially when they did not know I was listening – they made usual judgments and used general words to describe teaching, rather than use the metalanguage we used when they talked with me. For example, during a conversation about a lesson plan, a student began, "That sounds like a really good lesson. The game sounds like fun." Another group member added, "Yeah, very interesting. It's a really good idea." This does not surprise me. I believe it takes time to learn not to make judgments and to become more aware of our use of language when we talk about teaching. It also requires that we believe this is important to do. Most teachers and teacher educators, however, do not pay attention to their language and tend to use general words and judgments to talk about teaching. It is easy to join the mainstream, even when what it does is not as productive as it could be.

Finally, I see laughter as contributing to the course. There was a lot of laughter, some out of nervousness and as a way to reduce anxiety, especially during the first few microteaching sessions. But, the reasons for laughing changed as the teachers became more comfortable with the sessions. Participants' true personalities emerged, and some had a keen sense of humor. Joking and laughter not only helped us to relax, but also made the class more enjoyable. Several students told me that they enjoyed the class because they felt free to express their ideas and to be themselves.

For the most part, I believe the class was a success. Toward the end of the semester, however, I did receive feedback from the four mentors that I could have done more to support their efforts. With the exception of a few basic rules – for example, to discuss teaching in nonjudgmental language – I purposely gave them freedom to mentor as they saw fit. I basically left them alone with the teachers, having confidence in them to figure out how to work with them. This amount of freedom apparently was not always easy for them, and they had no mentor of their own to talk through their problems or consider new ways to work with the teachers. Consequently, the next time I set up support groups and include mentors, I will offer to have mentoring meetings throughout the semester.

I am humbled by this experience. I have seen how capable preservice teachers can be if given the opportunity. I have relearned that, for the most part, the teacher educator does not need to be the center of the experience: preservice teachers, with lots of support from their peers, can be the center. I also now understand how strongly I believe in the students. Although I have read about, even lectured on, how important it is to give students responsibility for their own learning, this experience truly made this clear for me. I feel privileged to have been a part of this class.

Task Break

The teacher educator, Jerry Gebhard, noticed that when student teachers and mentors talked, especially when they did not know he was listening, they made usual judgments and used general words to describe teaching, rather than use the metalanguage they used when they talked with him. For example, during a conversation about a lesson plan, a student began, "That sounds like a really good lesson. The game sounds like fun." Another group member added, "Yeah, very interesting. It's a really good idea."

Although the student teachers and mentors likely understand the value of not making judgments and in communicating through a common metalanguage, they still used judgmental and vague language to talk. If you were the teacher educator, would you try to convince these student teachers and mentors to use non-judgmental language and a common metalanguage? If so, how would you encourage them to do so?

What examples illustrate the self-observation experience?

We end this chapter by providing two illustrations of lesson plans and self-observations. The following two reports were written by Hyunhee Lee and Mio Hashimoto.

Self-observation report by Hyunhee Lee

LESSON PLAN

Objective.   The students will play *Yut*, a traditional Korean game that is usually played on New Year's Day.

Materials.   Game boards, tokens, watch, candies, handout with instructions to play *Yut*, and several blocks or die.

Teaching procedures:

1. Warm-up: Begin by saying the following – "Today I will introduce to you a traditional Korean game, *Yut*. Before starting the game, I will show you a picture and you have to tell me what you see in the picture." Then, ask: "What do you need to play *Yut?*" and "When do you think Koreans play *Yut?*"
2. Explain the rules: Using handouts, have students read the rules. As they read, I can demonstrate the game.
3. Play the game
   a) Divide students into four groups by giving play money to students. Each student gets a different amount of money. They will get together with two classmates to make a total of fifty dollars.
   b) Two teams in a group will compete against each other until one group wins the game.
4. Closure: "Did you have fun? What did you learn from the game? You have to be smart to win the game and respect other members' opinions. Korean culture is based on harmony with other people. So, I think this game also represents harmonious work. Thank you for your cooperative work."

DESCRIPTION, INTERPRETATION, AND ALTERNATIVES

Description.   Before starting the lesson, I asked students to push the tables toward the wall and to sit down on the floor while I prepared materials for the lesson. One of the students helped me to put things on the chalkboard. There were many materials to prepare, so I was busy finding materials and kept asking myself where I put them.

After everything was ready, I showed a color transparency reflecting a picture of playing *Yut* and asked the students what they could see in the picture. I called students by name to answer my questions. With a transparency, I explained basic tools to play the Korean traditional game. Then,

I distributed handouts and demonstrated how to throw the *Yut* in the air. In order to teach the rules of *Yut*, I had students read the rules and explained them by using the game board on the chalkboard. When I asked students whether or not they had any questions, one of the students raised her hand and asked, "Uh-oh, how can we finish the game? When you reach the last red dot of the game board?" I replied, "You mean here (pointing to the dot)? You have to go beyond this red dot."

After students had learned how to play *Yut*, I divided them into four groups to play. I gave each student a certain amount of money and let them make fifty dollars with two other students in order to make one team. Then, I gave each group a *Yut*, a board, and game pieces. Students started to play *Yut* and asked me questions. Most students clapped their hands, laughed, and shouted while they were playing the game. While they played, I walked around to take a look at how they were playing. After finishing the game, the winners got a box of candy as a prize. Then, I asked students whether they enjoyed the game and explained how important playing *Yut* is as a part of Korean culture.

Analysis and Interpretation.   I analyzed asking behaviors and movement patterns in order to see how I ask questions and how I move in the classroom. First, I used SCORE (Acheson & Gall 1997) to analyze my questioning behaviors, as Figure 9.1 illustrates.

As the tally marks show, I used general questions 14 times and individual questions 4 times. Whenever I called on a student, I got a response from that student. Compared to my former teaching, I tried to call on individual students this time. But I still had trouble calling on the students by name. As an interpretation of this behavior, I think that if I were an experienced teacher, I could often use individual questions. I realize that calling the students by name was very hard for me because the names did not come to me easily. Maybe I was so concerned about teaching itself that I could not remember my classmates' names, although I call them by name outside the classroom. I would interpret this behavior as a sign that I felt more comfortable using general questions than individual ones.

When it comes to the students' response behaviors, they responded to my individual questions. However, some students seemed unwilling to respond to general questions. I guess that these students were not comfortable enough to speak in front of the class because they were shy or they did not know the answers to the questions. An outlandish interpretation is that these students were waiting until their names were called, or they were not in a good mood because they were tired of their classmates' minilessons, as this

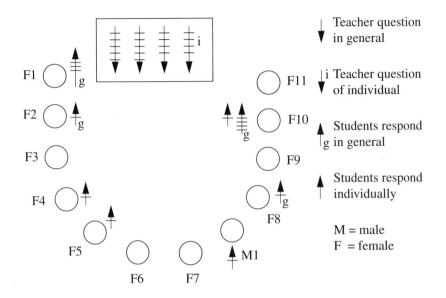

Figure 9.1

lesson was taught toward the end of the second set, and as such, they had already experienced eighteen such lessons before mine.

Besides my questions, I also wanted to take a look at how I moved during the lesson because I think the teacher's movements can influence the students' learning. Thus, I tallied my movements in each activity and checked how long it took to change seating arrangements between the activities.

In the first activity, I usually moved between the chalkboard and the inside of the circle so that I could explain the rules of *Yut*. Students did not move during my explanation. As Figure 9.2 shows, I moved more frequently (5 times) toward the chalkboard than the inside of the circle (3 times). Whenever I needed to throw the *Yut*, I approached the circle; otherwise, I remained standing next to the table. An interpretation about this movement pattern, I think, is that the game board was on the chalkboard and I needed to use it so that I could explain the rules better. What I realized from this analysis is that, as a preservice teacher, I tended to hesitate to come forward because I did not feel secure being in close proximity to the students. An outlandish interpretation about my movements is that I might be too shy. I wanted to get away from the students because I thought I might blush too much.

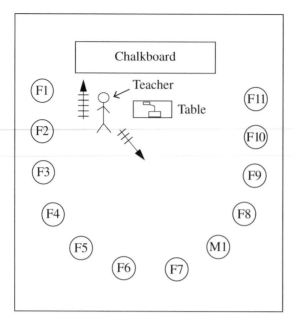

Figure 9.2

In order to see the movements of the teacher and the students during the activity, I drew another picture and analyzed it. I checked my movements to see how many times I visited each group and looked at how far the students moved from their original spots after I gave them the play money and task to form groups by finding two others who have enough money to make fifty dollars.

As Figure 9.3 shows, I approached Group B two times more frequently than I did Group A. Although I kept in mind that I would visit each group with the same frequency, I overvisited Group B. As an interpretation of this, I would say that student F5's position blocked me from going to Group A; thus, it was easier for me to go to Group B than to Group A. Another interpretation would be that Group B was more active than Group A, or that Group B drew my attention quite easily. An interpretation that I wish was outlandish, but could very well be true, is that I did not like one of the students in Group A and therefore, I did not feel like going to her group.

Figure 9.3 also shows how far the students moved from where they were in Figure 9.2 after the transition activity to match play money to form groups of three. Most students did not move from their first place (Figure 9.2), except students F5 and F7. When I asked students to move for the group work,

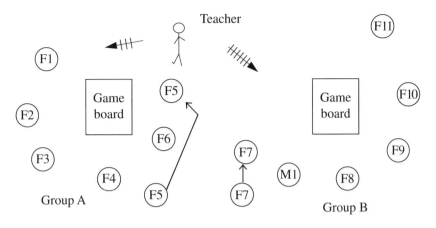

Figure 9.3

most did not. Instead, they talked and showed their play money to those students who were nearby. It took 1 minute 41 seconds to start the new activity. One interpretation of why students did not want to move is that they were sitting on the floor; although I urged students to stand up, to find their group members randomly, and to move far away from the first place, they did not want to move. Another interpretation is that the students could not understand what I wanted them to do. Therefore, they just sat and tried to figure out what to do. It is also possible that the students did not wish to move around during the lesson and that they were quite comfortable with those around them and in the spot in which they were sitting.

Alternatives.   I watched the videotape several times to think about alternatives for this lesson. First, I thought about the possibility of teaching *Yut* to language learners. I might use this game to teach numbers or the directions on the game board. While students are playing the game, they have to count numbers in order to see how many steps to move game pieces on the board. The repetition caused by playing the game would allow students to learn numbers easily. Moreover, students would not necessarily be aware of the repetition because of the amusement of the game.

Second, to start the class differently in the warm-up activity, I could use a videotape in which Koreans are playing *Yut* and ask students what they need to play the game and how it is played. Using a visual material – the videotape, might bring about students' active participation in the activity. In the actual lesson with my peers, I used a color transparency to raise the students' motivation; using the color transparency seemed to fit my intention, and the students responded well.

Third, as an alternative way of explaining the rules, I could have students throw the *Yut* and decide how many steps they can move so that students will learn it by touching the real object. Another alternative might be to use pictures instead of throwing the *Yut;* by preparing pictures of various outcomes when I throw the *Yut*, I could explain the different outcomes. Moreover, I could have students read handouts silently first after explaining the rules briefly while pointing to the pictures.

A fourth alternative would be to play *Yut* as a whole class instead of in small groups. I could assign students with different responsibilities: some of them could be charged with throwing the *Yut*, for example, while others take care of moving the game pieces.

Task Break

Can you think of other alternatives?

Self-observation report by Mio Hashimoto

LESSON PLAN

Objective.   Have fun learning how to ask and answer questions about Japanese foods and places. Practice Japanese while using a chantlike rhythm.

Materials.   Six pictures of Japanese foods and Japanese places. One handout with an example conversation.

Level of the students.   Most students are at a very beginning level. A few students have studied Japanese before. Two of the twelve students are native speakers of Japanese.

Teaching procedures:

1. Warm-up (4 minutes): "In Japan, there are many delicious foods and many beautiful places."
   a) Ask students what kinds of Japanese food they like (know), and introduce sushi, soba, and mochi by using pictures.
   b) Ask students which Japanese mountain, city and sea they like (know), and introduce Mt. Fuji, Tokyo, and the Okinawan Sea by using pictures.

c) Tell students: "We will learn how to ask and answer questions about Japanese foods and places in Japanese."

2. Presentation of new material

a) Dialogue 1 (4 minutes): Demonstrate the dialogue with my class-mate, Miyuki.

Mio: Nani tabetai?
Miyuki: Sushi tabetai.
Mio: Doko ikitai?
Miyuki: Umi ikitai.

Elicit the meaning of the dialogue through guessing, repetition, and translation. Give one hint: "tai" = want.

b) Dialogue Two (6 minutes): Demonstrate the rhythm we will use to practice the dialogues. Clap my hands in a rhythmic fashion to show the way we will practice saying the dialogues. The clap goes on every other syllable. Do dialogues in order from 2.1 to 2.6.

	Dialogue 2.1	*Dialogue 2.2*	*Dialogue 2.3*
Mio:	Nani tabetai?	Nani tabetai?	Nani tabetai?
Miyuki:	Sushi tebetai.	Soba tabetai.	Mochi tabetai.

	Dialogue 2.4	*Dialogue 2.5*	*Dialogue 2.6*
Mio:	Doko ikitai?	Doko ikitai.	Doko ikitai.
Miyuki:	Yama ikitai.	Machi ikitai.	Umi ikitai.

c) Practice: First, have students repeat after me. Second, divide the class into two and have the conversation between the two groups. Third, have students practice the dialogue in pairs. Have them practice using the special rhythm.

3. Activity (6 minutes): Form a circle. Ask and answer questions about the favorite foods and places in a rhythm as we walk around the circle. I will begin, "Nani tabetai? Nani tabetai? Nani tabetai?" The student behind me has to respond. For example, "Sushi tabetai. Sushi tabetai. Sushi tabetai." This student then asks a question; for instance: "Doko ikitai? Doko itkitai. Doko ikitai?" and so on.

DESCRIPTION, INTERPRETATION, AND ALTERNATIVES

My lesson plan is based on a presentation I saw at the TESOL convention in Orlando in March 1997. In the demonstration, the presenter, Noriko Taka-hashi, introduced a rhythmic way of teaching English to Japanese college students. For example, she taught, "What do you do?" in a rhythm combined with movement, such as walking. I thought I would like to teach in this way too. Students have fun with classmates in saying the phrases rhythmically while moving. I applied this way of teaching to my microteaching of Japanese. The purpose of using rhythm and action is for the students to memorize the phrases by repeating them again and again.

Description.   Students sat on chairs, forming a circle. I stood in front of them. In the warm-up, I told them that there are many delicious foods and beautiful places in Japan. I asked them if they were familiar with any Japanese foods. Several students answered, "sukiyaki," "sushi," "sashimi," and "mochi." I introduced three main Japanese foods – sushi, soba, and mochi – that I think are delicious, by showing pictures one by one. I then asked one student to tape them on the chalkboard. Next, I asked them if they knew some places in Japan. One student answered, "Tokyo."

Then, I changed the question to a more specific one. I asked if they knew some Japanese mountains. Some students answered, "Fuji" – the highest mountain in Japan. I showed the picture of Mount Fuji, on which I had drawn a national flag. I then had the students practice saying "yama" (mountain) and asked a student to put the picture of the mountain on the chalkboard. I asked what the biggest city in Japan is. Several students answered, "Tokyo." I showed the picture of Tokyo and had the students repeat the word "machi" (city) after me several times. I asked a student to tape the picture of Tokyo to the chalkboard. I asked what the most beautiful sea in Japan is, and there was a pause until one student answered, "Okinawa." I then asked a student who is from Okinawa if she agreed that this sea is the most beautiful, and she nodded in agreement. I then said the word "sea" and asked a student to put the picture of the sea on the chalkboard. As she did this, I told them that we would practice asking and answering questions about the delicious foods and beautiful places in Japan.

I put the conversation sheet with the dialogue on the board and asked one of the Japanese students to demonstrate the dialogue with me. Before the demonstration, I told the class that I would be asking questions and my partner would answer them. I then asked the students to guess the meaning of our conversation. Here is the dialogue:

Mio: Nani tabetai?
Miyuki: Sushi tabetai.
Mio: Doko ikitai?
Miyuki: Umi ikitai.

When Miyuki answered, she pointed to the food and the place that she mentioned. I let the students guess the meaning of the conversation and gave them a hint that the first half of the conversation has the word "sushi." One student (who I believe had no background in studying Japanese) guessed the meaning of "Nani tabetai?" by saying "What is your favorite food?" and another student said, "What are you eating?" I told them that they are close, and hinted, "She hasn't eaten yet." Then, one student said, correctly, "What do you want to eat?" After making sure that they had the meaning, I asked them to repeat after me "Nani tabetai?" twice. I then asked them what Miyuki's answer, "Sushi tabetai," means, and several students answered, "I want to eat sushi." Again, I had the class repeat the phrase after me.

Then, I asked the class about the second half of the conversation and gave them a hint. I pointed to the picture of the sea and said that "tai" has the same meaning as in the first question. I let them think about this lexical item by pointing to the "tai" at the end of each sentence; I wanted them to guess the meaning from its context. One student said, "You," which is incorrect, and another student answered, "want," which is correct. I repeated that "tai" means "want." I then attempted to teach the pronunciation of the word by comparing it to the word "Thai." I pointed out that this should be easy for Apinun, a Thai student in the class, and everyone laughed. I then explained the meanings of "tabetai" (want to eat) and "ikitai" (want to go). I suggested that they repeat the question part, "tabetai" and "ikitai," when they give their answers. I also told them that they should use rising intonation when they ask the questions and lower it when they answer them. I then pointed at the picture of the sea and asked them what they thought "Doko ikitai?" means, and several students said, "Where do you want to go?" After they said they were sure of the meaning of all of the sentences, I let them repeat the entire dialogue twice after me.

After the repetition, I said, "Good job." Then, I asked Miyuki to help me demonstrate another thing, and I told the students that we would have some fun, and started to laugh. I then demonstrated what they would be doing by asking them to help Miyuki and me by clapping their hands. I asked them to do it in a certain tempo and with a low sound so that they could hear our conversation. Miyuki and I demonstrated the way we would practice Dialogue 2 by using clapping to set the rhythm. After the demonstration, the students applauded us, and I said, "It's like music. You can learn Japanese through rhythm." I then had them repeat the dialogue after me while clapping their hands to set the rhythm.

Next, I divided the class into eight pairs and told one student to be A and play my part and the other student to be B and play Miyuki's part. I asked student A to ask the two questions alternately and asked B to answer by following the pictures on the board. I asked them to do it slowly, and to make two pauses between the questions and the answer. The students nodded, indicating they understood. I asked them to clap their hands. We practiced doing the dialogues in pairs for 2 minutes.

We then moved on to a whole-class activity. I said, "Let's do one more fun thing!" and asked them to stand up and form a circle. At this point, I explained the procedure as follows:

You move forward, clap your hands, and I will say, "Nani tabetai?" (said fast), "Nani tabetai?" (said fast), "Nani tabetai?" (said half as fast). Do this in rhythm. After that, turn inside the circle and the first person to the left answers the question. If this person wants to eat sushi, he or she should say, "Sushi tabetai" (said fast), "Sushi tabetai" (said fast), "Sushi tabetai" (said half as fast). Then move forward again, walking slowly while saying together, "Doko ikitai?" (said fast), "Doko itkitai?" (said fast), "Doko ikitai?" (said half as fast). Then, stop walking and turn inside the circle again. The person to the left of the last person that answered the question should answer. For example, if he or she wants to go to the sea, he or she should say, "Umi ikitai" (said fast), "Umi ikitai" (said fast), "Umi ikitai" (said half as fast). We will take turns in this way.

When I moved forward and clapped my hands, the students imitated my action. They laughed and followed my lead. I began, "Nani tabetai? Nani tabetai? Nani tabetai?" and stopped. We all turned into the center of the circle, and the student to my left pointed at the picture of sushi and said, "Sushi tabetai. Sushi tabetai. Sushi tabetai." Everyone laughed. The activity continued. When the students seemed to understand what to do, I asked them to go faster and faster. They walked faster and spoke faster and clapped faster. I said, "Do it fast!" and they accelerated the tempo. The last person did it the fastest, and everyone laughed. After the activity, everyone shouted and applauded. They then sat down and I concluded my lesson by saying, "That's all. Thank you very much."

Interpretation.   I interpret what was done in this lesson by raising two questions: (1) How did the activity provide students with chances to learn Japanese? And (2) How did the activity possibly block chances for students to learn Japanese?

Selected Aspect 1: Warm-up.   During the warm-up, I introduced Japanese foods and beautiful places in Japan by using pictures. I think that students became fascinated by these foods and places. I believe that the visual aids helped create this interest, and the pictures helped students memorize the Japanese words easily. They imagined what kinds of tastes and what kinds of places they were and related those concepts to the words.

It might also be interpreted as follows, however. I forced students to think about only the three foods and places that I came up with. This might have been boring to them, rather than fascinating. This could have made it hard for some students to learn the Japanese words.

An outlandish interpretation might be that students expected me to serve them the foods I introduced, because usually in our microteaching lessons, at least one student teacher prepared food for the class. However, I just showed pictures of food and made them hungry. The students may have been so hungry that they could not pay attention and did not feel like learning Japanese.

Alternatives.   I generated several alternatives:

- I could bring real food to the class. By actually eating them, students can know not only what the foods look like but also how they taste. Perhaps this would make it easier for students to memorize the words, because they can associate the word with a taste and a smell.
- I could do the opposite and not use pictures (or real food) to teach the names of the foods and places. Instead, I could be vague by verbally describing the food and places. I wonder if students can imagine the foods and places in their minds without the use of visual aids.

Selected Aspect 2: Whole-class activity.   During the whole-class activity, we formed a circle and asked and answered questions about what the students wanted to eat and where they wanted to go. We used clapping and rhythm to do this. This activity appeared to be a lot of fun for the students. It impressed them because they could repeat the sentences again and again and memorize them while having fun. Another interpretation, however, could be that some students did not like this activity because it was a version of the audiolingual approach to language learning. The students felt that simply repeating sentences over and over again is not a very productive way to learn a language, even though they were able to select from three foods they wanted to eat or three places they wanted to go.

Another possible interpretation, one that is partly outlandish and partly possible, is that some students found the activity boring and childish. Because they are grown-up and mature, they thought it stupid to walk in a circle while clapping. Their laughter was not because it was fun, but because they were embarrassed.

A fully outlandish interpretation is that all the students found the activity to be fun because they felt they were performing a musical in front of many people, and were being spotlighted. They viewed the person who videotaped the lesson as a cameraman. Therefore, they behaved as well as they could, moving forward while clapping and clearly projecting and articulating Japanese. They could not wait for their own solo part to answer the question. When it came to each one's turn, they showed off how well they could act.

Alternatives

- Instead of this activity, I could do another activity I call "performance competition." I could divide the class into three groups, each consisting of five people. The basic pattern is that the first person asks, "Nani tabetai?" and the second person answers, "Sushi tabetai." The second person says, "Doko ikitai?" to a third person, and she or he answers, "Yama ikitai." They continue until each group member asks and answers questions. They do it in a rhythm. Each group could have one focus for the performance: speed, action, or pronunciation. If one group focuses on speed, they should do it as fast as possible. If one group focuses on action, they should perform unique actions during the performance. If one group focuses on pronunciation, they should enunciate the words perfectly.

• Regarding exploration, I can do the opposite by letting the students structure their own learning. Instead of the teacher doing it, the students can create an activity to ask and answer questions about foods and places in Japanese. The teacher could ask them to give her the instructions for the procedure and see what kind of activity they create. They might not use rhythm or clapping. They might create even more impressive and enjoyable ways to teach the same content.

Task Break

• Both Lee and Hashimoto describe their teaching, but each uses her own unique way to do this. How are their descriptions of teaching different?
• What central awareness do you believe came out of the self-observation process that the teachers experienced?

---

10 Two action research projects

Helen Collins Sitler
Zubeyde Tezel

> Becoming a critically reflective teacher . . . involves the reali-
> sation that as second language teachers, we are both the pro-
> ducers and the creators of our own history.
> —L. Bartlett (1990: 206)

In this chapter, we provide reports on two action research projects, thereby illustrating the process for raising teacher awareness that was the subject of Chapter 4. The first project is by Helen Sitler, who was interested in evoking students' verbal response to instructions. The second is by Zubeyde Tezel, and is about getting students to talk during tutorials. Our action research questions, which guide the content of this chapter, were:

- How can I elicit students' verbal responses to my instructions?
- How can I get students to talk during tutorials?

We want to point out that both of us took a usual approach to action research by posing and seeking solutions to problems we were having in the class-room, and, through our action research efforts, we both gained considerable awareness about our teaching.

Project 1: How can I elicit students' verbal responses to my instructions?

Returning to graduate school brought with it a wealth of new experiences. Among them was the opportunity to study the teaching of ESL. Twelve years of teaching high school English and several semesters as a part-timer instructing freshman composition at the college level had exposed me only minimally to ESL students, and not at all to appropriate methodology. I had been unprepared to address adequately the needs of the ESL students who passed through my composition classroom and vowed that I would serve such students better in the future. Graduate courses were providing a necessary theoretical base for understanding second language acquisition, ESL pedagogy, and the teaching of reading and writing. However, I felt a gap; I wanted hands-on classroom experience. I requested an ESL internship.

The context of the project

Building on my experience, Jerry Gebhard assigned me to teach a summer session of intermediate-level writing at a university-connected language institute. Most of my students would be university students, either returning to their home universities or staying in the United States to continue their education abroad.

The prospect of teaching this course was both exhilarating and frightening. It had been several years since I was in a classroom at all. In the interim, my beliefs about effective teaching had changed substantially. I was eager to test methods I had never tried before.

I chose to design the course as a writing workshop modeled after Atwell (1987). Although workshop is a recommended model for teaching composition both to native and to nonnative speakers of English, it was a method I had never used. Not only would I be teaching ESL students for the first time, but I would be facilitating a writing workshop for the first time.

Intermediate Writing would meet each Tuesday and Thursday for 75 minutes during a 10-week session. Class would begin every day with a minilesson. During minilessons, I would model writing-workshop techniques, such as how to generate ideas for a paper, how to organize material in a paper, how to work with a peer to read and revise a draft, and how to solve nagging grammatical issues. Each minilesson would involve the whole group of fifteen students for 20 to 30 minutes. For the remainder of the class, students would work on their own writing projects.

The writing-workshop format places considerable responsibility on the student. Each student must come to class prepared to work on a chosen writing project. During workshop time, students may participate in a number of self-selected activities. They might confer with peers or with the teacher about their drafts, or they might work individually. My job during workshop time was to circulate among the students, conferencing with them individually about their current projects. I served as interested reader and responder during these conferences, encouraging students to focus on communicating their ideas to a reader. When ideas had been adequately communicated, then we could focus on grammatical issues in our conferences.

The process of conducting the action research project

The process included posing a problem, seeking knowledge about this problem, planning an action, implementing the action, observing the action, reflecting, and revising the plan.

POSING A PROBLEM

During these brief, daily writing conferences with students, I realized that I was more successfully communicating with individuals than with the class during the whole-group minilessons. In conferences, we were having conversations. Students were listening to me, comprehending my suggestions, and responding to my instructions. In turn, I was able to focus our workshop-writing conferences on the students' individual needs. This give-and-take dynamic is what I wanted for our whole-group interactions as well. I could not rely solely on individual conferences for my teaching; the minilessons were important. They were the foundation on which students would build their understanding of writing in the American classroom.

It was imperative that I change what I do in these whole-group sessions. One problem was that students were not consistently understanding or responding to my verbal instructions in minilessons; I made this the focus for my action research project, a requirement of my ESL internship. Eliciting student response to instructions during minilessons became the goal of the project. Preferably, the students' responses would be verbal, thus giving them additional language practice.

SEEKING KNOWLEDGE

Having identified an issue of concern, I now needed to discover more about the issue. Two means of doing so presented themselves: observing colleagues and videotaping my own class. I began by visiting the classrooms of two experienced ESL instructors who allowed me to observe their classes. During these visits, I observed the dynamic interaction that I wanted with my own students. Noting the methods these instructors used to generate the interaction was helpful.

One instructor constantly called students by name. She addressed questions and instructions to the whole group, but for specific comprehension checks, or to regain a student's wandering attention, she used individual names. The other instructor depended heavily on gestures, miming much of her conversation with the students. Both instructors used the board for vocabulary. When students asked for clarification of a word or when either instructor used a word she felt the students would not know, she wrote it on the board.

My next step was to videotape a minilesson that began each writing-workshop session. As Day notes, "Since more observation in teacher education programs [sic] concerned with the teacher, often the most useful results are obtained when the camera is focused on the teacher" (1990: 46). With this in mind, I kept the camera focused on myself. Later, viewing only that portion of the tape precluded the data overload that could have resulted had I attempted to focus on the entire 75-minute class period. It was sufficient to allow me to observe repeated patterns in my teaching behavior (Fanselow, 1987).

The videotape was revealing. As gestures and direct address of individual students had been effective strategies for the experienced instructors, I first watched the tape for my own use of these techniques. I discovered that my gestures were too minimal to assist students in comprehending and that I addressed a student by name only one time. I also noted two additional points: (1) I had spent 20 minutes talking without gaining any verbal response from the students; (2) reference to a colored paper elicited nonverbal responses, which indicated that students were comprehending what I was saying, even if they were not verbally responding.

Teacher instructions to students	Number of instructions	Students' response to instructions
Verbal to entire class	2	None
Verbal – with colored paper	1	Nod by several students indicating understanding; read page silently with me
Verbal – with transparency	1	None immediate; later, students did as I had asked them to do
Verbal and gesture – with white paper and pointing to a section on it	1	Read along on page with me
Verbal – address a student by name	1	Hands me the paper I ask for

The final example in the list above – addressing a student by name – occurred shortly after the 20-minute minilesson. I include it because it presents a contrast. This was a more successful strategy than when I had addressed the whole class, asking for any student to give me a copy of a particular paper. At that time, no one responded.

I noted that several strategies during the 20-minute minilesson prompted response from the students: the use of colored paper; gesturing to specific points on other papers; and addressing a student by name. None of these responses, however, were verbal. I had spent 20 minutes talking *at* the students rather than *with* them.

The videotape clearly indicated that I needed to adjust my methods if my goal was to elicit responses from the students, particularly verbal responses. If I was to involve them in actively using language, I had to provide them more speaking time. In addition, I realized that a serious mismatch had occurred between my goals for the class and my classroom practice (Fanselow 1988). My goal was a student-centered classroom where students had numerous communicative opportunities for active language use. Throughout the taped minilesson, students had had no communicative opportunities. Instead, they had listened to me lecture.

PLANNING AN ACTION

Based on this tape, I decided to take three steps:

1. talk less and let students talk more;
2. use more visual references – the board, gestures, colored paper;
3. call students by name.

Planning an action includes predicting possible outcomes. I predicted that students would respond to my instructions more easily if I took these three steps during a minilesson. I also predicted that if I were to have necessary materials already in place in the classroom, students would need less direction and could begin their minilesson task more quickly. Beginning the task more quickly would translate into more speaking time for them. They would have greater opportunities to talk with one another, and I would be able to cut down on my own speaking time.

Planning also involves deciding on a means of collecting and analyzing descriptions of the planned action. To accomplish this, I would do as I had with the initial investigation. I would videotape again and would transcribe the minilesson. In addition, I would again make a chart matching my instruction giving with the responses of the students. Finally, because speaking time for the students was a concern, I would tally the number of minutes each speaker, including myself, talked.

IMPLEMENTING THE ACTION

On this day, students would be working on a short small-group project during the minilesson. As planned, I arrived at the classroom early and arranged materials – poster paper and markers – at several stations around the class-room. I also wrote some key words and questions on the board. When class began, I videotaped. Because I had been regularly videotaping class sessions, not all of which were used for this action research project, the students had grown accustomed to having the camera in the room. As before, I kept the camera focused on myself.

I knew I needed to carry out this project in a deliberate way; however, changing my teaching style was easier in planning than in real time. I fell into my usual routine during the first minutes of the class. Communication was hindered by my whole-group questions. It required a conscious effort on my part to shift into the new strategies I had planned.

OBSERVING THE ACTION

The transcription of the videotape from this minilesson shows small changes in my teaching methods. Although I did, indeed, have some difficulty initiating the new strategies, I was able after the first 5 minutes to follow the actions I had planned. I moved into addressing students by name, pointing to key words on the board, pointing at the project question on the board and reminding students they had answered that question for homework, and gesturing that students should raise their hands to agree or disagree. The students responded. Careful advanced preparation had also helped. Once students moved to their small-group stations, their task was clear and each group was able to begin immediately with no further questions.

The following list indicates the pace of this minilesson. It clearly differs from the earlier minilesson to which students had difficulty responding.

Teacher cues to students	*Number of cues*	*Students' response to cues*
Verbal – to entire class	2	None
Verbal – call student by name	2	Move into groups; student gets Scotch tape to hang group's poster
Combined – writing on board, gesture	3	Raise hands to vote; begin brainstorming on today's topic; record responses on poster paper

In this minilesson, my primary goal had been accomplished. Students were able to respond to my instructions. In addition, students had greater opportunities for speaking to one another, in small groups and later to the whole class. In the earlier minilesson, I had spoken for a solid 20 minutes.

In this lesson, a bit longer at 35 minutes, the distribution of speaking time shows students' active language use. Our exchanges followed the following pattern:

Number of minutes	*Speaker and context*
5	Teacher talks.
10	Students work in small groups. Teacher circulates, talking briefly with each group.
1	Teacher talks.
4	Student presents group 1 brainstorm list.
2	Teacher interjects during student report.
3	Student presents group 2 brainstorm list.
2	Teacher interjects during student report.
2	Student presents group 3 brainstorm list.
2	Teacher talks.
1	Student asks question.
2	Teacher talks, summarizes.

Total speaking time
Students: 20 minutes   Teacher: 14 minutes

REFLECTING

The second minilesson elicited more student response to instructions, both nonverbal and verbal. Students moved quickly to the assigned small-group task. Key vocabulary and the day's project question on the board facilitated students' focusing and responding. The combination of written material on the board, my calling on individual students by name, and the use of gestures had effectively elicited students' responses. Further, the second minilesson, because it was a small-group task, generated greater student–student interaction. It allowed students to use language actively for extended periods.

REVISING THE PLAN

We were near the end of the 10-week summer session when I completed this action research project. No time remained for revising the plan and testing the revision. Had there been time, however, I could have begun a new cycle of action research by building on what I had learned. I could have continued to use the strategies of writing key information on the board, calling on students by name, and using broad gestures. I also learned that small-group work had been effective during the minilesson. I could have structured more minilessons to include group work. Finally, I wanted still more speaking time for the students. Rather than teacher response to small-group presentations, I could have asked the students in other groups to respond.

What I learned about action research

Bartlett (1990) urges teachers to become critically reflective by moving "away from the 'how to' questions . . . to the 'what' and the 'why' questions" as a means of "transforming our everyday classroom life" (p. 205). The action research project I completed during my summer ESL internship shifted my own focus significantly to the whys and whats: why weren't students responding, and what could I do to change this pattern in my classroom?

Our teaching patterns have been formed by the models through which we ourselves were taught (Allwright & Bailey 1991). In this first attempt to change the teacher-centered model so ingrained in me, the opportunity for self-observation was eye-opening. My research tools – observation of experienced ESL instructors and videotapes of my own teaching – forced me to reflect on my teaching philosophy and to scrutinize the ways in which my pedagogy served my teaching goals.

I was delighted with the outcome of this action research project. Teachers are trained in pedagogical methods; however, we are seldom trained to observe closely the effects of those methods. Action research gave me a means of doing this. I felt newly empowered to do investigations in my own classroom and to bring about positive change. No methods course had ever presented me with such a stimulating possibility.

Conducting the action research project did not require years of experience as a researcher. It only required curiosity and a sincere interest in exploring my teaching. Now, several years later, I still conduct action research projects in my classroom. I have learned the value of becoming aware of my teaching behaviors and of investigating their consequences for students' learning. I am simultaneously teacher and learner.

Task Break

To answer her question, "How can I elicit verbal responses to my instructions?" Helen approached her teaching as a problem-solving process.

- How did she do this?
- What are some advantages of looking at teaching as a problem-solving process?

- How can such a problem-solving approach to teaching limit us from gaining awareness of our teaching?

Project 2: How can I get students to talk during tutorials?

For many years, researchers have packaged methods and techniques for teachers to apply in their classrooms (Richards & Rodgers 1986). Those methods and techniques, which may change from year to year, have been imposed on teachers and students in the assumption that they would bring the best results in every context and with any group of students. Because they do not take into consideration the unique nature of each class, and the dynamic interaction between teacher and students in classes, what we hear or experience as teachers are comments such as: "Group work just doesn't work in my class," "I don't think my students like peer correction," "I don't think this technique works."

There are, in fact, useful methods and techniques; but what needs to be realized is that they may not work in every context, or at least not in the same way. Realizing this, I decided to make action research a part of my classroom practice. I believe that action research increases our understanding of classroom teaching and learning as it allows for a systematic investigation of our own classroom and students and gives us the power to make more informed decisions through observation and reflection on our teaching (Fanselow 1987, 1988; Gebhard 1991, 1996; Kemmis & McTaggart 1982; Nunan 1995; Richards & Lockhart 1994; Strickland 1988). As Good and Brophy (1997) indicate, action research provides an opportunity for teachers to discuss ideas, reflect on teaching, and extend their knowledge of alternative practices.

The context of the project

The action research project I report on here took place at an intensive language institute in an ESL context. The project was a part of the institute's teacher development program, which was supervised by the interim director of the institute. The group that participated in the program consisted of one supervisor and seven teachers, who were paid extra salary to conduct action research in their classrooms. The group met every 2 weeks for an hour to talk about the projects, to give reports, and to counsel one another.

The institute was an intensive English program that offered courses to increase the English proficiency of international students and to assist them in adapting to American culture, academic institutions, and social relations. The program included a tutoring system in which a tutor provided guidance and special help, in one-to-one sessions, to the students who needed assistance with their individual problems and specific learning goals.

The process of conducting the action research project

As with Helen Sitler's action research project, my process included posing a problem, seeking knowledge, planning an action, implementing and observing the action, and reflecting on the results.

POSING A PROBLEM

At the time I conducted this action research project, I was one of the tutors at the institute. The student population I worked with consisted of female students, and they were all advanced-level students. My students were from Thailand and Japan. Two of them were planning to attend a college in the United States in order to pursue graduate studies, and the other was an EFL teacher who wanted to improve her English. As these were tutorial sessions, I asked the students about language problems, and all three tutees indicated that they needed to improve their speaking skills the most. Because these were one-to-one sessions, the environment was not ideal for having various speaking activities. The books and other resources were quite limited in this sense and did not address the real problems I had in my tutorial sessions: what kinds of speaking activities would make my students speak more during these one-to-one sessions, and what would be the amount of time my students spent talking during these activities? Therefore, I decided to find out what activities would provide the best opportunities for the tutees to speak.

SEEKING KNOWLEDGE

After I posed the problem, the next step was to gather as much information as possible about the nature of the problem. I talked to group members and the supervisor during the meetings about the problems I was investigating. I did a library search to look at the various speaking activities and about possible variations to adapt to my one-to-one tutorial sessions. In the following meetings, I had the chance to get feedback from my colleagues and the supervisor about the activities I chose and adapted for my tutees.

PLANNING AN ACTION

The discussions in the action research group meetings helped me to create a plan of action. Colleagues suggested that I audiotape or videotape the sessions to refer back to the activities, the students' performance, and the amount of time they spent talking during each activity. I decided to audio-tape the sessions as this would be more practical and less distracting for the students. I decided to try the activities with each of my students, observe whether each activity would lead to communicative interaction between the students and me, as well as to see if the amount of time each student spent talking during each activity would vary and whether the source of interaction would be the student or myself. I also decided to take brief notes about the students' behavior, such as on their willingness and interest.

The speaking activities I decided to adapt for my research included the following:

Activity 1: cartoon strip stories.   In this activity, the student would be given a series of cartoons and asked to create a story based on the actions taking place in the cartoons.

Activity 2: movies.   For this activity, the student would select a movie to watch before coming to the session. During the session, she would first summarize the story in the movie, then reflect on it by talking about her re-actions, feelings, and opinions with regard to certain events or actions that took place in the movie.

Activity 3: songs.   The student would listen to a song; a cloze exercise would be given to fill in the blanks in the lyrics. Then, the student would be given an opportunity to talk about the theme of the song, the singer, and the type of music. I expected that the activity would lead to topics in which the student would talk about her favorite songs and singers.

Activity 4: ambiguous pictures.   A set of ambiguous pictures would be brought to the sessions. The student would be asked to describe what she was seeing in the pictures and asked to justify her descriptions.

Activity 5: diary.   The student would be asked to keep a diary at the be-ginning of the semester. This activity would involve her in talking about the issues she had written in her diary that particular week.

Activity 6: short stories/plays.   The student would be asked to select a short story, play, or novel to read. During the session, she would summarize the read-ing and give her opinion and feelings about the events and characters in it.

Activity 7: TV/radio news.   Before the session, the student would be as-signed to watch TV or listen to radio news and to take notes on at least three news items. During the session, she would first restate the news, and then talk about the issues mentioned in it.

Activity 8: interview.   Before coming to the session, the student would interview a native speaker about real issues, such as how to rent a house or apartment or any topic that she might be interested in and want to learn more about. Then, during the session, she would be asked to present the interview and talk about the topics she covered in the interview.

Activity 9: reading passages or dialogues in textbooks.   During or before the sessions, the student would be given a short passage or dialogue to read; she would then be asked comprehension questions. A discussion on the topic covered in the passage or dialogue would follow.

Activity 10: reproduction of a dialogue.   The student would be given a dialogue to study. Then she would be asked to reproduce useful parts of the dialogue during a conversation between the student and myself.

IMPLEMENTING AND OBSERVING THE ACTION

I applied all the activities for each student and audiorecorded the sessions. I also took notes about each student's overall interest in the topic and willingness to talk during each activity. The whole process took about 3 weeks to complete.

I also observed which of these activities involved the students in talking, whether or not the student initiated the conversation, and the amount of time each student spent talking. For this purpose, I reviewed the tapes and my notes. I transcribed sections from the tapes and analyzed each activity for each student in terms of the amount of time the student spent talking and who the initiator of the speaking act was.

Table 10.1 shows the total amount of time each student spent for each activity. "Initiator" indicates whether the teacher or the student initiated the speaking act. For example, Student 1 initiated and spent a total of 25 minutes engaged in the speaking act during activity 2. On the other hand, the same student spent a total of 5 minutes talking during activity 10, and it was the teacher who initiated the speaking act. The amount of time a student took for an activity and whether she initiated speaking were important to show that the student was interested in the activity, was willing to talk, and that the activity provided opportunities for her to talk.

The amount of time spent by each student on speaking changed greatly according to the activity. In the case of activities 1, 2, 3, 4, 5, 7, and 8, the

Table 10.1

Activity	Student 1		Student 2		Student 3	
	Time	*Initiator*	*Time*	*Initiator*	*Time*	*Initiator*
1	20 min.	Teacher	25 min.	Student	15 min.	Student
2	25 min.	Student	20 min.	Student	20 min.	Student
3	20 min.	Student	25 min.	Student	20 min.	Student
4	25 min.	Student	30 min.	Student	18 min.	Teacher
5	20 min.	Student	35 min.	Student	25 min.	Student
6	15 min.	Teacher	12 min.	Teacher	15 min.	Student
7	15 min.	Student	15 min.	Teacher	20 min.	Student
8	30 min.	Student	36 min.	Student	30 min.	Student
9	10 min.	Teacher	7 min.	Teacher	10 min.	Teacher
10	5 min.	Teacher	5 min.	Teacher	5 min.	Teacher

students seemed interested, initiated talk, and, while doing these activities, talked a lot. As the teacher, I rarely talked during these activities. For example, during the cartoon strip stories activity, I brought a series of cartoons and asked the students to describe what was happening in each picture and to create a story. The students appeared to love to look, examine, and make up stories based on the cartoons. They said that the cartoons were attractive and that made it easy to interpret and interact with them. Each student became quite imaginative and was able to create interesting stories.

During some tutorials when we used cartoon strip stories, I explored by trying slightly different techniques. For example, I wanted to see what would happen when I kept one of the last pictures in the strip and asked each student to guess what happened. It was a lot of fun to speculate on the possibilities about how the story ended and later match the original picture to their versions. Most important, a lot of speaking was taking place, and, as the teacher, I was reaching my goal of making just a few comments and giving the students a chance to talk.

Among other activities that provided meaningful contexts for the students to practice their speaking skills were movies (activity 2), diary (activity 5), TV/radio news (activity 7), and interview (activity 8). These activities actually went beyond the sessions as they engaged the students in the target language outside the classroom. For example, for activity 2, the student selected and watched a movie before coming to the tutorial session. I asked each student to take notes while viewing the movie in order to have a record of major events to summarize. One of the goals of this activity was to integrate listening and speaking skills. It also aimed at helping each student to expand her vocabulary.

All my tutees enjoyed watching their favorite movies and making comments on certain events and issues, how they felt about characters, the theme, the cinematography, and so on. They were eager to summarize the movie for me and see my reactions. Most of the time, the conversation went beyond the movie to talk about more general topics and issues. For example, I recorded the following in my observation notes: "Today I could really see the excitement in my student's eyes while she was trying to tell me what happened in the movie in a clear and orderly way. She said she cried at the end of the movie because she felt so happy for the main character; then she explained why."

REFLECTING

Developing speaking skills involves a two-way process between speaker and listener. The textbooks that emphasize developing oral communication skills usually include activities such as debates, role plays, and dramas. In this regard, it was a challenge for me to find appropriate speaking activities for my tutees during these one-to-one sessions, as there could not be student-to-student interaction, which is considered to be crucial for the development of oral communication skills. Activities such as debates, role plays, and dramas were out of the question. Yet, as the tutor, I had to meet these students' specific needs – that is, improving their speaking skills. My exploration by trying out alternative activities, such as cartoon strip stories, movies, songs, and ambiguous pictures, and observing how much talk by students these activities produced, along with whether or not the student initiated communication during these different activities, helped me choose the kinds of activities I could use with the tutees.

My search was especially useful as the results guided me to choose the type of activity that would address the specific needs and problems of my students. I had a clearer idea about what I needed to do during the rest of the semester. The process of exploring the consequences of different speaking activities on the talk time and interest of the tutees also had an impact on my attitudes toward tutoring: I became more confident about my decisions and more aware of my teaching. I believe I was a better teacher because I knew what helped my students improve their speaking abilities and because I felt that I individualized the instruction and fulfilled the objectives of the tutoring sessions.

What I learned about action research

The problem I had in the tutorial sessions could not be addressed realistically and effectively by the methods and techniques I read about in reference books or textbooks. Among all the theories, methods, and the latest developments in language, I felt confused and came to ask one main question: What would be my starting point, those nicely stated methods or my own students? By doing the action research in my class, I felt I addressed my students' needs much better because it helped to close the gap between the predetermined methods and my own class. I was able to choose what would work for my students rather than trying to apply the most recent and popular methods and activities.

Teachers in any context can greatly benefit from learning to derive the methodological principles and practices from the regular observation of their classroom teaching and learning processes. They can benefit from observing their students and analyzing the circumstances and conditions under which learning experiences are accomplished. The teacher should not be concerned with searching for the best method but, rather, should be concerned with the students and trying to find out what works for them. This forms the basis for creating student-centered classrooms.

If we conceptualize teaching a second language only in terms of methods, we accept a static view of the teaching environment because the methods already determine the teacher's and students' roles, activities, and procedures. However, we know that the classroom is dynamic and interactional, and we are and should be aware of our students' changing needs during their development in the target language. Through action research, not with a predetermined method, teachers can meet the demands of a dynamic class and students' changing needs, as action research allows for a systematic analysis of our classroom and students. Teachers can address the real issues and problems in class.

In conclusion, we can list the following reasons for teachers to do action research:

- Teaching can be accomplished if teachers follow students, not the packaged methods, to structure the learning/teaching process. As Atwell (1991) explains, the teaching methods should take a back seat to allow our students to become our focus.
- Action research can narrow the gap between researchers and teachers (Lieberman 1986; Nunan 1995).
- I agree with Tim Gillespie's words when he states how teachers feel:

> Teachers are victims of so many theories or strategies or activities or programs or reading series that are abstractions of the messy realities of the classroom. . . . So much happens in educational thinking and scholarship and research; so many ideas keep coming and they just wash over us. I mean from a classroom teacher's perspective, it feels like you're standing in the ocean and a wave

comes and then another wave comes – the latest pedagogical trend or movement. (In Hubbard, 1991: 36)

Through the use of action research, teachers can find their own way among
all those methods and theories and texts.
- The real issues and problems in the classroom can be addressed (Nunan
1990).
- Action research is a part of professional development. It provides a means
for teachers to become more aware and reflective in their teaching.

Task Break

Based on your knowledge from reading Chapter 4,
how do the two action research projects described in
this chapter exemplify what action research is? What
could either or both of the two teachers do to further
expand their awareness through action research?

---

11 *How yoga was taught*
Connecting my student and teacher selves

Jerry G. Gebhard

> Each of us yearns to create and recreate for ourselves what has already been created by others for themselves.
> —J. F. Fanselow (1997: 167)

This book ends with a story that is another illustration of exploring and gaining awareness of teaching. My experience in learning yoga also illustrates the central point presented in Chapter 7, where Robert Oprandy explored the process of connecting our personal and professional lives. My questions reflect the reflective and personal nature of my quest to connect who I am with who I am as a teacher:

- How did I search for a suitable yoga class?
- What connections have I made between who I am and who I am as a teacher?

How Did I Search for a Suitable Yoga Class?

A number of years ago, while living in Hawaii, I decided to study Hatha Yoga. Being a novice and physically not very flexible, I was rather shy about joining a class; instead, I found a tutor. "How lucky," I thought, "no way to embarrass myself in front of other students." But, although I was not embarrassed and at first took the weekly lessons and daily home practice

A version of this chapter was published in *The Language Teacher* (special issue on Second Language Teacher Education), volume 16, number 12. I would like to thank the editor of *The Language Teacher* for granting me permission to reprint parts of the original article.

seriously, I soon quit. I guess I just could not handle all the directives: "Hold that pose for exactly 1 minute"; "Always meditate after you practice!"; "Change your bicycle peddles to rubber ones. You will destroy the nerves in your feet. Listen, these nerves are connected to every part of your body." Being young and a little rebellious at times, the day I quit I rode my bicycle in my bare feet, metal peddles and all!

I did learn to breathe, stretch, and meditate, however, and I liked the way doing these activities made me feel. Therefore, I continued my search for a class. Some months later, I joined a yoga class at a community center in Honolulu. At first it was engaging. The students came from all walks of life, and the yoga instructor never talked. Instead, he modeled the warm-up stretches and poses without a word. He would even exaggerate his movements, letting the fifty or so students see each step in the process of getting into a particular pose. Some students seemed to follow him very well, getting into and holding poses as long as the instructor did. Others, like me, were lost. We had trouble getting into poses and could not hold them. I once tried to ask a student how to get into a pose, but he whispered that we were not allowed to talk. I had no idea if I was doing the pose correctly. Doing the pose perfectly seemed to be important, although no one ever said it was. Eventually, my solution was to stop, sit, and practice my breathing exercises and meditation techniques. Visions of riding my bicycle in my bare feet would pop into my head. I soon stopped going.

My third attempt to find a yoga class was in Tokyo. I liked much about the yoga club I had joined. The hours were flexible, and the teacher and his assistants gave one-to-one instruction. The class even went on trips to Kamakura for sports competitions on the beach, which were always fun. But, the lessons at the club were always the same. The instructor would tell me to begin my routine and verbally correct me when I made an error. Each week he would explain a new pose, step me through it, have me practice it, and give me verbal feedback on whether I was doing it correctly or not. I did not mind the feedback. In fact, I wanted it. But, it was always done in the same way through verbal explanation, and I never seemed to get the pose right. One time I asked the instructor to show me how he did the pose; but he explained it instead. Then, when I did not quite get the new pose right, he told me to listen more carefully. The harder I tried to listen, the worse I seemed to do. My meditations at the end of the sessions usually included visions of riding my bicycle in my bare feet.

My fourth try at finding a suitable yoga class was at a yoga center in Bangkok, and I was delighted. The center had beautiful wood floors and only three walls, leaving the front view open to a beautiful garden. There were pictures of people doing yoga on the side walls, and the back wall was lined with full-view mirrors in which students could watch themselves and others do poses. I also found the students and the instructor to be friendly and easy to approach. Most of all, however, it was how this instructor approached teaching that made all the difference for me and others I talked to in this class.

When I first arrived, I had a fairly high level of anxiety. After all, I had been through three previous experiences, all of which I had quit out of disappointment. I told the instructor that I could not get rid of this anxious feeling, and his response was exactly what I needed. I can still recall his words:

Everyone arrives with different abilities. Some can stretch easily and others can't. Some have balance. Some don't. I notice that you can control your breathing. Others still have to learn this. Everything takes time and practice. Let your yoga emerge. It will happen if you practice and pay attention to it.

I now realize that his nonjudgmental verbal and nonverbal behavior also helped to reduce my anxiety. For example, he did not tell (or nonverbally indicate to) a student that a pose is getting better (or worse), and he rarely used words such as "good," "bad," "better," or "worse." Rather, he would point out a different way that a student could get into a pose or hold a pose longer. When I was learning to do a headstand and could hold the pose for only a few seconds, for instance, he simply tapped my elbows as I was getting into the pose, indicating that I should move my forearms further apart. It worked. I held the pose for minutes. More important, perhaps, he did not tell me I was doing the pose wrong or badly and then explain how I should be doing it, as instructors in the past had done. Likewise, when I was able to hold the pose, he did not tell me I was doing the pose better. This lack of judgmental behavior, I believe, made it easier for me to focus on doing a pose, as I did not have to get emotionally involved in the judgments.

Upon reflection, I also liked the variety of ways he gave feedback to students. He would try one way, and if it did not work, he tried another. For example, I remember expressing dissatisfaction with how I was doing a certain pose. So, the instructor did it with me, stepping me through it. When I still did not feel comfortable with it, he had me look at a picture of the pose, then look at myself in the mirror as I did it. He then asked me what the person in the picture was doing that I was not. I saw that my back was not arched in the same way, changed it, and felt much more comfortable with the pose.

My personal success in part resulted from the instructor's way of giving feedback. However, I also believe that I gained in my ability to do yoga because he provided opportunities for me to take responsibility for my own development, as well as showed me how I could do this. For example, he taught me how to observe myself and others doing yoga in the mirror. He would point out that the mirror provided instant feedback on seeing the form of the pose, as well as a way to become comfortable with myself as a practitioner of yoga. He also whispered that it is a great way to observe what others are doing.

Likewise, he gave me many chances to explore different aspects of yoga. He encouraged me to study the pictures he had on the walls of famous yogi in different postures. After a few months at his center, he invited me to join special Saturday morning demonstrations, for example, on how to clean phlegm from one's air passage. From time to time he also gave me, along with others, chances to talk about yoga and doing yoga, benefits we seemed to be gaining, and problems we were having with certain poses. He also provided chances for me to read about aspects of yoga and to relate the ideas in the readings to my practice.

Because I had a consistent interest in learning to do different breathing exercises, for example, he lent me a book that included a chapter on the breathing practices of yoga. This chapter impressed on me that the way I breathe is a consequence of habit and that the purpose of practicing and mastering different ways of breathing is to have more control over the way I breathe and the consequences of this on my intellectual and emotional state. I also realized that I could practice different breathing exercises anytime I wanted, not just at the yoga center, and that it was possible to use breathing as a way to refresh myself physically and mentally even while walking down the street.

Something the instructor said also had a tremendous impact on how I see myself as a student and the way I approach the development of my yoga. When I told him that I was impressed by the way a particular student did yoga and that I wanted to become like him, he told me that there are correct and incorrect ways to do yoga, in that there are ways that bring benefits to the body and mind and ways that do not, but there are certainly degrees of variation in the ways yoga can be done and that this varies from person to person and comes from within the person. He added that my focus needs to be on observing how experienced practitioners do yoga so that I can take this knowledge inside myself, interpret how they do yoga, and relate this knowledge to my own development as a practitioner of yoga. The goal is not to be like them; it is to make use of their knowledge to build my own yoga values and practices.

In short, I believe that I learned to both appreciate and do yoga because of the multiple opportunities this instructor provided for me. Unlike the other yoga classes I had attended, he did not judge the way I did yoga as being good or bad, but rather focused on describing what I could do to change the way I do it. Likewise, he did not go through each lesson in a lockstep kind of way, but rather paid attention to the consequences of his actions on my unique way of doing yoga, for example, on whether or not I changed my yoga behavior to match my own concept of an ideal posture based on his feedback. He also focused on providing opportunities for me to take on the responsibility for my own yoga development by showing me how to use pictures and a mirror image as a way to observe, as well as to relate ideas to my own practice through reading and talk.

While practicing yoga with this teacher, I no longer had visions of riding my bicycle in my bare feet.

Task Break

What connections do you think I made between who I am and who I am as a teacher? See if you can predict my connections. Then, read the next section.

What connections have I made between who I am and who I am as a teacher?

Reflecting on my personal learning experiences with different yoga teachers has given me the chance to connect more closely my experiences with who I am as a teacher and teacher educator. My reflection on these experiences has given me fresh awareness of the learner. Some learners are, as I was, rebellious. They sometimes do not want to be told what to do and how to do it. They want to figure things out for themselves. Of course, some learners can be the opposite, and do not want to take much responsibility for their own learning.

Reflecting on my own experiences with anxiety and apprehension while studying yoga has made me much more sensitive to the affective states of the students who study with me. I can more fully understand that students often arrive in our language classes with a variety of learning experiences. Some of these experiences are quite negative, even to the point of students feeling threatened and anxious about being in the language class. As a result, when students enter my language classes, I want to learn much about their language-learning histories. My goal is to discover their stories about being a language learner, join them in their appreciation of the things they love about learning a language and the strategies that work or do not work well for them, learn about their fears and anxieties about learning a second language, work with them to overcome these inhibiting feelings, and celebrate their accomplishments. The same is true for teachers who study in my teacher-education program. I am interested in their language learning and formal and informal teaching experiences and stories, their fears and anxieties, and their accomplishments.

Reflecting on these yoga experiences, I also am reminded that I need to focus consistently on the way I give feedback to students so that they do not feel the way I did. My first yoga teacher in Honolulu was very prescriptive and somewhat judgmental in her feedback, which annoyed and even angered me. The second teacher gave no direct feedback. The only way I could get feedback was to watch the teacher model each pose and compare that with my own posture, and this left me confused and irritated. At the yoga club in Tokyo, the teacher used the same verbal techniques over and over again. These techniques did not work for me, and I was not able to change my posture through primarily verbal feedback and felt that I was inadequate and being negatively judged.

In contrast, my positive experiences at the Bangkok yoga center gave me ideas for providing feedback to students and teachers. I deeply believe that feedback can be enjoyable when the teacher does not constantly make judgments about performance. Rather than saying that performance is good or bad, better or worse, I am reminded through my yoga experiences that as a language teacher I can offer description and alternatives. For example, a judgmental way of interacting with a student is to say to him or her (while frowning and shaking one's head back and forth in a disappointed way), "No! No! Don't say, 'I *have* 23 years.' You should say, 'I *am* 23.' How many times do I have to tell you this!" A nonjudgmental descriptive way to interact with this same student is to say (with an encouraging facial expression and neutral body language), "You said, 'I have 23 years.' Let's see. I'll write down three sentences. You read them aloud to me. Then, tell me which one you said and which one is standard English." I believe that such nonjudgmental verbal and nonverbal behavior reduces threat. Without threat, students do not have to filter their language development through emotional turmoil. They will be free to focus attention on their use of language, explore learning, and find, at least at times, that language learning can be great fun and not all that difficult.

Like the first three yoga teachers I experienced, some language teachers limit the way they offer feedback. Like the teacher in Bangkok, however, it is possible to be quite creative in the way we offer feedback. For example, that yoga teacher used a combination of visual techniques to give me feedback on my poses. He had me view myself and others in a mirror, showed me pictures and photos, had me draw the posture, had me read about postures, and demonstrated the pose. He also explained how to get into the pose and used touch to indicate how to change a posture. Through a combination of these visual, auditory, and tactile techniques, I was able to develop my yoga consistently.

Reflecting on my yoga experiences in Bangkok, my belief is reinforced that language students can greatly benefit from processing their language through multiple activities. At the yoga center, I was able to practice getting into different poses, observe others doing yoga, talk with the teacher and other students about yoga, attend special Sunday morning demonstrations, read about yoga, and more. Through such varied activities, I was able to develop my yoga. Like the Bangkok teacher, who provided multiple activities for me to process my yoga, I like to provide many ways for language students to process their second language. For example, if a student expresses interest in learning English related to photography, I will talk with the student about photography, give her newspaper clippings or magazines on the topic, introduce her to others who have the same interest, point out a photography show at a nearby museum and encourage her to go, and encourage her to write an essay on an aspect of photography.

As discussed in Chapter 1, teachers can become more aware and develop their teaching by processing an interest or need through multiple activities. For example, if a teacher is interested in learning more about questioning behaviors, as his teacher educator, I might give him a few readings on the topic, introduce the topic for discussion during a seminar, and encourage him to do self-observation, journaling, or an action research project. I am convinced that through connected multiple activities, teachers can develop their teaching interests and the beliefs and practices associated with these interests.

As my yoga teacher in Bangkok told me, I too tell my students, whether they are language students or teachers, that they need to take on the responsibility for their own learning. As language learners, students can listen to advice and participate in language-learning activities. But, ultimately, the learner is the one who does the learning. The more responsibility the learner accepts for his or her own learning, the more likely the learner is to make progress in mastering the second or foreign language. This is not easy for some learners to do, especially in foreign language settings and if they are in a system in which the teacher dictates what and how they should learn. Nevertheless, many foreign language students do succeed in taking some control of their own learning. Motivated EFL students, for example, accept responsibility for doing reading outside teacher assignments, join English clubs where they have a voice in deciding the English they will use and learn, decide to go to English-language movies that are not dubbed in their native language, watch CNN or CNBC, write to a pen pal in English, write in an English journal or diary, and so on. I do not hesitate to show interested students how they can take on more responsibility for their own learning, no matter what the learning context.

Making connections: Thoughts on time, knowledge, and reflection

Sometimes past experiences, such as the ones I had with yoga, gain their true value as a tool for reflection when we are able to gain distance from them through time and filter them through additional experience. This chapter is based on reflection back to an earlier time in my life; the yoga experiences lasted from 1974 to 1980. Since then, I have completed a doctorate, gained additional experience as an ESL and EFL teacher and teacher educator, had a variety of satisfying language-learning experiences, married, and lived a life in which I interact daily with people from a variety of cultures. All these cumulative experiences have provided me with knowledge through which I can creatively reflect on the value of my earlier experiences in relation to my present teaching beliefs and practices.

While reflecting on my yoga experiences, I more clearly grasped that some of the students who enter my language classes (and teacher-education classes) have had previous experiences that might have resulted in their feeling anxious or even threatened about being in my class. I believe that this awareness has been heightened because I have gained, in a phenomenological sense, other experience since 1980 that has been useful when reflecting on my past yoga experiences. For example, while studying for my doctorate, I had the privilege of reading the work of such humanistic educators as Charles Curran (1976, 1978), Earl Stevick (1976, 1980, 1982), and Jenny-belle Rardin (1977), as well as taking classes on Counseling-Learning and talking with others who had been experiencing humanistic methodologies. I was also introduced to theories of second language acquisition, including the ideas of Krashen (1981, 1982) and Krashen and Terrell (1983) on lowering the affective filter that blocks many students. Through the years, I have also focused on anxiety in the language classroom through research. For instance, I was involved with a research project done by Jacinta Thomas (1992, 1993) on the affective states of students in an ESL writing class. Her in-depth study gave me much to think about. Such experiences have impressed me with the importance of paying attention to the affective side of language learning, including how teachers can be sensitive to the emotional needs of students who enter our language classrooms. All these educational experiences built up knowledge that allowed me to reflect creatively on the value of my earlier experiences with yoga in relation to my present teaching beliefs and practices.

Another example comes from my studies for several years with John Fanselow (at Teachers College, Columbia University), whose nonjudgmental, descriptive way of looking at teaching has had a tremendous influence on my beliefs about teaching and learning. While studying with him, I read (1977a, 1978) and offered feedback (1987) on his written work, and participated in many discussions with him and with others about his work. In addition, I studied others' ideas on judgment and description as well, such as the work of Simon and Boyer (1974) and Gallwey (1974). After graduating and taking on responsibility in a second language teacher-education program, I have asked both novice and experienced teachers to consider Fanselow's ideas, including those in his more recent publications. These experiences, like those concerning humanistic education mentioned earlier, have provided me with a wealth of knowledge that has allowed me imaginatively to reflect on the value of my earlier yoga experiences in relation to my present teaching beliefs and practices.

All this leads me to a question about reflection: How does the sum total of our experiences lend itself to the development of the beliefs we have about teaching and learning? There is no simple one-to-one relationship in my mind. Everything is cumulative as well as recurrent.

To conclude, I have been making connections between who I was and am as a practitioner of yoga and who I am as a teacher. To explore this connection, I selected a set of learning experiences from my past, reflected on these experiences by writing down and organizing my thoughts and feelings about them, attempted to make links between them and my present teaching beliefs and practices, and considered the complexity of reflection itself. I am happy that I did this because I have made connections between who I am and who I am as a teacher – perhaps the most important awareness of all in our professional, as well as personal, exploration.

Task Break

What personal experiences have helped you to make connections to your teaching?

Bibliography

Abbs, P. 1986. The poisoning of the Socratic idea. *The Guardian* (January 13).

Acheson, K. A., & Gall, M. D. 1987. *Techniques in the clinical supervision of teachers: Preservice and inservice applications* (2nd ed.) New York: Longman.

Acheson, K. A., & Gall, M. D. 1997. *Techniques in the clinical supervision of teachers: Preservice and inservice applications* (4th ed.) New York: Longman.

Adler, P. A., & Adler, P. 1994. Observational techniques. In N. K. Denzin and Y. S. Lincoln (Eds.), *Handbook of qualitative research* (pp. 377–392). Thousand Oaks, CA: Sage.

Agar, M. A. 1980. *The professional stranger: An informal introduction to ethnography*. New York: Academic Press.

Agar, M. 1985. *Speaking of ethnography*. Beverly Hills, CA: Sage.

Akamine, M. 1993. Exploring vocabulary teaching techniques: Check list. *Okieiken Review, 3*, 67–81.

Allen, P., Fröhlich, M., & Spada, N. 1984. The communicative orientation of language teaching: An observation scheme. In J. Handscombe, R. A. Orem, and B. P. Taylor (Eds.), *On TESOL '83: The question of control* (pp. 231–253). Alexandria, VA: TESOL.

Allwright, D. 1988. *Observation in the language classroom*. London: Longman.

Allwright, D., & Bailey, K. M. 1991. *Focus on the language classroom*. New York: Cambridge University Press.

Arcario, P. 1994. Post-observation conferences in TESOL teacher education programs. Unpublished Ed. D. dissertation, Teachers College, Columbia University, New York.

Atwell, N. 1987. *In the middle: Writing, reading, and learning with adolescents*. Portsmouth, NH: Boynton/Cook Publishers.

Atwell, N. 1991. Wonderings to pursue: The writing teacher as researcher. In B. M. Power and R. Hubbard (Eds.), *Literacy in process* (pp. 227–244). Portsmouth, NH: Heinemann.

Bailey, K. M. 1983. Competitiveness and anxiety in adult second language learning: Looking at and through the diary studies. In H . W. Seliger and M. H. Long (Eds.), *Classroom oriented research in second language acquisition* (pp. 67–102). Rowley, MA: Newbury House.

Bailey, K. M. 1990. The use of diary studies in teacher education programs. In J. C. Richards and D. Nunan (Eds.), *Second Language Teacher Education* (pp. 43–61). New York: Cambridge University Press.

Bailey, K. M., Bergthold, B., Braunstein, B., Fleischman, N. J., Holbrook, M. P., Truman, J., Waissbluth, X., & Zambo, L. J. 1996. The language learner's autobiography: Examining the "apprenticeship of observation." In D. Freeman and J. C. Richards (Eds.), *Teacher learning in language teaching* (pp. 11–29). New York: Cambridge University Press.

Bailey, K. M., & Nunan, D. (Eds.). 1996. *Voices from the language classroom.* New York: Cambridge University Press.

Bakhtin, M. M. 1981. Discourse in the novel. In M. Holquist (Ed.), *The dialogic imagination: Four essays by M. M. Bakhtin* (pp. 259–422). Austin: University of Texas Press.

Barnes, D. 1976. *From communication to curriculum.* Harmondsworth, England: Penguin.

Barnes, D. 1992. *From communication to curriculum* (2nd ed.). Portsmouth, NH: Boynton/Cook Publishers.

Bartlett, L. 1990. Teacher development through reflective teaching. In J. C. Richards and D. Nunan (Eds.), *Second language teacher education* (pp. 202–214). New York: Cambridge University Press.

Beattie, M. 1995. New prospects for teacher education: Narrative ways of knowing teaching and teacher learning. *Educational Researcher, 37,* 53–70.

Bellack, A. A., Kliebard, H. M., Hyman, R. T., & Smith, F. L. 1966. *The language of the classroom.* New York: Teachers College Press.

Berliner, D. C. 1986. In pursuit of expert pedagogue. *Educational Researcher, 15*(7), 5–13.

Berne, E. 1964. *Games people play: The psychology of human relationships.* New York: Grove Press.

Braun, C. 1976. Teacher-expectation: Sociopsychological dynamics. *Review of Educational Research, 46,* 181–182.

Brinton, D. M., & Holten, C. A. 1989. What novice teachers focus on: The practicum in TESL. *TESOL Quarterly 23,* 343–350.

Brinton, D. M., Holten, C. A., & Goodwin, J. M. 1993. Responding to dialogue journals in teacher preparation: What's effective? *TESOL Journal, 2*(4), 15–19.

Brock, M. N., Yu, B., & Wong, M. 1992. "Journaling" together: Collaborative diary-keeping and teacher development. In J. Flowerdew, M. N. Brock, and S. Hsia (Eds.), *Perspectives on second language teacher education* (pp. 295–307). Hong Kong: City Polytechnic of Hong Kong.

Brophy, J., & Evertson, C. 1981. *Student characteristics and teaching.* New York: Longman.

Buckheister, P. E., & Fanselow, J. F. 1984. Do you have the key? In J. Handscombe, R. A. Orem and B. P. Taylor (Eds.), *On TESOL '83: The question of control* (pp. 223–230). Washington, DC: TESOL.

Burns, A. 1996. Collaborative action research and curriculum change in the Australian Adult Migrant English Program. *TESOL Quarterly, 30*, 591–598.

Burns, A. 1997. Valuing diversity: Action researching disparate learner groups. *TESOL Journal, 7*(1), 6–11.

Burns, A., & Hood, S. (Eds.). 1997. *Teachers' voices 2: Teaching disparate learner groups.* Sydney, Australia: National Centre for English Language Teaching and Research.

Cardoza, L. F. 1994. Getting a word in edgewise: Does "not talking" mean "not learning"? *TESOL Journal 4*(1): 24–27.

Cazden, C. 1988. *Classroom discourse: The language of teaching and learning.* Portsmouth, NH: Heinemann.

Cohen, L., & Manion, L. 1985. *Research methods in education,* (2nd ed.). London: Croom Helm.

Collier, V. 1987. Age and rate of acquisition of second language for academic purposes. *TESOL Quarterly, 21*, 617–641.

Collier, V. 1989. How long? A synthesis of research on academic achievement in a second language. *TESOL Quarterly, 23*, 509–531.

Collins, M. 1992. *Ordinary children: Extraordinary teachers.* Charlottesville, VA: Hampton Roads.

Connelly, F. M., & Clandinin, D. J. 1990. Stories of experience and narrative inquiry. *Educational Researcher 19*, 2–14.

Corey, S. 1952. Action research and the solution of practical problems. *Educational Leadership, 9*(8), 478–484.

Corey, S. M. 1953. *Action research to improve school practices.* New York: Teachers College Press.

Crookes, G. 1993. Action research for second language teachers: Going beyond teacher research. *Applied Linguistics, 14* (2), 130–144.

Curran, C. A. 1970. *A need for listeners.* East Dubuque, IL: Counseling-Learning Publications.

Curran, C. A. 1976. *Counseling-learning in second languages.* East Dubuque, IL: Counseling-Learning Publications.

Curran, C. A. 1978. *Understanding: A necessary ingredient in human belonging.* East Dubuque, IL: Counseling-Learning Publications.

Dantonio, M. 1995. *Collegial coaching: Inquiry into the teaching self.* Bloomington, IN: Phi Delta Kappa.

Day, R. R. 1990. Teacher observation in second language teacher education. In J. C. Richards and D. Nunan (Eds.), *Second Language Teacher Education* (pp. 43–61). New York: Cambridge University Press.

Dewey, J. 1938. *Experience and education.* New York: Macmillan.

Diaz-Rico, L. T. 1995. Issues of power in the teacher education classroom. *TESOL Matters, 5*, 9.

Edge, J. 1992. *Cooperative development.* Essex, England: Longman.

Elbow, P. 1973. *Writing without teachers.* New York: Oxford University Press.

Fanselow, J. F. No date. Unpublished observation guides. New York: Teachers College, Columbia University.

Fanselow, J. F. 1977a. Beyond Rashomon: Conceptualizing and observing the teaching act. *TESOL Quarterly, 11,* 17–41.

Fanselow, J. F. 1977b. The treatment of learner error in oral work. *Foreign Language Annals, 10,* 583–593.

Fanselow, J. F. 1978. Breaking the rules of the classroom game through self-analysis. In R. L. Light and A. H. Osman (Eds.), *Teaching English as a second language and bilingual education: Themes, practices, viewpoints* (pp. 145–166). New York: NYS ESOL BEA.

Fanselow, J. F. 1982. "What kind of flower is that?" – A contrasting model for critiquing lessons. In H. Eichheim and A. Maley (Eds.), *Papers from Goethe Institute – British Council Seminar on Classroom Observation.* Paris: Goethe Institute.

Fanselow, J. F. 1987. *Breaking rules: Generating and exploring alternatives in language teaching.* White Plains, NY: Longman.

Fanselow, J. F. 1988. "Let's see": Contrasting conversations about teaching. *TESOL Quarterly, 22*(1), 113–130.

Fanselow, J. F. 1990. "Let's see": Contrasting conversations about teaching. In J. C. Richards and D. Nunan (Eds.), *Second language teacher education* (pp. 182–197). New York: Cambridge University Press.

Fanselow, J. F. 1991. A lesson in observation. *Practical English Teaching, 12*(2), (December), 12–13.

Fanselow, J. F. 1992a. *Contrasting conversations.* White Plains, NY: Longman.

Fanselow, J. F. 1992b. Opera and role play. *Practical English Teaching, 12*(4) (June), 15–16.

Fanselow, J. F. 1997. Post card realities. In C. P. Casanave and S. R. Schecter (Eds.), *On becoming a language educator* (pp. 157–172). Mahwah, NJ: Lawrence Erlbaum.

Fanselow, J. F., & Light, R. L. (Eds.). 1977. *Bilingual, ESOL, and foreign language teacher preparation: Models, practices, issues.* Alexandria, VA: TESOL.

Farrell, T. S. C. 1996. A qualitative study of four experienced EFL teachers as they reflect on their work. Unpublished doctoral dissertation, Indiana University of Pennsylvania.

Fattah, A. 1993. The influence of dialogue journals and other practicum activities on the writing proficiency and pedagogical knowledge of EFL student teachers. Unpublished doctoral dissertation, Indiana University of Pennsylvania.

Forsdale, L. 1981. *Perspectives on communication.* Reading, MA: Addison-Wesley.

Freeman, D. 1989. Teacher training, development and decision-making. *TESOL Quarterly, 23*, 27–45.

Freeman, D. 1991. "To make the tacit explicit": Teacher education, emerging discourse, and conceptions of teaching. In D. C. Li, D. Mahoney, and J. C. Richards (Eds.), *Exploring second language teacher development* (pp. 1–20). Hong Kong: City Polytechnic of Hong Kong.

Freeman, D. with Cornwell, S. (Eds.). 1993. *New ways in teacher education.* Alexandria, VA: TESOL.

Freeman, D., & Richards, J. C. (Eds.). 1996. *Teacher learning in language teaching.* New York: Cambridge University Press.

Fuller, F. F. 1969. Concerns of teachers: A developmental conceptualization. *American Educational Research Journal, 6,* 207–226.

Fuller, F. F., & Brown, O. H. 1975. Becoming a teacher. In K. Ryan (Ed.), *Teacher education: The seventy-fourth yearbook of the National Society for the Study of Education* (pp. 25–51). Chicago: National Society for the Study of Education.

Gaies, S., & Bowers, R. 1990. Clinical supervision of language teaching: The supervisor as trainer and educator. In J. C. Richards and D. Nunan (Eds.), *Second language teacher education* (pp. 167–181). New York: Cambridge University Press.

Gallwey, W. T. 1974. *The inner game of tennis.* New York: Random House.

Gallwey, W. T. 1976. *Inner tennis: Playing the game.* New York: Random House.

Gardner, H. 1991. *The unschooled mind.* New York: Basic Books.

Gardner, R., & Lambert, W. E. 1972. Attitudes and motivation in second language learning. Rowley, MA: Newbury House.

Gattegno, C. 1976. The common sense of teaching foreign languages. New York: Educational Solutions.

Gebhard, J. G. 1984. Models of supervision: Choices. *TESOL Quarterly, 18,* 501–514.

Gebhard, J. G. 1985. Interactional arrangements in a teacher preparation practicum: Providing and blocking opportunities for change. Unpublished doctoral dissertation, Teachers College, Columbia University, New York.

Gebhard, J. G. 1990. Interaction in a teaching practicum. In J. C. Richards and D. Nunan (Eds.), *Second language teacher education* (pp. 118–131). New York: Cambridge University Press.

Gebhard, J. G. 1991. Language teacher supervision: Process concerns. *TESOL Quarterly, 25,* 738–743.

Gebhard, J. G. 1992. Awareness of teaching: Approaches, benefits, tasks. *English Teaching Forum, 30*(4), 2–7.

Gebhard, J. G. 1996. *Teaching English as a foreign or second language: A teacher self-development and methodology guide.* Ann Arbor: University of Michigan Press.

Gebhard, J. G., & Duncan, B. 1992. EFL teacher education curriculum development as inquiry. In J. Flowerdew, M. M. Brock, and S. Hsia (Eds.), *Perspectives on second language teacher education* (pp. 319–335). Hong Kong: City Polytechnic of Hong Kong.

Gebhard, J. G., Gaitan, S., & Oprandy, R. 1987. Beyond prescription: The student teacher as investigator. *Foreign Language Annals, 20,* 227–232.

Gebhard, J. G., & Oprandy, R. 1989. Multiple activities in teacher preparation: Opportunities for change. *ERIC:* ED 307 813.

Gebhard, J. G., & Ueda-Motonaga, A. 1992. The power of observation: "Make a wish, make a dream, imagine all the possibilities!" In D. Nunan (Ed.), *Collaborative language learning and teaching* (pp. 179–191). Cambridge: Cambridge University Press.

Gitlin, A., & Price, K. 1992. Teacher empowerment and the development of voice. In C. D. Glickman (Ed.), *Supervision in transition.* Washington, DC: Association for Supervision and Curriculum Development.

Glausiusz, J. 1998 (June 22). Growing disaster? Science and Environment. *Pittsburgh Post-Gazette.*

Good, T. L., & Brophy, J. E. 1997. *Looking in classrooms* (7th ed). New York: Addison Wesley Longman.

Greene, M. 1973. *Teacher as stranger: Educational philosophy for the modern age.* Belmont, CA.: Wadsworth.

Holten, C. A., & Brinton, D. M. 1995. You shoulda been there: Charting novice teacher growth using dialogue journals. *TESOL Journal, 4*(4), 23–26.

Hornberger, N. H. 1994. Ethnography. *TESOL Quarterly, 28,* 688–690.

Hubbard, R. 1991. On paying attention to the magic: An interview with Tim Gillespie. In B. M. Power and R. Hubbard (Eds.), *Literacy in Process* (pp. 32–38). Portsmouth, NH: Heinemann.

Jackson, P. W. 1968. *Life in classrooms.* New York: Holt, Rinehart and Winston.

Jarvis, G. A. 1972. Teacher education goals: They're tearing up the street where I was born. *Foreign Language Annals, 6*(2), 198–205.

Jarvis, J. 1992. Using diaries for teacher reflection on in-service courses. *ELT Journal, 46*(2), 133–142.

Jersild, A. T. 1955. *When teachers face themselves.* New York: Teachers College Press.

Jimenez-Aries, I. 1992. A descriptive study of error treatment in ESL settings. Unpublished M.A. thesis, Indiana University of Pennsylvania.

Johns, A. M. 1985. Some principles of materials design from the world around us. *TESOL Newsletter, 19,* 1–2.

Johnson, K. 1992. The instructional decisions of pre-service English as a second language teachers: New directions for teacher preparation programs. In J. Flowerdew, M. Brock, and S. Hsia (Eds.), *Perspectives on second language teacher education* (pp. 115–134). Hong Kong: City Polytechnic of Hong Kong.

Johnson, K. 1999. *Teachers understanding teaching.* Boston: Heinle and Heinle.

Jorden, E. H., & Noda, M. 1987. *Japanese: The spoken language*. New Haven: Yale University Press.

Kagan, D. M. 1992. Professional growth among preservice and beginning teachers. *Review of Educational Research, 62*(2), 129–169.

Kemmis, S., & McTaggart, R. 1982. *The action research planner*. Victoria, Australia: Deakin University Press.

Kohl, H. 1984. Growing minds: On becoming a teacher. New York: Harper and Row.

Kornblau, B. 1982. The teachable pupil survey: A technique for assessing teachers' perceptions of pupil attributes. *Psychology in the Schools, 19*, 170–174.

Krakauer, J. 1997. *Into thin air*. New York: Villard.

Krashen, S. 1981. *Second language acquisition and second language learning*. Oxford: Pergamon Press.

Krashen, S. 1982. *Principles and practice in second language acquisition*. New York: Pergamon Press.

Krashen, S. D., & Terrell, T. D. 1983. *The natural approach*. New York: Pergamon Press.

Kumaravadivelu, B. 1994. The postmethod condition: (E)merging strategies for second/foreign language teaching. *TESOL Quarterly, 28*, 27–48.

Lacey, C. 1977. The socialisation of teachers. London: Methuen.

Lange, D. L. 1990. A blueprint for a teacher development program. In J. C. Richards and D. Nunan (Eds.), *Second language teacher education* (pp. 245–268). New York: Cambridge University Press.

Lewin, K. 1948. *Resolving social conflicts*. New York: Harper and Brothers.

Lewin, K. 1952. Group decision and social change. In T. M. Newcomb and E. L. Hartley (Eds.), *Readings in social psychology*. New York: Holt.

Li, D., Mahoney, D., & Richards, J. C. (Eds.). 1994. *Exploring second language teacher development*. Hong Kong: City Polytechnic of Hong Kong.

Lieberman, A. 1986. Collaborative research: Working with not working on . . . *Educational Leadership, 43*, 28–33.

Lisle, L. 1980. *Portrait of an artist: A biography of Georgia O'Keeffe*. New York: Washington Square Press.

Long, M. H. 1987. Native speaker/non-native speaker conversation in the second language classroom. In M. H. Long and J. C. Richards (Eds.), *Methodology in TESOL* (pp. 339–354). Rowley, MA: Newbury House.

Lortie, D. C. 1975. *Schoolteacher: A sociological study*. Chicago: University of Chicago Press.

May, N., & Sigsworth, A. 1987. Teacher-outsider partnerships in the observation of classrooms. In R. Murphy & H. Torrance (Eds.) *Evaluating education: Issues and methods* (pp. 257–273). London: Harper and Row.

McDermott, R. L., Gospodinoff, K., & Aron, J. 1978. Criteria for an ethnographically adequate description of concerted activities and their contexts. *Semiotica, 24*(3/4), 245–275.

McDonald, J. P. 1992. *Teaching: Making sense of an uncertain craft*. New York: Teachers College Press.

McDonough, J. 1994. A teacher looks at teachers' diaries. *ELT Journal, 48*(1), 57–65.

McFaul, S. & Cooper, J. 1984. Peer clinical supervision in an urban elementary school. *Journal of Teacher Education, 34*, 34–38.

Mead, M., & Bateson, G. 1942. *Balinese character*. New York: New York Academy of Sciences.

Mehan, H. 1979. *Learning lessons: Social organization in the classroom*. Cambridge: Harvard University Press.

Murphy, J. M. 1992. An etiquette for nonsupervisory observation of L2 classrooms. *Foreign Language Annals, 25*, 215–225.

National Center for Research on Cultural Diversity and Second Language Learning. 1992. Instructional conversations. *ERIC Digest*, EDO-FL-92-01. Washington, DC: Center for Applied Linguistics.

Neubert, G. A., & Stover, L. T. 1994. *Peer coaching in teacher education*. Bloomington, IN: Phi Delta Kappa.

Numrich, C. 1996. On becoming a language teacher: Insights from diary studies. *TESOL Quarterly, 30,* 131–153.

Nunan, D. 1988. *The learner-centered curriculum*. Cambridge: Cambridge University Press.

Nunan, D. 1989. *Understanding language classrooms: A guide for teacher initiated action*. London: Prentice-Hall.

Nunan, D. 1990. Action research in the language classroom. In J. C. Richards & D. Nunan (Eds.), *Second language teacher education* (pp. 62–81). New York: Cambridge University Press.

Nunan, D. 1995. Closing the gap between learning and instruction. *TESOL Quarterly, 29*, 133–158.

Oprandy, R. 1988. A conceptual base for the analysis of ESOL listening materials. Unpublished doctoral dissertation, Teachers College, Columbia University, New York.

Oprandy, R. 1993–1994. By wheelchair to Birmingham Jail. In D. Larson (Ed.), *All the rest is just peanuts: An IDIOM supplement on peace education and teaching English to speakers of other languages. IDIOM 23,*(4) (winter), 20–23.

Oprandy, R. 1994a. Enriching input from a variety of sources. In J. D. Macero & V. Chesser (Eds.), *Student-centered perspectives and practices: Selected papers from New York State Teachers of English to Speakers of Other Languages 1990–1992* (pp. 49–57). New York: New York State TESOL.

Oprandy, R. 1994b. Listening/speaking in second and foreign language teaching. *System, 22*(2), 153–175.

Perrone, V. 1991. *A letter to teachers: Reflections on schooling and the art of teaching*. San Francisco: Jossey-Bass Publishers.

Phenix, P. H. 1964. *Realms of meaning: A philosophy of the curriculum for general education.* New York: McGraw-Hill.

Rardin, J. 1977. The language teacher as facilitator. *TESOL Quarterly, 11*, 383–387.

Rardin, J., & Oprandy, R. 1985. Teacher as listener: Listening skills through an understanding relationship. *TESOL Newsletter, 19*, 19–21.

Rardin, J., Tranel, D., Green, B., & Tirone, P. 1988. *Education in a new dimension: The Counseling-Learning approach to community language learning.* New York: Counseling-Learning Publications.

Richards, J. C. 1998. *Beyond training.* New York: Cambridge University Press.

Richards, J. C., & Ho, B. 1998. Reflective thinking through journal writing. In J. C. Richards, *Beyond training* (pp. 153–170). New York: Cambridge University Press.

Richards, J. C., & Lockhart, C. 1994. *Reflective teaching in second language classrooms.* New York: Cambridge University Press.

Richards, J. C., & Nunan, D. (Eds.). 1990. *Second language teacher education.* New York: Cambridge University Press.

Richards, J. C., & Rodgers, T. 1986. *Approaches and methods in language teaching: A description and analysis.* New York: Cambridge University Press.

Richardson, V. 1994. Conducting research on practice. *Educational Researcher, 23*, 5–10.

Roderick, J. A. 1986. Dialogue writing: Context for reflecting on self as teacher and researcher. *Journal of Curriculum and Supervision, 1*(4), 305–315.

Rogers, C. R. 1983. *Freedom to learn for the 80's.* Columbus, OH: Charles E. Merrill.

Rosenthal, R., & Jacobson, L. 1968. *Pygmalion in the classroom: Teacher expectation and pupils intellectual development.* New York: Holt, Rinehart and Winston.

Roth, J. 1984. So you're being observed tomorrow? Some nightmare avoidance strategies. Presentation at New York State TESOL Conference.

Rowe, M. B. 1974. Wait time and rewards as instructional variables: Their influence on language, logic and fate control. *Journal of Research in Science Teaching, 37*, 81–94.

Rowe, M. B. 1986. Wait time: Slowing down may be a way of speeding up. *Journal of Teacher Education, 37*, 43–50.

Rubin, H. J., & Rubin, I. 1995. *Qualitative interviewing: The art of hearing data.* Thousand Oaks, CA: Sage.

Saryusz-Szarska, M. In process. Jumping into the learner's shoes: An ethnographic study of the classroom language learning experience. Doctoral dissertation, Indiana University of Pennsylvania.

Schön, D. A. 1983. *The reflective practitioner: How professionals think in action.* New York: Basic Books.

Schön, D. A. 1987. *Educating the reflective practitioner: Toward a new design for teaching and learning in the professions*. San Francisco: Jossey-Bass Publishers.

Schulman, L. 1987. Knowledge and teaching: Foundations of the new reform. *Harvard Educational Review, 57*, 1–22.

Shiomi, K., & Dalton, J. 1990. *Enjoy listening*. Tokyo: Eichosha Company.

Showers, B. 1985. Teachers coaching teachers. *Educational Leadership, 42*(7), 43–48.

Silliman, M. 1995. A case study of two consecutive self-studies of a TESOL master's degree program. Unpublished doctoral dissertation, Teachers College, Columbia University, New York.

Simon, A., & Boyer, E. G. 1974. *Mirrors for behavior III: An anthology of observation instruments*. Philadelphia: Research for Better Schools.

Smith, D. 1992. Anthropology of education and educational research: CAE presidential address. *Anthropology of Education Quarterly, 23,* 185–198.

Smith, F. 1988. *Joining the literacy club*. Portsmouth, NH: Heinemann.

Spada, N. 1990. Observing classroom behaviors and learning outcomes in different second language programs. In J. C. Richards and D. Nunan (Eds.), *Second language teacher education* (pp. 293–310). New York: Cambridge University Press.

Spradely, J. 1979. *The ethnographic interview*. New York: Holt, Rinehart and Winston.

Stevick, E. 1976. *Memory, meaning, and method*. Rowley, MA: Newbury House.

Stevick, E. W. 1980. *Teaching languages: A way and ways*. Rowley, MA: Newbury House.

Stevick, E. W. 1982. *Teaching and learning languages*. New York: Cambridge University Press.

Strickland, D. S. 1988. The teacher as researcher: Toward the extended professional. *Language Arts, 65*, 754–764.

Suzuki, S. 1970. *Zen mind, beginner's mind*. Tokyo: Weatherhill.

Takahashi, N. 1997. Helping Japanese learners with English pronunciation. Presentation at the Thirty-First Annual TESOL Convention, Orlando, Florida.

Tanizaki, J. 1967. *In praise of shadows* (translation by T. J. Harper and E. G. Seidensticker). New Haven: Leete's Island Books.

Thomas, J. 1992. The affective experience of ESL writers. Unpublished Ph. D. dissertation, Indiana University of Pennsylvania.

Thomas, J. 1993. Countering the "I can't write English" syndrome. *TESOL Journal, 2*(3), 12–15.

Thorne, C., & Wang, Q. 1996. Action research in language teacher education. *ELT Journal, 50*(3), 254–262.

Tirone, P. 1990. The structure of directionless talk: The interactional management of equality and hierarchy in the discourse of a school staff meeting. Unpublished doctoral dissertation, Teachers College, Columbia University, New York.

Ullmann, R., & Geva, E. 1982. *The target language observation scheme (TALOS)*. New York Board of Education, Core French Evaluation Project. Ontario Institute for Studies in Education, Toronto.

van Lier, L. 1993. Action research. Paper presented at the PeruTESOL conference.

van Lier, L. 1996. *Interaction in the language curriculum: Awareness, autonomy and authenticity*. London: Longman.

van Manen, M. 1977. Linking ways of knowing with ways of being practical. *Curriculum Inquiry, 6*, 205–228.

Vygotsky, L. 1978. *Mind and society*. Cambridge: Harvard University Press.

Waite, D. 1993. Teachers in conference: A qualitative study of teacher-supervisor face-to-face interactions. *American Educational Research Journal, 30*(4), 675–702.

Wajnryb, R. 1992. *Classroom observation tasks*. Victoria, Australia: Cambridge University Press.

Wallace, M. 1996. Structured reflection: The role of the professional project in training ESL teachers. In D. Freeman & J. C. Richards (Eds.), *Teacher learning in language teaching* (pp. 281–294). New York: Cambridge University Press.

Wallace, M. J. 1998. *Action research for language teachers*. Cambridge: Cambridge University Press.

Waller, W. 1967. *The sociology of teaching*. New York: Russell and Russell.

Watson-Gegeo, K. A. 1988. Ethnography in ESL: Defining the essentials. *TESOL Quarterly, 22*: 575–592.

Widdowson, H. G. 1993. Innovation in teacher development. *Annual Review of Applied Linguistics, 13,* 260–265.

Woods, P. 1995. *Creative teachers in primary schools*. Buckingham, England: Open University Press.

Author index

Subject index